D0975418

"Topgrading must be a continuous process of raising the bar in the identification of top and bottom players to enhance overall organizational vitality."
—Bill Conaty, former Senior Vice President of
Human Resources, General Electric

"During the last three years of the recession we have continued to grow revenue, we've been one of Utah's fastest growing companies, and we've won multiple awards as a 'best place to work.' Having 94+% A Players at Access is one of the key reasons for this success. Topgrading has been the foundation to help us attract, hire, and retain these A Players."
—Larry Maxfield, CEO, Access Development

"Of course Argo is more successful as a company because Topgrading has resulted in a higher percentage of A Players. But also a more interesting thing happened, and that is, once we had a number of very good people, we didn't need as many people."
—Mark Watson, CEO, Argo Group

"In my IT department efficiency has increased tenfold and productivity is much improved. The only way we could have achieved those results is with Topgrading."
—Bruce Leidal, CIO, Carestream Health IT Department

"With over $70 billion in assets . . . Topgrading is key to our strategies, and . . . the strategies that have generated the majority of our profits would not have been possible without Topgrading."
—Ken Griffin, CEO, Citadel

"After implementing Topgrading for all new hires and promotions, I am thrilled. Our organization has embraced the philosophy and process and we are seeing the results . . . the right people in the right positions."
—Tim Tevens, President and CEO, Columbus McKinnon

"Topgrading has given our team the quality people to keep us winning despite today's economic challenges. Our peers in the region have seen layoffs and eroding sales with this tough economy. But our A Players have kept us focused and on plan over the past two years. Our team of top performers is poised and positive about the future. We're playing offense and we're winning."
—Vic Oenning, Senior Vice President,
Sales and Operations, Corwin Beverages

"Topgrading has been an invaluable tool for DenTek in recruiting and retaining high-level performers. Over the past six years we have blossomed into a world-class consumer goods company with explosive growth and great opportunities, due largely to the hard work of A Players recruited through the Topgrading process."
—David Fox, President, DenTek Oral Care

"Brad Smart is the #1 thought leader in the world on hiring best practices. As the global talent leader for a publicly traded top medical technology company, I know of no other hiring method that comes close to what Topgrading achieves if you want to hire 'A' level, high performers at every pay level."

—John H. Dickey, Sr., Vice President,
Corporate Support, Hillenbrand

"The company emerged from Chapter 11 one of the strongest automotive suppliers, and Topgrading contributed to that success. Topgrading is a central part of our culture and the most important of our core competencies. We can't win if we miss on people. I urge you to Topgrade so you too can get an edge on your competition."

—Curtis Clawson, President, CEO, and Chairman, Hayes Lemmerz
(recently retired since acquisition by Maxion in 2012)

"Topgrading has allowed us to triple the projected sales for the office. A Player caregivers impress clients, who refer us, and A Players refer other A Players for us to hire."

—Michael Steinberg, Franchise Owner,
Home Instead Senior Care

"Brad's second opinion interviews and Topgrading methodology have helped us pick the right executives, which is key to making money in private equity."

—Earl Powell, Founding Partner and
Chairman Emeritus, JLL Partners

"Topgrading is the #1 reason for our company success."

—Scott Mesh, CEO,
Los Niños Services

"There's nothing that's done more for our company than Topgrading. Marine-Max is a huge fan of Brad Smart's Topgrading system. We began the process in 2002 and we're totally convinced Topgrading has significantly improved our bottom line. We are in the people business, and now with Brad's gift, Topgrading is the heart of our culture and a primary focus of MarineMax."

—Bill McGill, CEO, MarineMax

"We've grown from one to forty-six locations and have experienced 50% to 100% growth annually since Topgrading."

—Ken Sim, Founder, Nurse Next Door

"Although in a recession in which all sales forces in the industry were selling less, I'm confident that our Topgraded sales force sold much more than if we hadn't Topgraded."

—Regional Sales Director,
Anonymous Fortune 500 Pharmaceutical Company

"Topgrading has definitely made Red Door Interactive more successful. With more A Players, we can achieve higher margins on our services. And clients appreciate the results driven by the high caliber of people we hire and retain. All we have to sell is people."　　　　—Reid Carr, CEO, Red Door Interactive

"There is no doubt about it—the company as a whole has performed better because of Topgrading. A Player executives do a better job of setting direction, four times as many A Player store directors of course get better results, and when we've Topgraded entry employees and the social media rave about how positive and energized the whole store is, record sales no longer surprise us!"
　　　　—Bob Mariano, CEO, Roundy's

"Having used many recruiting processes and methodologies in the past, I can honestly say that Topgrading is the best investment for ensuring that your company hires A player talent."
　　　　—Gidgett Ingalls, HR Manager, Sigma Marketing

"Synergetic is definitely more successful because of Topgrading."
　　　　—Fred Mouawad, Chairman and CEO, Synergetic One

"Topgrading has definitely enabled Triton to perform better as a total company."　　　　—Frank Evans, CEO, Triton Management Group

"Of all the changes I've made to improve our company, none has been more important than Topgrading. *Topgrading* is the single most valuable business book I've read. I'd recommend it for every executive, in every company! What I would say to any CEO starting out on Topgrading is to be prepared for the corporate antibodies that are going to tell you it's just another fad, it's just another program. It's not; this one works. This one will pay dividends."
　　　　—Jon A. Boscia, Chairman and CEO (retired),
　　　　Lincoln National Corporation

"Topgrading is not just desirable but essential for organization success in this competitive world. Brad has helped me grow, and has helped DSC evolve from a warehousing company to a growth-oriented, leading-edge supply-chain management company."　　　　—Ann Drake, CEO, DSC Logistics

"I have used Brad for years in my ongoing efforts to build and enhance our own A team. Topgrading represents the kind of breakthrough I would expect from Dr. Smart. I will use it as standard practice here at DCM. American industry, I believe, will adopt Topgrading as a necessary human resource optimization process in order to be competitive and survive on a global basis."
　　　　—David Gottstein, President, Dynamic Capital Management

"The author's focus on talent as the sine qua non for prosperous organizations is cradled persuasively in a savory introduction and practical, valid methods."
—Robert Perloff, Distinguished Service Professor Emeritus of Business Administration and Psychology, Katz Graduate School of Business, University of Pittsburgh

"In a previous start-up I worked for, hiring was done haphazardly. At Mint.com, I've had very rigorous hiring. We use a technique called Topgrading, which reveals patterns in behavior. In the history of Mint, I've fired only two people and one left voluntarily." —Aaron Patzer, Founder of Mint.com

"With Topgrading, Labsphere more than doubled sales and quadrupled profits in less than three years. Oh yes, one other thing, I was promoted from my old job as CEO of Labsphere to become CEO of Ocean Optics, another Halma company that's about three times larger than Labsphere."
—Kevin Chittim, CEO, Ocean Optics, Labsphere

"We started applying Topgrading three years ago in one of the roughest business environments in the world—Venezuela, where crime, corruption, and social deterioration are rampant. Thanks to Topgrading, we've transformed the company and our community."
—Alberto C. Vollmer, CEO, Ron Santa Teresa

"There is no doubt that Topgrading contributed a lot to our 3000% growth since we began Topgrading." —Jim Twining, CEO, Southern Tide

"Brad narrows the target and then tells you how to hit it. For anyone who believes good people make a difference, this is excellent reading."
—Leslie G. Rudd, CEO, LRICO

TOPGRADING

Smart, Bradford D., 1944
Topgrading : the proven
hiring and promoting met
c2012.
33305226126120
sa   11/21/12

THE PROVEN HIRING AND PROMOTING METHOD
THAT TURBOCHARGES COMPANY PERFORMANCE

Third Edition

Bradford D. Smart, Ph.D.

PORTFOLIO / PENGUIN

PORTFOLIO / PENGUIN
Published by the Penguin Group
Penguin Group (USA) Inc., 375 Hudson Street, New York, New York 10014, U.S.A. •
Penguin Group (Canada), 90 Eglinton Avenue East, Suite 700, Toronto, Ontario, Canada
M4P 2Y3 (a division of Pearson Penguin Canada Inc.) • Penguin Books Ltd, 80 Strand,
London WC2R 0RL, England • Penguin Ireland, 25 St. Stephen's Green, Dublin 2, Ireland
(a division of Penguin Books Ltd) • Penguin Books Australia Ltd, 250 Camberwell Road,
Camberwell, Victoria 3124, Australia (a division of Pearson Australia Group Pty Ltd) •
Penguin Books India Pvt Ltd, 11 Community Centre, Panchsheel Park, New Delhi – 110 017,
India • Penguin Group (NZ), 67 Apollo Drive, Rosedale, Auckland 0632, New Zealand (a
division of Pearson New Zealand Ltd) • Penguin Books (South Africa) (Pty) Ltd, 24 Sturdee
Avenue, Rosebank, Johannesburg 2196, South Africa

Penguin Books Ltd, Registered Offices:
80 Strand, London WC2R 0RL, England

This third edition published in 2012 by Portfolio / Penguin,
a member of Penguin Group (USA) Inc.

1   3   5   7   9   10   8   6   4   2

Copyright © Penguin Group (USA) Inc., 1999, 2005
Copyright © Bradford D. Smart, 2012
All rights reserved

Photograph on page 91 used by permission of Shutterstock Images.

LIBRARY OF CONGRESS CATALOGING IN PUBLICATION DATA
Smart, Bradford D., 1944–
Topgrading : the proven hiring and promoting method that turbocharges
company performance / Bradford D. Smart. — 3rd ed.
p.   cm.
Includes index.
ISBN 978-1-59184-526-3
1. Industrial management. 2. Leadership. 3. Employees—Recruiting. 4. Teams in the
workplace—Training of. 5. Mentoring in business. 6. Employee retention. I. Title.
HD31.S5776 2012
658.4—dc2   2012006927

Printed in the United States of America
Set in Minion Pro Regular with Helvetica Neue LT Std
Designed by Daniel Lagin

No part of this book may be reproduced, scanned, or distributed in any printed or electronic
form without permission. Please do not participate in or encourage piracy of copyrighted
materials in violation of the author's rights. Purchase only authorized editions.

*This book is appropriately dedicated to the hundreds of clients
and thousands of managers who have, indirectly, written this book.
Here's a toast to you, terrific clients, for modifying Topgrading methods
in innovative ways, sharing problems and asking for solutions, and offering
your insights to others by providing your case studies.*

CONTENTS

TOPGRADING WILL MAKE YOUR COMPANY MORE SUCCESSFUL

After decades of studying thousands of successful and failed careers, and hundreds of successful and failed companies, we at Smart & Associates have found that the one factor accounting most for individual and organizational failure is not flawed strategy, insufficient capital, lack of government protection or bailouts, bad luck, corruption, or technology. More important than all of these factors combined is a failure to embed sufficient talent in the organization.

The single most important driver of organizational performance and individual managerial success is *human* capital, or *talent*. The ability to actually do what every company and every manager wants to do—hire and promote the best people available at every salary level—is what distinguishes premier companies, large and small, from mediocre firms. And the ability to hire and promote the best talent available at every salary level accounts for why managers enjoy highly successful versus more ordinary careers.

Consider two examples: In the face of increasing international and domestic competition, two senior managers in similar companies vie to outperform the other. Both strive to improve their teams' performance because both have studied the latest management trends and have attempted some version of quality and process improvement—Six Sigma, lean manufacturing, or Toyota manufacturing methods. Using the latest technology, they have discovered and rediscovered their customer base, and both use social media to make their organizational culture more positive and attractive for recruitment. The companies are equivalent in financial and geographic resources. However, the companies differ in one respect. One manager has a team of 25% high performers, 50% "adequate" but mediocre performers, and 25% low performers. The other manager has a team of almost 90% high performers. *Which manager would you bet on to win?* It doesn't make much difference if the organizations are Global 100 companies, grocery stores, or high-tech start-ups, because the company with better talent is bound to win.

The trouble is, throughout the world most companies do *not* have superior talent because they are poor at picking talent. They simply can't figure out how to solve three huge problems in hiring:

1. rampant *dishonesty* by weak candidates who easily get away with fudging their résumés and faking their interviews,
2. *insufficient information,* because most companies use superficial hiring methods that enable candidates to control and hide what they share about themselves,
3. lack of *verifiability,* as most reference checks are practically useless. Since most reference checks are fact checks with Human Resouces, not done at all, or conducted with the candidates' buddies as references, even the weakest candidates can get away with problem #1, dishonesty.

As you look back at your career, what percent of your frustrations, mistakes, headaches, failures, and disappointments have been caused by your having too many mediocre and low performers? As you reflect on your painful and costly people mistakes, do you instinctively sense the whole hiring system is broken because weak candidates you hired got away with being *dishonest, sharing insufficient information,* and not permitting you to *verify* what they told you in reference calls with their former bosses?

While we're wallowing in the misery of talent headaches, here is some more evidence that you are not alone if you are frustrated with talent challenges:

- I've conducted 65,000 oral case studies with managers, covering all aspects of managers' job histories. In 95% of those case studies, the managers said the "least enjoyable" aspects of the job were problems caused by their mis-hires.
- I met with just the #1 Human Resources executives of Global 100 companies, and they completed a survey revealing 80% of the managers they *hire* turn out to be mis-hires because their hiring methods are flawed. And they said that 75% of the people *promoted* turn out to be underperformers, mistakes they made because, again, their methods for picking talent are flawed. The non-Topgraders in this elite group

hired people—or rather mis-hired 80%—by screening from résumés (that don't screen out C Players whose résumés are deceptive), conducting a series of 45-minute competency or behavioral interviews (which produce insufficient information and are simple for C Players to fake), and only doing reference calls with people the candidate chooses (and C Players list their buddies, not former bosses, as references).

- Human Resources is disappointing CEOs for failing to deliver talent. *McKinsey Quarterly* (January 2008) published an article ("Making Talent a Strategic Priority") in The War for Talent series, showing how the image of HR is mediocre and declining. Line managers say the so-called best practices of HR just don't work, and they complain that HR is not accountable for high *quality* of hires.

- Two hundred CEOs reported to us that they felt they got their money's worth from executive search firms only 21% of the time. (There are A Player executive search executives and you'll learn how to find them.)

- The American Productivity and Quality Center (APQC) conducted a study of quality of hires* in which nineteen companies participated as case studies, sponsors, or both. Only one company, a Topgrading company, stood out for both measuring success accurately and for achieving more than 75% success hiring and promoting not just "okay" performers but high performers. Several global companies that had initially offered to participate dropped out of the study when it became clear that their hiring and promoting methods produce mediocre results. The full report is available at www.APQC.org.

As you can see, talent headaches are universal; you're not alone!

TOPGRADING SOLVES THE THREE BIGGEST HIRING PROBLEMS SO PROFOUNDLY, MANAGERS GET SUPERIOR TALENT AND THEIR ORGANIZATIONS PERFORM BETTER

Now for the good news. In this book you will read of the treatment and cure for your talent headaches, and it's not a pill. It's Topgrading methods that are revolutionary in infusing hiring with honesty, thoroughness, and verifiability of candidate information, producing 75% and even 90%+ success.

---

* APQC, "Recruiting, Selecting, and Retaining Talent," Summary of Key Findings (2007).

That is such a dramatic improvement in talent at every level of every organization that dozens of CEOs quoted in this book state that Topgrading has definitely made their company more successful. Hence the subtitle of this edition of *Topgrading.*

How Does Topgrading Solve the Three Biggest Hiring Problems?

High performers basically are truthful in their résumé and interviews, but low performers too often hype positives and hide negatives. Topgrading hiring has a "truth serum," replacing commonplace falsehoods in résumés and interviews with refreshing honesty. That "truth serum" is candidates understanding that eventually they will have to arrange reference calls with former bosses.

Topgrading hiring has a "truth serum," replacing commonplace falsehoods in résumés and interviews with refreshing honesty.

The Topgrading Interview cures the "lack of information" headache because it covers the total career—every success, failure, key decision, and key relationship, for every job. And Topgrading cures the "lack of verifiability" headache by requiring candidates to arrange reference calls with former bosses and others *you* choose. Aah . . . Topgrading brings truth and honesty, complete information on the candidate's career, and, as frosting on the cake, everything a candidate claims will be verified through reference checks that the candidate arranges.

Topgrading will permit you to double, triple, or even quadruple your success hiring and promoting high performers. That simple fact will then permit you to dramatically change your organizational culture—to raise the performance bar for everyone. And Topgrading coaching methods will help you develop and retain top talent. The result, as the CEOs of our case studies state, is improved organizational performance.

On an individual manager level, Topgrading will pack your team with high performers, which will assure your improved personal performance and greater career success. And there is frosting on the cake for you personally: because you will be able to delegate to more A Players, you will be able to enjoy that elusive thing . . . that dream of . . . what is it called, oh yeah— work-life balance.

What's New in the Third Edition of *Topgrading*

A *lot* is new—so much that I completely rewrote the book.

- **As the subtitle suggests, this edition proves that Topgrading companies perform better.** The first edition (1999) of *Topgrading* said, "Here are the methods I've used professionally, and companies improved their talent because I picked the winners, and by the way, maybe you can copy what I do and improve your results." Only a few managers seemed to do it. The second edition (2005) said, "I've taught leading companies such as General Electric, Honeywell, and American Heart Association how to use Topgrading, and they are hiring and promoting a lot more high performers, so you can, too." Preparing for this third edition I asked, "So what? Does better talent really make a difference?" "Of course," Topgraders unanimously say. However, to my knowledge there has never been a book or article that, like this book, cites dozens of CEOs and heads of HR who say, "I'm certain our sales, profits, market share, etc., are significantly better because of Topgrading." This edition quotes dozens of CEOs who say Topgrading has made their company more successful.
- **Topgrading is for all companies, large and small.** Tiny, small, and medium-size companies can afford fewer mis-hires than big companies, and *all* of the Topgrading methods work perfectly well in *all* companies. It was my fault that the image of Topgrading became "big company." In earlier Topgrading books I cited many leading companies that embraced Topgrading, and of course they are very big companies. They dominated the 2005 edition of *Topgrading*. This edition showcases extremely diverse organizations—big, small, growth, entrepreneurial, domestic, and international—in well over 100 countries.
- **Human Resources can launch Topgrading!** Until very recently Human Resources could not be the prime driver of Topgrading. Topgrading historically has started at the top, with the CEO engaging Smart & Associates to assess and coach the top team, and screen replacements. All managers, starting with the top team, participated in 2-day Topgrading Workshops. The company invested in a license to use all the Topgrading forms and guides, and boom! Topgrading was launched.

The CEO continued to use Smart & Associates (they still do) for "second opinion" interviews of finalists for C-suite jobs, and internal managers paired off for tandem Topgrading Interviews of candidates below the top team. But the head of Human Resources almost never was the driver of Topgrading, because if peers balked at Topgrading and ran to the CEO, and if the CEO did not support HR's wanting thorough Topgrading Interviews or candidate-arranged reference calls (or whatever), the legs were cut out from under HR. Today HR can launch Topgrading. So can any department head. The Topgrading Lite steps you will soon learn can be implemented today, and better hiring results will occur almost immediately. Topgrading is the surest way Human Resources can regain the lost respect the aforementioned *McKinsey* article chronicles. I have interviewed and coached hundreds of heads of HR, and after years—no, decades—of their asking that we come up with some version of Topgrading they can implement to improve talent, without relying much on the CEO, we finally can help.

- **There are now 12 very clear, very proven Topgrading Hiring Steps.** This book fully explains why all 12 steps are crucial to better hiring and how to implement them.
- **Abbreviated, simplified Topgrading methods enable companies to dramatically improve hiring for** *entry-level jobs.* Several case studies share their abbreviated forms and guides.
- **A lot of advice comes from CEOs and heads of Human Resources.** In previous books, 98% of advice came from the author (that would be me). In this edition, CEOs and heads of HR offer hundreds of suggestions for how to successfully roll out Topgrading. And they give their opinions regarding which Topgrading methods can be tweaked and how to do so for unique situations. Who'd a-thunk it?—executives implementing Topgrading might be smarter and have deeper insights than the author.
- **Dozens of case studies show "how to do it."** The executives in these case studies are named, and you'll read their words explaining how Topgrading made each of their companies more successful. Instead of half a dozen case studies (typical for a best-practices book), there are case studies in 40 companies, encompassing businesses of all sizes, diversified industries, and regions all over the world. You should have no difficulty finding several Topgrading case studies that are very much like your organization.
- **Case studies are presented in a unique way.** In this book (chapter 5) there is a Master Chart showing talent improvements in current and

former case studies, and an appendix has half-page mini summaries of all the case studies. Here's what's unprecendented: we've launched a Web site, www.TopgradingCaseStudies.com, where long versions of the case studies are not only available but will be revised and updated indefinitely. So in 2020, for example, a reader of this book might be interested in a case study, and realize, "I can go to www.Topgrading CaseStudies.com to get the 2020 version!" You can access www.Top gradingCaseStudies.com using this QR Code:

- **There is the totally new Topgrading Snapshot.** It's a one-page multi-color picture ("snapshot") of a candidate's career, making it possible to literally screen someone in or out, accurately and validly, in seconds. It may seem tacky to sell a book that sells a product—sorry, but we are convinced the Topgrading Snapshot will prove to be the most valid, powerful, simple-to-use, and least expensive preselection tool on the planet. (And you can get some Topgrading Snapshots free.)
- **Fifty competencies are now color coded.** Topgrading professionals agreed on which competencies are difficult to improve at or overcome, and we've color coded them: green (relatively easy for people to improve; e.g., experience); red (relatively hard for people to improve; e.g., integrity, passion); and yellow for competencies that fall in between the extremes (e.g., Topgrading). So now hiring managers can rate candidates on various competencies with an instant reminder of whether low-rated competencies are those they can probably help the candidate improve.
- **This edition is shorter than the almost 600 pages in the second edition.** Are you a busy, somewhat hyper manager who prefers to skim reading material? I am, too, so I cut the book to (333 pages). One of the reasons for pushing a lot of support material into www.Topgrading CaseStudies.com was to shorten the book.
- **A lot of free resources.** These resources include the Topgrading Snapshot, a 50-page e-book, videos, invitations to bimonthly "Chat with a

Topgrader" conference calls, and more. My personal goal in revising *Topgrading* is to help every reader, anywhere in the world, enjoy a more successful career by adopting Topgrading methodologies. If you are a not-for-profit, call us to discuss the huge discounts available. In addition to what is listed in the Topgrading Resources section (page 331), additional free (and other) resources are constantly being added at www.Topgrading.com, which can be accessed with the following QR Code:

- **Fun anecdotes.** Finally, to add a little human interest, I've sprinkled in some snippets of some of the strangest Topgrading Interviews I've had professionally, including with a murderer, a mobster, political leaders, someone who attempted to overthrow a country, and a few others of note.

However, most of this book is dead serious, and I've done my best to chop what would have been an 800-page tome (with 40 case studies) down to 333 pages of the most practical and useful information you need to Topgrade your team and your organization, and to enable you to not "just" have more talent, but to have a more successful organization and career.

Chapter 1

TOPGRADING BASICS

Mediocrity knows nothing higher than itself, but talent instantly recognizes talent.

—Sir Arthur Conan Doyle

A "tipping point," the title of the best seller by Malcolm Gladwell, is the point at which a buildup of small changes constitutes a breakthrough such that "everyone's doing it." There are clear signs that Topgrading is steadily becoming not just the best practice for hiring and promoting domestically but also globally. In this chapter I'll lay the foundation for your journey through this book by explaining why all companies can and should Topgrade, dispelling common myths like "Topgrading is for big companies," or "Topgrading is firing C Players," or "Topgrading is ranking and yanking people." I'll also briefly explain the history of Topgrading, give you a Topgrading Lite course (so you can begin Topgrading today), and suggest that for all these reasons, the Topgrading tipping point is near.

Every Organization Can Topgrade

When originally published in 1999, *Topgrading* offered a radical vision. Topgrading techniques for hiring, promoting, assessing, and coaching people had enabled hundreds of companies to achieve 75% and even 90%+ success picking not just "okay" performers but rather true high performers. In order to build credibility for Topgrading, I cited companies in both the 1999 and 2005 editions that were mostly huge companies like General Electric, American Heart Association, AlliedSignal/Honeywell, and Hillenbrand. Thus I was responsible for what I call Topgrading Myth #1: Topgrading is only for big companies. Not so! Topgrading is arguably *more* important to small and medium-size companies in which just a couple of mis-hires could cause the business to fail.

Hundreds of new Topgrading success stories have emerged since 1999, and this edition includes dozens of case studies showing that Topgrading works everywhere in the world, in every type of organization, and in every size organization. About half of the 40 case studies in this book are companies with less than 500 employees; several have fewer than 100 employees. You'll meet entrepreneurs (whose businesses, as you know, create most new jobs) and learn in their words how they Topgraded. And you'll read of the experiences of large companies, not-for-profits, and even individual managers who got special permission to deviate from company hiring policies and initiate Topgrading.

Every Organization *Should* Topgrade

Okay, if every type of company on the planet *can* Topgrade, why *should* they?

Our experience and research show that about 25% of managers hired or promoted turn out to be high performers, A Players, in every type of company. Topgraders achieve 75%, 90%, and even greater success picking high performers—that's why every company *should* Topgrade.

In the dozens of case studies reported in this book, the companies and senior executives are identified. (A couple are not because the company does not want competitors to know about, and perhaps emulate, their Topgrading competitive advantage.) And the average result across all the 41 companies is to improve hiring and promoting success from 26% high performers to 85% high performers, with one-third achieving 90%+ high performers hired or promoted. Looking ahead to the fourth edition of this book, I note that Topgrading companies are increasingly pushing their supply chain to Topgrade. Do you want to be supplied by vendors who have mostly A Players or the typical mix of As, Bs, and Cs?

Dozens of case studies are reported in this book, with companies and senior executives named, and the average result across all the 41 companies is to improve hiring and promoting success from 26% high performers to 85% high performers.

But Should Companies Topgrade During Economic Downturns?

Yes! Are you becoming all too familiar with recessions? In the 1990s, a decade in which premier companies Topgraded, lesser companies could sometimes perform spectacularly for a while without a lot of A Players, but from 2000 to 2002 there were annual declines in the stock market. Ouch! Companies with flawed business plans and not enough high performers faltered. Companies that hung on to marginal performers too long did what an increasingly competitive, Darwinian marketplace guaranteed: they went out of business. Then from 2002 to 2008 the economy was strong, and many businesses got fat with too many marginal performers.

From boom to the 2008 *bam!*—the severe global downturn arrived, with a U.S. market decline of 36% in 2008. Although stock markets recovered in 2009 and 2010, unemployment and debt globally lingered on and on and on. Hundreds of thousands of companies failed, and a major factor was hanging on to too many people, including too many weak performers. Most companies naturally cut head count, starting with "fat," but this time the Great Recession had forced companies to figure out they can be more successful with fewer people. The CEOs of many case studies in this book report that their companies perform better with fewer people, but those fewer people are A Players.

Companies That Topgrade Are Much Better at Picking High Performers Than Companies That Don't

The primary reason companies and managers don't achieve A teams, don't perform well, and sometimes fail is that they don't have enough high performers . . . and the main reason is that they fail to use accurate methods to assess candidates for hire or promotion. Use of the Topgrading methods has proven far superior to all other methods. Forgive me for repeating certain facts throughout this book; I've learned over the years that a lot of readers are high-powered and fast-paced, so they skim a lot and sometimes miss such key points as:

Topgrading solves the hiring problems of dishonesty, incomplete information, and lack of verifiability, problems that typically result in 75% mis-hires. The Topgrading methods you'll learn have, for many companies cited, produced a *success* rate of even 90% A Players hired and promoted.

Why It *Was* Smart for Managers to Keep Some "Marginal but Adequate" Performers

For most managers *not* exposed to Topgrading, all that frustration, wasted time, headaches, lessened job performance, and high costs of mis-hires is very understandable. Huh? Seventy-five percent mis-hires is "understandable?"

Let me explain. Suppose your mixture of talent is typical, and only 25% of the people you hire or promote turn out to be high performers. It was (and still is) smart for you to give your high performers a lot of support, coaching, challenge, and financial rewards in order to retain them. And it was (and still is) smart to replace your chronic low performers, the ones that cause your biggest headaches and keep you awake at night. And it was (until you learned about Topgrading) smart to retain your "adequate," "marginal," "deficient" performers because you were only 25% successful picking high performers. It would be too risky for you to replace low performers if there is a 75% chance your replacements will be no better, and there is a 25% chance your replacements will be *worse performers*. Does this make sense?

It would be too risky for you to replace low performers if there is a 75% chance your replacements will be no better, and there is a 25% chance your replacements will be *worse performers.*

Aah, but this scene changes when you're a Topgrader. When 75% to 90% of the people you hire and promote turn out to be *high* performers, it's smart and rational to replace not only low performers but also marginal performers. When you achieve 90% success, you will *know* it's smart to also replace marginal performers who lack the potential to become high performers.

Topgrading Lite

Since this edition is written for very busy people, allow me to give you a "preview of coming attractions," a brief synopsis of Topgrading methods you can use right away and improve your success picking high performers.

- **Use the TORC Technique.** The Threat of Reference Check (TORC) convinces candidates to reveal the whole truth. Simply tell candidates, at every step in the hiring process, that *they* will have to arrange personal reference calls with former bosses and others just prior to a job offer. This is a powerful "truth serum," solving one of the biggest problems in hiring, and that is that underperfomers get away with portraying themselves, in their résumé and interviews, as high performers.
- **Use the Topgrading Career History Form, which produces the Topgrading Snapshot.** The Topgrading Career History Form becomes your application form; it has the TORC Technique truth serum in the instructions and asks for the usual application form information plus a LOT more. It's a long form that candidates complete online, and when they click Submit you will receive it, but you will also receive the Topgrading Snapshot, a multicolor picture of the most revealing aspects of the person's career. The Topgrading Snapshot shows you at a glance crucial information such as dates and job titles, the candidate's full compensation history, accurate boss ratings, and true reasons for leaving each employer. The Snapshot enables you to screen candidates in, and out, in seconds. This is the easiest, least expensive way to get started Topgrading, and this tool will definitely help you hire better. See Topgrading Resources, Appendix H (page 331), for how to try out the Topgrading Snapshot free.
- **Use the Starter Topgrading Interview Guide.** The Topgrading Interview is the most powerful hiring tool. Use the simple Starter Topgrading Interview Guide, Appendix E (page 293), and when you graduate to the full Topgrading Interview Guide, a free training video (in the Topgrading Shop at www.Topgrading.com) will help you in this transition.

  Whether you use the Starter or Full Topgrading Interview Guide, all you do is read the questions, take notes, ask follow-up questions, and turn the page when it's full. Use the Guide to ask the candidate, who is now motivated to tell the truth, to describe every job in chronological order and specifically to describe every success, failure, key decision, and key relationship, including guesses as to how all bosses will rate them.

- **Use two interviewers.** When two trained interviewers are used, managers like you achieve results almost as good as results Topgrading professionals achieve. Two heads are *way* better than one. Using the Topgrading Interview "solo," managers at leading companies achieved about 50% high performers hired, double what they achieved pre-Topgrading. Not bad! But adding the tandem interviewer enabled many to achieve the results in the case studies in this book—an average of 86% high performers.
- **Ask candidates to arrange personal reference calls with their former bosses and others you choose.** No telephone tag. A Players get their former bosses to talk. You and your tandem partner each call half of those references. Then the two of you share your notes, discuss them, consider all the information gleaned from Topgrading methods, and decide whether or not to extend a job offer.

There you go! That's most of what I've learned in decades, and you can literally begin taking these steps today. Just use the Career History Form (with the TORC Technique in the instructions) and the Topgrading Snapshot to give you honest and complete information to screen candidates and invite only sharp candidates in for interviews. Then use the Starter Topgrading Interview Guide, with a tandem interviewer, to get total information on every success, failure, key decision, and key relationship in the candidate's career. Next ask finalist candidates to arrange reference calls with former bosses, and finally, you and your tandem partner call those references—the references you chose to talk with.

HISTORY OF TOPGRADING

How did Topgrading come about, and where is it today, as described in this book? For decades I was a lone practitioner using Topgrading to screen executive candidates for hire or promotion and to coach managers. I never made a sales call because CEOs and heads of Human Resources told their peers that almost everyone I recommended for hire or promotion turned out to be a high performer. (Sorry, that's immodest, but true.) Although clients occasionally asked me to conduct workshops to teach their managers to hire better, most of them didn't achieve better than 50% hiring success because their interviewing skills weren't good enough. I suggested to many CEOs that because their managers lacked the experience of a Topgrading professional, if they'd pair off and use a tandem interviewer, the tandem interviewers would cover for each other's inexperience and do just fine. No one accepted that advice, until years later.

In the 1980s and 1990s, while regularly consulting with General Electric, we figured out how high-performing managers, trained thoroughly in Topgrading, could double, triple, and even quadruple hiring and promoting success. Jack Welch, GE's CEO at that time, accepted my recommendation for tandem interviews, and the results at GE, and other leading companies that copied GE, were impressive: managers who had found that only 25% of the people they hired turned out to be high performers boosted their success to 70%, 80%, and 90%+. Showing that trained managers could do so well helped both editions of *Topgrading*, first published in 1999 and revised in 2005, become top sellers.

At GE we learned that one-day Topgrading Workshops were not thorough enough, because managers trained simply didn't have time to conduct a full tandem Topgrading Interview. Subsequently, we began conducting two-day Topgrading Workshops, and we found that a year after workshops almost all those trained are successfully practicing Topgrading. Day #1 consists of Topgrading content and exercises, and on Day #2 the attendees conduct a full Topgrading Interview. That is, the tandem interviewers study the Topgrading Career History Form and Topgrading Snapshot of their interviewee, get four hours of coaching as they conduct the full Topgrading Interview, analyze the data, write a report, and conduct a real coaching session, just as if their interviewee were a recently hired A Player. Convinced that they got the best insights into an interviewee *ever*, managers don't just *think* they can become Topgraders, they *know* it.

If you read the Dedication for this edition of *Topgrading*, you know that for years clients have been invaluable in helping us to refine, streamline, simplify, and improve Topgrading methods and how we educate managers to use those methods. In a nutshell, Topgrading has become the unrivaled best practice for hiring and promoting only because of an unending interplay in which A Player managers, passionate about talent, shared their great ideas and insights with us.

We're exploring ways to help Topgraders communicate directly with other Topgraders; today there is a LinkedIn Topgrading Group (for everyone) and we're starting groups for CEOs/Presidents and for heads of

Human Resources. Finally, we're donating Topgrading intellectual property to World Vision, Feed the Children, American Heart Association, Arthritis Foundation, Jane Goodall Institute, and other not-for-profits.

The Smart & Associates mission is simple: to "Topgrade the World," for we passionately believe that every manager, from a mega company to a five-person company in Bangladesh, can perform better with the improved talent that comes from Topgrading.

TWO MORE MYTHS ABOUT TOPGRADING

In the beginning of this chapter I mentioned Topgrading Myth #1: Topgrading is just for big companies. Please allow me to dispel two more myths about Topgrading.

Topgrading Myth #2: Topgrading Is Getting Rid of C Players

I'll go into more detail in subsequent chapters, but for now please do *not* interpret what you read to equate Topgrading with firing underperformers. If you're a CEO and want to roll out Topgrading, the best way to be sure your organization will fight you every step of the way is to suggest that Topgrading means firing a bunch of people. Do yourself a favor and instead emphasize the feel-good practices for hiring the best, promoting the best, and coaching to help everyone develop. Your performance-management system should deal with poor performers, who should fire themselves for failing to achieve the accountabilities they committed to.

Topgrading Myth #3: Topgrading Is "Rank and Yank"

Forced distributions can be unfair, and they are cousins to "rank and yank," forced ranking systems with automatic firing ("yanking") of those ranked at the bottom. This has *never* been part of Topgrading, but that myth has prevailed, mostly because Jack Welch, former General Electric CEO, *seems* to advocate it. GE, with CEO Jack Welch, was a major client that worked with me to make Topgrading methods successful for all managers.

Before elaborating on this myth, I want to express my admiration for Jack Welch. Surveys showed him to be the most admired CEO in the world. Jack continues to be the most powerful advocate I know of for driving high performance standards. He is the single most talented and effective CEO I've known, and the only one who could successfully run 200 companies all at once, making decisions about everything from global strategy to engineering and labor contract details. I love Jack's energized, messianic, nonstop preaching the importance of having only high performers in the company.

But we Topgrading professionals, and especially I, constantly explain, "Jack doesn't mean you should fire people in the bottom 10% *if they are A Players;* GE is one of those few companies that have high performers in the bottom 10%, and neither Jack Welch nor current CEO Jeffrey Immelt has, to my knowledge, fired high performers just because they were in the bottom 10%."

Jack and I gave speeches at a global conference and we discussed our differences on this practice. I said to Jack that I thought we agreed that:

- People should fire themselves for failing to achieve the accountabilities they committed to.
- The goal of Topgrading is to have *all* high performers, so if you force-rank your team and have A Players at the bottom, you should celebrate, and certainly *not* fire any As.
- A company firing the bottom 10% every year would have a horribly political culture, with people motivated to undercut and diminish their peers.
- After the forced ranking system was implemented at GE, my recollection is that the bottom 10% were scrutinized—that's okay because everyone's performance was scrutinized at GE—but no one in the bottom 10% who *met* their performance goals and competency goals was fired. No one I was aware of.

The good news is that Jack agrees that high performers should never be fired. "But," he said, "99% of the people in audiences where I give speeches should fire the bottom 10%." I responded, "Yes, Jack, that's probably true. But in my experience companies can take one round of removing underperformers, but if the bottom 10% are fired yearly, the company will suffer a death from 1,000 cuts."

When Jacques Nasser was chairman of Ford he tried to copy a lot of things Welch did, but he totally messed up on "rank and yank," and thankfully did *not* call it Topgrading. (His head of HR called me several times to consult with Ford but I didn't have the time.) Nasser required forced ranking, and no matter how good the bottom 10% were, they had to lose their bonus in the first year and get fired the second year. When it became obvious that even high performers ranked at the bottom could be fired, Ford managers sued and the company lost and paid over $10 million to settle. So their version of forced ranking was abandoned; it never should have been rolled out!

Confusion over "rank and yank" is so widespread, leading to questions every time I give a speech, that I'll now go into a fair amount of detail. Some companies use a performance-management system in which there is a forced ranking with 20% A Players, 70% B Players, and 10% C Players; in my opinion *that is nuts* when clearly there are *not* 20% As, 70% Bs, and 10% Cs. Shoving, say, 100 people into a curve *is* desirable because it really forces managers to avoid giving Exceeds Performance Expectations ratings to too many people who don't deserve it. But labels such as A/B/C Player had better match the percentages in those groups, or an A Player told, "Sorry, we have to call you a B Player because we have so many As and you're a lower-level A" will be furious. How would you feel if you were shoved into the B group? Right—you'd feel lousy, and I've interviewed managers who felt so unfairly labeled that they quit.

What is the goal of your talent systems? You want the top 20% *and* the middle 70% *and* even the bottom 10% to *all* be A Players, right?

Bill Conaty, retired head of Human Resources at General Electric, and I recently talked for an hour and a half about this topic and he explained that forced distributions of talent at GE are sometimes misunderstood. There have been a lot of versions of the forced distribution at GE: 1 through 10; A/B/C Players; Top 20%/Middle 70%/Bottom 10%; and other versions. He told me that currently GE has a forced disctribution of Top 30%/Middle 60%/Bottom 10%. Why? Because these percentages reflect reality—that there are roughly 30% outstanding managers in the group labeled "Top 30%."

The forced distribution percentages reflect the *real* percentages of A/B/C Players.

As head of HR, Bill would ask, "What percent are *actually* high performers?" When executives at GE responded with 27%, Bill and the CEO decided to make the top group 30%, in order that the forced distribution percentages reflect the *real* percentages of A/B/C Players. Bill said, "You *don't* want your top performers to be shoved into a group with a lower designation than what they are—it insults them and it's unfair. There is no substitute for good judgment and common sense. The GE CEO ultimately makes the judgment of what are the percentages in the company, then requires managers to slot their teams into that distribution, but the top executives would always say to managers, 'Don't let us force you to put someone in a category where they don't belong.'"

Bottom line, at GE if someone truly has 100 high performers and can prove it, none would be fired, according to Conaty.

And consistent with that common sense, what happens if a manager of, say, 100 people claims that no one belongs in GE's Bottom 10% group? Is he forced to fire anyone? Nope. Bottom line, at GE if someone truly has 100 high performers and can prove it, none would be fired, according to Conaty.

Forced Distribution with Accurate A, B, C Ratings

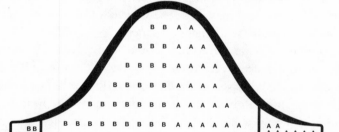

Please look at the bell curve above. It shows a forced distribution that accurately portrays a hypothetical reality in which the team consists of half As, half Bs, and no Cs. Suppose the company has been Topgrading for a couple of years and used to have a bunch of Cs, but no more. Back when they had 20% Cs, calling the Bottom 20% Cs made sense. Now they have half As and half Bs, so the distribution should reflect that reality, which the bell curve does. Just to take this to the extreme to make the point, if your company has all 100 A Players and you have a forced distribution of Top 20%, Middle 70%, and Bottom 10%, it's okay if you place all 100 As in that bell curve, as long as you either don't have labels for the categories or you have accurate labels such as "Top A Player," "Middle A Player," "Bottom A Player."

Okay, I'm going overboard to dispel the "rank and yank" myth, so let's just leave with this bottom-line advice: Use a forced ranking system annually to help measure talent, but do not require the removal of any high performer JUST because they are ranked close to the bottom.

TOPGRADING CAN BE LED BY THE CEO, HUMAN RESOURCES, OR ANY TALENT-ORIENTED MANAGER

There is a radical change taking place in the Topgrading world, NOT one that is obvious when you read the 40 case studies. For more decades than I like to admit, my career has focused on helping CEOs pack their teams with A Players . . . and Topgrading filtered down to lower levels with the CEO driving it. In almost all the case studies in this book, the CEO is the driver of Topgrading. But as I type these words, a sea change is taking place in which Human Resources and individual managers are increasingly taking the lead. For Human Resources, the vehicle to launch Topgrading is the Topgrading Snapshot. For individual managers, the vehicle is their dogged determination to pack their teams with high performers.

I just quoted Bill Conaty, recently retired head of HR at General Electric and probably the most respected HR executive in the world; Bill has said, "Topgrading has to be driven by the CEO, not HR." In the past it made a lot of sense: in Corporate or any division of a company, the head of HR has peers, some of whom will fight Topgrading (though not for good reasons). So, suppose HR has launched Topgrading with a passive CEO, and suppose success hiring was measured and the head of Sales has a terrible record of impulsive mis-hires. Suppose after going through training and learning Topgrading disciplines, the head of Sales wants to hire a fraternity buddy and not conduct the Topgrading Interview or ask the candidate to arrange reference calls with former bosses. HR might push to maintain the Topgrading disciplines, but if the head of Sales runs to the president and persuades the president to override HR . . . you know the end of the story. HR is powerless. Put not so delicately, it's highly unlikely a company will embrace Topgrading launched by HR and achieve 75%+ high performers if the CEO is a softy, unwilling to reinforce the Topgrading disciplines and overly willing to let managers hire and retain low performers.

The biggest trend starting now is for the Topgrading world to be turned on its head, with Human Resources initiating Topgrading every day, successfully. HR is not necessarily advocating Topgrading the top team, which might be a threat to some of their peers. No, HR is quietly introducing the

Topgrading Snapshot to improve hiring at all levels; the Topgrading Snapshot tool threatens no one, is extremely easy to understand and use, saves a huge amount of screening time, and instantly produces significantly better candidates for interviews. Hiring managers are impressed, and HR gets accolades for helping improve talent. My prediction is that CEOs will continue to be the main initiators of Topgrading, but heads of HR and other managers will increasingly take the lead.

Case studies in this book show that the "boss" who Topgrades the entire team doesn't have to be the CEO. Read the Carestream case study in which Bruce Leidal, head of Information Technology, Topgraded his organization. He got permission from Corporate Human Resources, who is pleased with his results. He didn't need a CEO to drive Topgrading. There are hundreds of individual managers who have Topgraded their division or function, but there is a caution: in large companies Corporate Human Resources does not want "loose cannon" managers deviating from approved hiring methods. So either a manager (like Bruce Leidal) gets permission to add Topgrading methods or quietly implements "stealth Topgrading," which at least includes the TORC Technique, the tandem Topgrading Interview, and candidate-arranged reference calls.

WHAT EVIDENCE IS THERE THAT
THE TOPGRADING TIPPING POINT IS COMING?

The talent world today reminds me of a super-modern medical facility that, unfortunately, is lax on cleanliness. There are too many germs and consequently few patients get well. In the mid-1800s Dr. Joseph Lister invented and perfected antiseptic surgical procedures. Lister (that's right, Listerine is named after him) killed germs with antiseptics, and more than 80% of his patients with compound fractures survived. Surgeons not using antiseptics had patients with compound fractures that got infected, and so the survival rate of these patients was low. Similarly, Topgraders commonly pick talent with a better than 80% success rate, whereas the rest of the world stumbles along with a 25% success rate. Remarkably, the non-Topgraders intuitively know they should assess talent better, but, stuck in their old ways, they don't overcome the obstacles to Topgrading; they are like surgeons who fail to use antiseptics. Just as the doctors who embraced antiseptic procedures early on saved 80%+ of their patients, managers who rely on Topgrading Interviews find that more than 80% of the people they hire and promote turn out to be A Players.

The trouble is, it took many years for the antiseptic tipping point to arrive; old docs, set in their ways, had patients with compound fractures who mostly died. Their patients were carried into the surgical room, were treated without antiseptic, and a few days later left in a body bag. In the same hospital, Dr. Lister was down the hall, using antiseptic on the fractures, and his patients survived. It was frustrating for Lister to see how slowly the medical communities in Europe and the United States abandoned their ineffective methods. Ditto for me and Topgrading, but some indications the Topgrading Tipping Point is near are as follows:

- There are now several dozen Topgrading professionals, and the number is increasing every year. Soon there will be hundreds "spreading the message" globally. The number of Topgrading clients served is in the thousands, the number of managers trained is well over 100,000, and hundreds of thousands have purchased Topgrading books and videos, attended Topgrading Workshops, and observed Topgrading speeches.
- Since some of our clients are global, Topgrading is now successfully implemented in over 100 countries.
- Technology, specifically the ability to conduct webinars with superior quality, has made international Topgrading training easier and cheaper.
- Topgrading forms and guides are all digitized, and the online Topgrading Snapshot promises to be the most popular preselection instrument in the world.
- Smart & Associates has three affiliate programs (in Topgrading Resources, Appendix H), enabling people interested in better serving their clients through Topgrading to
  - sell or refer Topgrading products and services (Basic Affiliation Program),
  - become certified to conduct Topgrading Workshops and offer Topgrading consulting (Certified Trainer Affiliate Program). Our plan is to have over 100 certified Trainers within two years,
  - join our team of Tograding professionals. Most have a Ph.D. in psychology and 10+ years of experience Topgrading. They have their own consultancy, and I refer clients to them and peer review their Topgrading Interview reports.

- A global HR consultancy is on the verge of partnering with Smart & Associates and promoting Topgrading to the largest companies in the world. Topgrading visability will increase a lot with a large, professional team of sales representatives calling on leading companies all over the world with one strong message: Topgrading is by far the best hiring/promoting method.

- My son Geoff is CEO of ghSMART, an executive assessment and coaching firm that has achieved great prominence using Topgrading methods; there are two Harvard case studies on Geoff's company, his book *Who* is a best seller, and ghSMART was featured prominently in *The Art of Managing Professional Services: Insights from Leaders of the World's Top Firms* (Broderick).

- A university is seriously considering launching a series of doctoral and master's theses on Topgrading.

- More and more Topgrading companies are not just encouraging but demanding that their vendors embrace Topgrading. As a tiny company, when I needed a software vendor, I used my Networks, who referred me to Tim Yandell at inetUSA. I was prepared to check them out and then make a contract contingent upon their Topgrading, but as it turned out, Tim had been in the audience when I had given a speech years earlier and had already Topgraded his company. Not many CEOs I know would be satisfied explaining disappointing results to shareholders with this message: "Our supply chain had too many C Players."

These are indicators that Topgrading is not a fad. As I stood in the British Museum last year and studied the Joseph Lister exhibit, I identified with how long it took for antiseptics to catch on. Lister's exhibit has furniture from his lab, equipment, notebooks, and vials that presumably contained carbonic acid, his antiseptic. My fantasy has a future Topgrading exhibit in the museum, with pictures on the wall of the Topgrading Interview Guide and the Topgrading Snapshot. Okay, forget that fantasy.

In the meantime, this edition provides 40 case studies with almost all named companies and named CEOs saying Topgrading made their companies more successful; perhaps this book will bring the tipping point a bit closer.

Chapter 2

ALL ABOUT A PLAYERS

The ability to make good decisions regarding people represents one
of the last reliable sources of competitive advantage, since very few
organizations are very good at it.

—Peter Drucker

There is an ever-growing body of research highlighting the impact of talent:*

- Paper plants managed by A Players have 94% higher profits.
- More talented investment banking associates are twice as productive as those average in talent.
- Return to shareholders for companies with top talent practices averages 22% above industry means.
- Top 3% of programmers produce 1,200% more lines of code than the average; top 20% produce 320% more than average.
- Top 3% of salespeople produce up to 250% more than average; top 20% produce up to 120% more.

Proactively seeking and employing the most talented people can have a multiplier effect on the creation of other competitive advantages. High performers—A Players—contribute more, innovate more, work smarter, earn more trust, display more resourcefulness, take more initiative, develop better business strategies, articulate their vision more passionately, implement change more effectively, deliver higher-quality work, demonstrate greater

---

* Ed Michaels, Helen Handfield-Jones, and Beth Axelrod, *The War for Talent* (Boston: Harvard Business School Press, 2001).

teamwork, prevent more problems, attract more A Players, and find ways to get the job done in less time with less cost. It's no coincidence that A Player managers embrace Topgrading so they can attract and retain more A Players who want to be part of organizations that succeed. But you know all of this; I'm probably preaching to the choir.

Topgrading companies throw out statistics such as "We tripled our hiring success" or "We improved our success promoting from 25% to 80%," and while the numbers are impressive, what do they really mean? At the end of this chapter you'll read where all those stats come from, but for "bottom liners," here they are:

- Typical companies find that only 25% of the people they *hire* turn out to be high performers . . . but Topgrading companies achieve 75%, 85%, and even 90%+ success.
- Typical companies find that only 25% of people they *promote* turn out to be A Players . . . yet Topgrading companies achieve 75%+ success.
- CEOs and heads of Human Resources provide case studies and testimonials confirming those hiring/promoting results.
- Typical companies have only 25% to 40% high performers in management . . . yet Topgraded companies achieve 75% and even 90%+ high performers.
- Topgrading companies can improve from 25% high performers in their ranks to 90%, with Topgrading methods.
- The costs of mis-hires, in money and wasted time, are astronomical and avoidable.

Topgraders refer to A Players and high performers, but what exactly are the definitions? And by the way, what exactly is the definition of Topgrading?

WHAT IS TOPGRADING?

Top·grade (täp′grād) *v.* -graded, -grading, -grades, -er. 1. To fill at least 75% of positions in the organization with high performers (A Players) by hiring and promoting people who turn out to be high performers at least 75% of the time.

The word "Topgrade" came from a frustration that the commonly used "upgrade" was lame. If I have 10 C Players and replace one with a B Player, sure enough, I've "upgraded" my team . . . which is still a team that does not perform. Even in the largest, most sophisticated companies, executives talked about "upgrading talent," but no one seemed to have a word that conveyed packing the team with almost all A Players. My son Geoff and I spent endless hours reflecting on my experience helping companies hire and promote better, and co-creating key Topgrading concepts; he and I co-authored an article entitled "Topgrading the Organization,"* which was the first time the word *Topgrade* occurred in print. We needed a more potent word than upgrade. The actual creation of the word came from a brainstorming discussion that went something like this: "Upgrade is weak . . . how about 'better grade'?" . . . "*Hmmm*, no . . . how about 'A team builder'?" . . . "Nope . . . somehow the term has to convey getting almost all top talent in a team." . . . "Hey, how about 'Topgrade'?"

Why Is the Range of 75% to 90% the Standard for Topgrading?

Every Topgrader I know has the goal of 100% high performers for their individual team or, from the CEO's perspective, the entire company. Individual managers have achieved 100% As, but only a couple of companies have (that I know of, and one is a case study in chapter 5) achieved 100% As, and they have less than 100 employees. In previous books 90% As was the cutoff for case studies, because enough leading companies had achieved it to make 90% a high but realistic goal. In this book I lower the cutoff for inclusion to 75% because I don't know of any CEO or manager who has achieved 75% high performers and then says, "That's good enough." And a few of the case studies show less than 75% success because their improvement was nevertheless spectacular or they are just getting into Topgrading, a "work in progress," sure to improve their results. Even companies with 90% or close to 90% success are not satisfied.

For example, a case study client, North American Nursing Education (one of the few cases with a fictitious name), more than tripled their success hiring school deans (from 19% to 87%) but theirs is a work in progress, and their goal is 90%+ for deans . . . and then they will focus on hiring at least 90% A Player instructors. Like other Topgraders, NANE will never be satisfied, even when they have 95% As throughout the company.

Talent is addictive, and when managers are confident that they will

---

* Bradford D. Smart and Geoffrey H. Smart, "Topgrading the Organization," *Directiors & Boards*, 1997.

make only one hiring mistake in four, they are dedicated Topgraders, determined to make only one mistake in 10.

Achieve 75% As hired and promoted, and you'll strive hard to achieve 90%+.

THE NEED FOR TOPGRADING

Forgive me, but the following scenario will be repeated throughout the book, just in case a reader might skim certain chapters and miss the fundamental assumptions underlying Topgrading. Managers enter a new job, review their talent, and—I've heard this thousands of times in oral case studies—those managers decide they have inherited

- 25% high performers and those with high performer potentials;
- 50% "okay," "adequate," but marginal performers who lack the potential to be high performers and are *not* as good as others available for the same pay; and
- 25% chronic underperformers.

Is the glass half empty or half full? If you add 25% high performers to 50% "okay" but not high performers, then you have 75% "okay" or better. That's the "half full" reality most companies live with. But when it comes to talent, A Players consider that particular glass half empty—75% lack even the potential to be high performers, and that is not good enough.

Among the 6,500 executives I've assessed and coached, the A Players were and are not satisfied with that glass half full, so they do everything they can to keep their As, and they replace the chronic low performers. In the meantime, the A Players work extra hard to cover for the inadequacies of the Bs and Cs. Too bad the As spend a lot of time "carrying" lesser performers rather than fully unleashing their own talent!

Thousands of Topgraders have teams that look this:

Topgraders have a "batting average" hiring and promoting that is so much better than 25% that it is smart for them to not be satisfied until almost all on the team are A Players or at least A Potentials.

So, Topgrading means achieving 75%+ A Player/A Potentials by using

- Topgrading hiring methods to bring in high performers;
- Topgrading methods to promote people who turn out to be A Players;
- Topgrading coaching methods to develop A Potentials into A Players (chapter 3 explains methods to develop people and, where impossible, to coach chronic low performers to leave).

DEFINITION OF A PLAYER

The simple definition of A Player is "high performer." Throughout this book I use the terms *A Player* and *high performer* interchangeably, but "high performer" is a bit simplistic. As I mentioned, my son Geoff and I created a more complex definition, and it's worth learning and using in order that you become fully "calibrated," able to distinguish among A Players and others:

A Player: someone in the top 10% of the talent pool available. B Players are in the next 25%, and C Players are in the bottom 65%.

That sounds simple enough, but it has subtle complexities. An A Player is "best of class," in the top 10% of talent available, but what does that mean? "Available" means willing to accept a job offer

- at the given compensation level,
- in that specific company, with a certain organizational culture (family friendly? dirty politics? fast-paced? Topgraded and growing?),
- in that particular industry,
- in that location,
- with specific accountabilities,
- with available resources, and
- reporting to a specific person (A Player candidates are more available to you if you are a positive A Player, not a negative C Player).

Every one of these factors affects "availability," though "at the given compensation level" is the most important. To help you understand some subtleties in the definition, here's a hypothetical scenario: Suppose you had an opening for, say, Systems Manager, paying $75,000. You did a massive recruitment, and 100 candidates sent in their résumé. Suppose further that you hired all 100, one at a time for one year, for a 100-year experiment. At the end of each year, the clock would be wound back one year and you would relive that same year, but with a different Systems Manager. (Does this remind you of the Bill Murray movie *Groundhog Day*?) And at the end of the 100-year experiment, you would look back and rank all 100 of the Systems Managers, from #1 to #100. The top 10% talent, the top 10 in proven value of contribution during the one year, were by definition the A Players. The next 25 (25%) were B Players, and the rest were C Players. Does this make sense? But "high performer" and "top 10% available" require a little more explanation.

INSTEAD OF PAYING MORE FOR A PLAYERS, FOCUS ON GETTING A PLAYERS FOR EVERY JOB, NO MATTER WHAT THE PAY

Topgrading turns the typical hiring logic on its head. Typically, when there is a perceived talent shortfall, Human Resources will be asked to recruit "above the midpoint." That is, following a job analysis and preparation of a job description, a salary range is established, and rather than aim for the midpoint in the range, the company aims higher, to attract the higher level of talent needed. So, it might target candidates at the seventy-fifth percentile of the salary range. "You get what you pay for" is the rationale.

Trouble is, most companies *don't* get what they pay for. With a 75% mis-hire rate, companies are paying for A Players and too often getting B/C Players. Topgrading embraces a different perspective:

Regardless of what you pay people, be sure to get top talent for the salary you can afford.

Topgraders are not cheap; indeed, circumstances described in this chapter might justify paying above the *entire* accepted salary range. But the Topgrader is more rigorous than the non-Topgrader—more thorough in assessment, and more certain to "produce what we pay for."

The Only Good Designations Are A Player and A Potential

Companies that Topgrade initially designate A, B, and C Players, but within about a year they focus on the designations that are most practical, most actionable:

- A Player,
- A Potential, and
- Non-A Player.

Topgraders regard a chronic B Player (unable, despite training and coaching, to rise to A Player status and not judged to be capable of being an A in a different job) as undesirable as a chronic C Player. Neither is good enough. Both C Players without A Potential and B Players without A Potential must be replaced.

An "A Potential" is someone who is predicted to achieve A Player status, usually within 6 to 12 months.

CONDUCT COMPENSATION SURVEYS

If an A Player is someone in the "top 10% of talent available" for the compensation, you (or Human Resources) must do compensation surveys. Google "compensation survey companies" and you will see expensive and inexpensive ("quick and dirty") options.

The amount of compensation necessary to attract a certain level of talent of course varies as talent supply and demand factors change. During the buildup to the Iraq and Afghanistan wars, military engineers were in high demand. In general, during boom times engineering salaries shoot up, and in economic downturns, or when military budgets are cut, they decrease.

Paradoxically, organizations that Topgrade do *not* necessarily pay more for talent than their competitors. Topgraders, in comparison with others, tend to look harder to find talent, screen harder to select the right people, and act more quickly to confront nonperformance.

Organizations that Topgrade do *not* necessarily pay more for talent than their competitors.

For example, suppose you have a team of 10 people (two As, four Bs, and four Cs), with an average comp of $50,000. If you were to Topgrade, maybe you'd replace the four Cs and two Bs with four As, so your team would consist of A Players, still at the $50,000 salary level. Your total comp for the group was cut from $500,000 to $300,000. But Topgraders everywhere would tell you that the benefits are far more, that the chances are the group would be *far* more productive because of course As just are more productive, but also because of another reason. In typical teams with Bs and Cs, the As devote a huge amount of time to preventing and fixing problems of the low performers. So the As perform even better without having to "carry" Bs and Cs.

In typical teams with Bs and Cs, the As devote a huge amount of time to preventing and fixing problems of the low performers.

If you need A Players at a higher salary level (more experienced, to match the competition, or whatever the reason), Topgrade and you might actually be able to cut total comp *and* pay more. Cass Wheeler, former CEO of the American Heart Association and author of *You've Gotta Have Heart,* is persuasive in his argument stating that not-for-profits *can* pay salaries competitive with private industry if they have mostly high performers and not a mixture of As, Bs, and Cs. Wheeler explodes the notion that not-for-profits have to settle for low performers, but his point pertains to for-profits as well. As a hypothetical example, instead of paying 10 people (two As, four Bs, and four Cs) $50,000 per year, or $500,000 total team comp, Topgrade and pay seven A Players an average of $71,000.

Topgrade and you might actually be able to cut total comp *and* pay more.

Topgrading companies, in contrast to their competitors, get disproportionately better talent for the total compensation dollars they spend. A company that begins a serious Topgrading effort finds it easier to recruit top talent because the company suddenly has a brighter future.

A Players are talent magnets.

A Players are the most cost-effective employees, since their talent, the value of their contribution to the organization's performance, exceeds the value contributed by Bs and Cs for exactly the same pay. This is true for all jobs, at every compensation level. Picture two sales organizations with the same budget; the Topgrader has five sales reps, all high performers and highly paid, and the competitor has the same budget spread across 12 sales reps—three As, six Bs, and three Cs. Which sales force would you want?

For the foreseeable future companies will be lean, and people at all levels are now expected to do what two or three people did previously. C and B Players simply can't cut it. Lean companies must have A Players to perform well in increasingly demanding jobs and you will read many case studies in this book that confirm that truism. Despite doing the work of one or two others, A Player managers (with some exceptions) can still enjoy work-personal balance because they can delegate to A Players who avoid most problems and who quickly fix the few problems that occur.

A PLAYERS, BY DEFINITION, EXIST AT ALL SALARY LEVELS

And so do C Players. Why would a board of directors pay a C Player CEO $900,000? They didn't intend to hire a C Player, but the mis-hired CEO turned out to be below the thirty-fifth percentile of executives available at $900,000. The board blew it. And why would an A Player accept a $30,000 job as Night Manager? Perhaps that A Player understands that her night manager job at a fast-food store is the highest-paying job where she qualifies among the top 10% of talent available. If she somehow were hired to manage a restaurant, a job paying $75,000, her lack of experience and training would likely doom her to C Player status, and she would likely fail. For now, she's smart to take a job where, as an A Player, she can succeed and incrementally build her credentials for bigger, higher-paying management positions in the future.

Topgraders like to say that theoretically everyone can be an A Player. Almost everyone can be a top 10% performer in some job, though not necessarily in the job or at the salary level they want. But when people develop to their maximum potential, marvelous career success can result. An extreme example is a woman I know who has Down syndrome. She lives on her own (her parents taught her to be resourceful and independent), and I'll bet that for the (fairly low) pay she receives, she is an A+ Player.

If a supervisor can be an A Player and a CEO of a multi-billion-dollar company can be a C Player, how do we apply a common standard? You simply have to define the "league" they are playing in, the salary range that makes sense, and then determine how much talent can be attracted for that price. A conversation between two hiring managers might go like this:

> Hiring manager 1: "Sally is an A Player director of marketing, at an $85,000 base."

> Hiring manager 2: "You think she's promotable to Vice President Marketing, which has a $110,000 base?"

> Hiring manager 1: "No, I'm sure she's among the top 10% of directors of marketing available at her pay, but she definitely is not in the vice president league yet, not an A Player at $110,000."

Notice that these managers use job titles to define what job falls into what salary range. Another way to pin down how much talent can be attracted to a specific job, in a specific industry/location/company for a specific pay range, is to go online and pay for a salary survey.

WHAT ARE A PLAYER COMPETENCIES?

Figure 2.1 provides an abbreviated set of competencies to give you a feel for how A Players differ from Bs and Cs. This particular example includes competencies for division president; very different competencies would be appropriate for different jobs. Keep in mind that to qualify overall as an A Player, one need not meet all of the A Player competencies. Plenty of C Players, for example, are very intelligent, honest, and customer-focused but short on drive, leadership, and resourcefulness.

That explains a theoretical definition of A/B/C, but it will take some work to make it practical, for you to be "calibrated," to distinguish among them in a Topgrading Interview. It's relatively easy to judge salespeople in most industries, just as it is easy to determine who are top 10% professional athletes: performance is relatively objective. (Maybe not; in every sports bar in the world there are loud disagreements about who are the A, B, and C Players on our team vs. the opposing team.) But for most jobs, you must immerse yourself, finding many ways to judge how much talent you can get for the compensation. To accurately distinguish among A, B, and C Players for, say, systems manager, you might:

- create a Job Scorecard that specifies numeric accountabilities for performance and numeric minimum ratings (in surveys) on key competencies;
- run ads, collect résumés, and interview candidates for systems manager;
- collect information on your competitors' systems managers by asking vendors about them;
- in Topgrading Interviews of IT directors, follow the Topgrading Interview Guide and get appraisals of their subordinates, including systems managers;
- participate in professional organizations, to meet systems managers;
- perform compensation surveys (Google "salary surveys");
- ask all your IT managers to offer opinions on how much pay attracts how much talent for systems manager; and
- ask recruiters to do a talent assessment of systems managers, utilizing their files and their skills at getting people in companies to give them information. One client asked a search firm to do a total analysis of competitors' executive teams.

Figure 2.1
Summary of Critical Competencies for Upper-Level Manager

	High Performer A Player	Adequate B Player	Low Performer C Player
Overall Talent Level	Top 10% of those available at this salary level.	65th–89th percentile available at this salary level.	Below the 65th percentile available at this salary level.
Problem Solving	A "quick study" able to rapidly perform complex analyses.	Smart; "average" insight.	Has difficulty coping with complex situations.
Leadership	Executes needed change; highly adaptive and able to inspire the organization.	Favors modest change; so there is a lukewarm "followership."	Prefers the status quo; lacks credibility so people don't follow.
Energy/Passion	Very high energy level; fast-paced; 55 (+) hour workweeks (plus home e-mail); driven to succeed.	Motivated; energetic at times.	Dedicated; inconsistent pace.

Resourcefulness/Initiative	Impressive ability to find ways over, around, or through barriers; can-do attitude.	Occasionally finds a solution; relies on others to "figure it out."	Defeated by obstacles; constantly "delegates" to supervisors.
Topgrading	Selects high performers and employees with potential; redeploys chronic underperformers.	Selects a few high performers.	Selects mostly underperformers; tolerates mediocrity.
Training/Development/ Coaching	Coaches and trains each team member to turboboost performance and personal/career growth.	Performs annual performance reviews; "spotty" coaching.	Inaccessible; hypercritical, stingy with praise; late/shallow with feedback.
Team Building	Creates focused, collaborative, results-driven teams.	May want teamwork but does not make it happen.	Drains energy from others; actions prevent synergy.
Track Record	Consistently excellent performance.	Meets some (not all) key constituency expectations.	Sporadically meets expectations.
Integrity	"Ironclad."	Generally honest.	"Bends the rules."
Communication	Excellent oral/written skills.	Average oral/written skills.	Mediocre.

As managers become calibrated, they inevitably make judgments about the talent reporting to them. Topgrading involves not just hiring and promoting As, but after the performance-management system identifies chronic underperformers, redeploying them. As a practical matter, we as outside professionals and experienced Topgrading managers develop a keen sense of which people internally are truly As or not. Managers in general are confident their high performers *are* A Players when they say

- high performers we hire from competitors say our reputation is that we have superior talent;
- our performance-management system is solid, with stretch goals, a culture of real accountability, and top bonuses only for truly outstanding performance;
- managers are given top performance ratings when rated by A Players;

- our annual talent reviews have integrity because they identify high and low perormers; and
- someone we consider an A Player has no fatal flaws—all critical competencies, such as integrity, resourcefulness, Topgrading, etc., are given high ratings.

As you can see, there is no one, single, perfectly valid way of designating someone an A Player. A pole-vaulter clearing the bar at 20 feet (close to the world record) is certainly among the top 10% in the world. A candidate who has exceeded performance expectations in the past three jobs may be an A Player in your company, but only if the Job Scorecard matches the person's talents, if the person's career goals are apt to be realized in the job, if there will be a good culture fit, and . . . oh, yeah . . . if you will be a highly respected boss. The bad news is that whether a candidate will be an A Player in your job depends on so many things. The good news is that Topgrading methods address every one of those "many things."

RESOURCEFULNESS IS
THE MOST IMPORTANT COMPETENCY

Resourcefulness is a composite of several competencies. It's energy, passion, analytic skills, and persistence wrapped into one. In common terms, resourcefulness is the brains and drive to figure out how to get over, around, or through barriers to success. A Players *all* exude resourcefulness, in spades. They just don't give up, and when challenged by opportunities or seemingly hopeless setbacks, their mind is going, 24/7, to somehow snatch success out of the jaws of defeat.

My daughter Kate and I wrote a book called *Smart Parenting: How to Raise Happy, Can-Do Kids.** Actually the original title was *Resourcefulness Parenting*, but resourcefulness just isn't an exciting word. The book is full of fun exercises, tested over 30 years, to help kids become can-do kids, leaders, responsible decision makers in all aspects of their lives. It's kind of like what you want in your team: you want them to be resourceful and come up with ways to prevent problems and fix them when they occur, rather than running to you, expecting you to make decisions. So you coach them to look ahead, anticipate opportunities and problems, and to figure out how to make things successful.

---

* You can order this at the Topgrading Shop at www.Topgrading.com.

Certainly managers have to be a lot more resourceful than grocery clerks, but for almost all individual contributor jobs (teacher, programmer, engineer, sales rep), resourcefulness is the most important competency for their job, too. So in Topgrading Workshops, just before people get into tandem teams and conduct a Topgrading Interview, we advise them, "In every response to every question, look for indications of resourcefulness." Sometimes resourcefulness doesn't kick in and become a strength until well into an A Player's career, perhaps when they finally report to someone who encourages and rewards it. C Players never seem to develop it. Constantly take notes on how resourcefulness is exhibited—or not—and you'll see that winners, people who earn excellent performance ratings, always describe how they accomplished things by using resourcefulness.

The trouble with resourcefulness, as everyone knows, is that it can be directed to achieve immoral, unethical, or illegal ends. Watch a TV special on business crooks and you'll marvel at how resourceful the crooks were and wonder, "Why didn't they use that resourcefulness to achieve success honestly?"

BRAD'S STRANGEST CLIENT (COUP ATTEMPT, BRIBE ATTEMPT, TORTURED SIX MONTHS, WORTH $.5 BILLION, JAIL TIME)!

Okay, you're starting to get brain cramps sorting through all these Topgrading distinctions, so it's time for some mental chewing gum. If you aren't interested in my strangest interviews, I won't be offended if you skip ahead. But this is a story of a highly resourceful bad guy. Of all my in-depth Topgrading Interviews, Juan's is the strangest and most interesting.

Juan headed a global financial services company (since his company was a client, I changed names and also used a fictitious industry) generally considered to be the most innovative in the world. As a child Juan was reared to prepare to overthrow the dictator, and at 20 years of age, he made the attempt, but failed. He and his friend were strung up, the dictator sliced off his friend's private parts, and when the dictator was about to do the same with him, he urinated in the dictator's face. Or so he told me.

The dictator decided to torture rather than immediately kill Juan, so he put Juan in a box similar to a coffin, and he was kept barely alive. An artist from Juan's country painted a modern picture portraying Juan in the box, with the lights of truth and freedom cascading off of the box, and I bought the painting (which is now in someone's basement). The dictator was overthrown six months later, Juan was hospitalized another six months, and 20 years later founded his company, with offices in 150 countries. To emerge from the torture box to mold a respected global company must have required resourcefulness, drive, brains, and guts. You're thinking, "Brad, this guy sounds like a hero, so where's the negative?" You'll see.

Juan hired me to help Topgrade the top three levels of his company, a three-year project. Juan was the only senior executive not to go through the Topgrading process with me. I told him that he should go through the Topgrading process, so I could help build teams that would work best for him. "You might find out something I don't want you to know, Brad," he said. Indeed!

Early in my consulting engagement Juan invited me to go to Las Vegas, promising that we'd make $250,000 his secret way, and we'd have fun ("private jet, penthouse suite, no wives—just the guys, heh-heh"). I'd heard Juan "fooled around a lot," but not with women inside the company. I was curious as to why Vegas hotels would pay all our expenses and then write us checks for $250,000, but didn't ask. Needless to say, I declined Juan's offer and he never asked me again. It didn't occur to me that Juan had a gambling addiction, because he showed me his net worth (in an estate document)—a half billion dollars.

Juan had a huge personality and ego. I witnessed his ordering a U.S. senator to "get your ass over here now." I sat in on a meeting with 50 participants plus eight translators, and Juan masterfully molded the opinions of the group so that he would get exactly what he wanted. In a champagne event where anyone else would toast three heads of state with grace and poise, Juan got away with an outrageous dirty joke. I would have loved to put Juan though a Topgrading Interview and talk to people who had known him over the years, because he was unique and fascinating. But it never happened. The Topgrading engagement was packing the organization with talent and Juan was doing well as the leader, so it didn't occur to me that Juan's idiosyncrasies might include stealing from the company.

When my Topgrading assignment was over, we had a final dinner in Washington, DC, at the Watergate Hotel. We toasted each other and said good-bye, with my wondering what the heck I didn't know about Juan.

Two weeks later the FBI marched into Juan's offices, and just as in the first *Wall Street* movie, he did the perp walk. Juan had bribed 10 consultants, contractors, and others to give him kickbacks on their contracts, apparently to support his gambling. He'd take them to Las Vegas, get them girls, and persuade them to participate in kickback schemes. The consultants didn't do much work, which caused them some legal problems. I was the only one of the consultants and contractors who was never even called by the FBI, I guess because there were so many of my reports that showed I actually did the work for which I invoiced them.

Juan tried to frame someone to take the fall for stealing, but it didn't work. He went to jail, was released three years later, returned to his home country, came back to the United States, and was arrested and jailed again for some additional illegalities.

Phew! Why, when I suspected that Juan was a sociopath, didn't I walk away from the engagement? I didn't know he'd bribed anyone, taken kickbacks, or had broken any laws, and I'd only heard vague rumors of the details of his Las Vegas trips and his marital difficulties. And as mentioned, he showed me the figures in the huge estate he managed. But somehow, when the truth came out, I wasn't shocked. I wonder how much of Juan's darker side I might have seen had he participated in the full Topgrading process.

SEPARATE A/B/C DESIGNATIONS FOR THE CURRENT JOB FROM A/B/C DESIGNATIONS FOR PROMOTABILITY

Large companies, and all companies in a fast-growth mode, are naturally interested in screening talent not just for the present but for future jobs, promotions. They want enough promotable people to fill a lot of positions with internal candidates, but not so many promotable people that many promotables are not promoted fast enough and quit. It's in your best interest to hire enough promotable people, but not everyone is equally promotable, so you can use the following scale:

A1: A Player, probably promotable two levels
A2: A Player, probably promotable one level
A3: A Player, but probably not promotable

A Topgraded organization expecting rapid growth has almost all A Players, including a lot more A1s and A2s than A3s. Some companies don't have a need for A3s—A Players who are not promotable. In CPA firms, for example, typically the policy is "up or out," and if someone is judged to lack partner potential, they eventually will be let go. However, fast-growth companies need A1s and A2s, but also some A3s. A company's succession plan usually includes a chart indicating who the A1s, A2s, and A3 Players will be for the next three to five years. Line managers must be able to look at the charts and say, "It will be impossible to achieve our strategic goals because we lack the bench strength." Or, "Okay, all of our managers are A Players, but only 20% are promotable. That's fine, because we are not going to be adding management jobs for several years."

An added value in defining an A Player as top 10% of talent available at all salary levels is *not* demeaning lower-level people just because they are not promotable. A Players are not just the future superstars, future presidents, or #1 salespeople. Everyone in the company should be an A Player, and proud of it. A terrific store manager may not be promotable, but why demean her by saying, "She's not an A Player"? You don't see a Walmart greeter awarded an "Employee of the Month" pin saying, "C Player Greeter."

B Players as Portrayed in the Media Are Usually A3s

Since 2003, articles have appeared extolling the virtues of B Players. The common theme is, "There are too many neglected B Players, super capable middle managers, reliable workers who know how to get things done, who regularly go the extra mile for the company. They don't have the fancy MBA and will never be a top executive, but they are terrific, valuable employees." Hey, you just described not a B Player, but an *A Player, an A3*, who may not be promotable but who is among the top 10% of talent available within the pay scale for a mid-manager.

Why B Players Are Not as Valuable as A3 Players

B Player	A3 Player
Not promotable	Not promotable
Works medium hard	Works very hard
Delivers marginal results	Delivers A results for exactly the same compensation as the B Player

Most companies must hire some promotable people, do succession planning, and build talent "benches." But companies failing to Topgrade this year waste their time talking about having all A Players in five years. It starts *now*, or "it ain't" Topgrading. The great Topgraders say *now* is the best time to use Topgrading methods to hire and promote the best. Managers who delay and eventually roll out Topgrading always wish they'd started sooner.

PERFORMANCE-MANAGEMENT SYSTEMS IN TOPGRADING COMPANIES MAKE "MEETS PERFORMANCE EXPECTATIONS" THE STANDARD FOR A PLAYERS

High performer is a term most people can relate to, but in a lot of performance-management systems an employee who receives an "Exceeds Expectations" rating is considered a high performer, and one who receives a "Meets Performance Expectations" rating is *not*. Topgraded companies eventually raise the performance bar so that "Meets Performance Expectations" is for A Players, high performers. It makes no sense for "Exceeds" to be used for As, and "Meets" for Bs, when the goal is for *everyone* to be a high performer.

Think of what it means when "Meets Performance Expectations" is for high performers, not so-so performers. Topgrading is not some simple project, sending managers to Topgrading Workshops to learn more thorough hiring methods. It changes the DNA of a company—eventually as more and more A Players inhabit the company, all the people systems change, including training and development, compensation, and succession planning, because a high level of performance is expected of everyone. Annual talent reviews are most meaningful and useful when "Meets" = "High Performer."

Can A Players Be Incompetent?

Yes. One reason could be that you've set the compensation too low. Suppose you own an NFL team and you're crazy enough to set the maximum salary at $25,000. Suppose you nevertheless got 500 applications from guys who are all out of shape and never played football, but applied anyway. No matter what screening system you used, the low pay that only attracted incompetent candidates would assure that you would not hire enough talent to win even one game.

You *must* hire A Players at the right salary level—in the right (compensation) league.

Another way you can wind up with a poor-performing A Player is if the person is stifled by the boss; or if a product or project is canceled, rendering the job of the A Player who ran it unnecessary; or if the performance bar is set so high that no one, not even the #1 A Player in the universe, could succeed; or if the person is a "square peg in a round hole."

We Topgrading professionals sometimes are asked to assess and coach management teams, and we find many more managers with A Potentials than CEOs thought they had. The A Potentials who had not been performing well quickly perform at the A level when put in a job better matching their talents, or assigned to a boss who will unleash rather than stifle them.

You can use Topgrading Audit methods (see chapter 6, "The Art of Topgrading") to actually help some Bs and even Cs move into the A category.

A PLAYERS CAN BECOME B AND C PLAYERS IN FAST-GROWING COMPANIES

When the company had $10 million in sales, paying $50,000 for an operations manager was sufficient to attract and hold the necessary A Player talent. The company grew to $100 million in three years. Naturally, mid-managers' salaries rose. The operations manager job became more complex and the operations manager is paid $100,000, not because he is worth it but because the job is now running three plants and it's worth paying that much for. But what if the company outgrew the manager? It happens all the time, so an A Player can drop to B Player, and drop to C Player—not because their absolute level of talent has diminished, but because their talent has declined *in relation* to the salary they are paid, for the more complex and difficult job.

The typical solution is to narrow the person's scope. So, the A Player sales rep who, in the fast-growing company, was promoted to Vice President Sales, qualified as an A Player. But with rapid growth in the company he was promoted to Vice President Sales and Marketing, and is performing at a B or C level. When assessed using Topgrading methods, he is "in over his head." It might be clear that the person is weak in marketing, so becoming Vice President Sales once again is best, and the company finds a vice president marketing.

When to Overpay A Players

Forward-looking, growing companies will *hire for the talent and compensation level needed three years from now.* We have a client (a biotech company) that grew from $2 million to $500 million in five years. Luckily they were prepared: they had sensibly hired senior managers for the $500 million level when the company was founded.

Another situation in which it may be wise to "overpay" for an A Player at a high level of absolute talent is in a turnaround situation. Your pool of candidates may be too small and undertalented, due to the unattractiveness of the employment prospects of joining a troubled company. Therefore, you may decide to pay a higher level of compensation in order to be able to attract sufficiently talented A Players.

Private equity companies sometimes buy a company cheap and try to turn it around. They parachute in a talented CEO, and offer equity as an incentive. Perhaps a CEO of a $150 million company in the industry would be paid a base of $250,000 plus bonus, but the private equity company offers a $750,000 package. Their goal in "overpaying" the CEO is to dramatically increase the value of the company, to turn it into a $500 million growth company, and when they succeed, because the CEO succeeded, the CEO wasn't "overpaid" at all. A lot of companies have to "overpay" necessary talent to compensate for an unattractive location, a declining industry, or Chapter 11 bankruptcy status. All those quotation marks mean that even though someone might be paid considerably more than is typical for a job, the unique circumstances might totally justify the pay.

Not to raise a sore point, but if you have a negative reputation as a boss, you'll have more difficulty attracting top talent; sharp candidates will ask questions and find out from vendors, competitors, and your team that you are difficult to work for. Let's put this in a positive way: some of the case study CEOs converted their "difficult" leadership image and style into a very positive style, with the result that they have been able to attract and hold far better talent. And they would say their company is a lot more successful and that Topgrading was more successful because they improved their leadership style.

In many situations people are overpaid in relation to their skills and marketability in general, but are *not overpaid* in relation to what the company requires, given the negative facts. Granting a 50% signing bonus plus additional "battle pay" to work in difficult circumstances might be exactly what the company needs to attract and hold A Players at the talent level necessary to succeed.

When to Pay Less for A Players

You can pay less for talent when there are economic downturns; more talent is available (cheap), and low performers expect to be let go. But be careful! Don't underpay your people too much, or when the economy turns around your high performers who felt taken advantage of are apt to leave.

A top salesman in a client company earned $1.6 million just before the dot-com bubble burst, and was happy to earn one-fifth that amount a year later because that was what he was worth in the downturn. It's your challenge as a Topgrader to stay on top of this issue, to adjust what you pay in relation to economic circumstances.

Early retirees sometimes offer a lot of talent, cheap. Many A Players 55 years of age take the parachute along with C Players, but are bored not working. The A Players typically do not want to fully retire and would be delighted to take an easier job, for less pay. There is an emerging industry that provides part-time and short-term (six months?) full-time engagements for executives. This is a great opportunity for highly talented former high-powered executives who are bored with retirement, maybe could use some extra cash, or who would just love "getting back in the game" but do not want to work full-time.

Some talented people want part-time jobs to raise kids or pursue other lifestyle preferences, and increasingly companies want to avoid pension and health-care costs by outsourcing. You know this—very often you can get more "talent for the buck" using contractors rather than full-time employees.

**If a permanent full-time job isn't warranted,
get a lot of talent for fewer bucks by hiring a part-timer.**

Entire industries, retailing for example, favor part-timers to lessen health-care costs. Outsourcing is on the rise, essentially institutionalizing what the techies predicted—that many would become "free agents," accepting "engagements" instead of "permanent" full-time jobs. As a management psychologist I frequently hear managers say, "There's no way I'll get approval to add that (marketing assistant, recruiter, strategy analyst) job." I say, "How about using your Networks to find a freelancer or contractor to do that project?" After that you may determine that they are worth hiring.

"Try Out" People Who Are Unemployed Before Hiring Them Full-Time

Particularly in a down economy there are a lot of very talented people out of work. As a Topgrading professional, I almost always recommend, "Hire So-and-So as a consultant, to do some project for a few months, to be sure the person will be an A Player who fits the culture." Tony Hsieh, CEO of

Zappos, does this for entry workers; they are in training for several weeks and then sent home (with a nice check) if they don't work out.

When to Hire Underqualified People

Occasionally firms hire high-potential people who will be superior performers in future roles but may seem underqualified initially. For their pay (not much) they have a lot of talent but need to be trained. So the new hire may be a B Player initially with the potential to become an A Player. For example, a CPA firm might hire a recent college graduate who has a limited technical background but exceptional intelligence, energy, and tenacity. The company believes that the new recruit will be a B Player auditor in the first year, but become an A Player in the second year. At the time the entry-level auditor is hired, should she be referred to as a B Player or an A Player? Clients have all labeled such people "A Potential."

Another example: When companies are dissatisfied with prospects within their industry, they appropriately recruit outside their industry, seeking candidates with superior talent and potential but who will have to experience a learning curve as they transition into a new industry. Usually they initially appear underqualified in relation to their high pay, but later when their results shine, they prove they were A Potential all along.

My rule of thumb is this: If the person was a B Player but became an A Player within a year, A Potential is the correct designation.

Get "Calibrated" to Correctly Judge A/B/C Players

This chapter has been devoted to ways you can become "calibrated." Validly judging if someone is an A, A Potential, B, or C Player requires never-ending research. Performing a compensation survey is useful but not sufficient to make you "calibrated." If you are a manager who must consider investing in new equipment or software, it's your job to get calibrated, to accurately judge the value of your investments. Purchasing professionals and financial analysts devote a lot of time and energy to become calibrated in equipment expenditures. It's exactly the same with people. Topgraders say:

**Managers *must* become calibrated as a Topgrader
in order to qualify as an A Player.**

To summarize, become calibrated by asking recruiters and vendors to assess your competition and your team, doing compensation studies, using Topgrading Interviews to assess people, recruiting possible replacements, joining organizations, and doing annual talent reviews. You can get Topgrading training and then conduct Topgrading Interviews in tandem; since two heads are better than one, your combined perspective is apt to be pretty good. To broaden your perspective and accelerate your becoming "calibrated" to judge A/B/C Players, interview more candidates, from more companies than necessary.

Finally, if you are a senior executive, consider asking a Topgrading professional to conduct Topgrading Interviews; for no additional charge you can be the tandem interviewer and accelerate your becoming calibrated by observing the professional, getting feedback and suggestions from the pro after the interview, and learning how to sort the "wheat from the chaff" in all the interview notes by having thorough discussions of candidates afterward.

TALENT STATISTICS: WHERE DO ALL THESE STATS COME FROM?

I don't want to bore you with too much information, but you keep reading about how companies have 25% hiring and promoting success prior to Topgrading and improve up to 90%+ with Topgrading, and perhaps you'd like some more information on where those numbers come from. You may not want all this information, and if that's the case, skip to the next chapter.

In Typical Companies Only 25% of Managers Hired Turn Out to Be A Players

For decades Topgrading professionals have been accumulating statistics on the success managers have hiring and promoting people. Here are the results from:

- **65,000 case studies.** I interviewed over 6,500 senior managers, with an average of 10 jobs each, and I asked them for every job what percent of the people they hired turned out to be high performers. That's 65,000 oral case studies, and they said only 25% of the people they hired in fact turned out to be A Players. (If you've followed Topgrading, you realize that the number 6,500 has not changed much in years. Why? I assess or coach only a handful of people annually—CEOs/presidents and candidates for those jobs—these days. I'm devoting more of my energies to educating managers in Topgrading. Smart & Associates Topgrading professionals, however, continue to serve clients by offering a "second opinion" on candidates for executive jobs, where mishires are extremely expensive.)

- **Workshop attendees.** In hundreds of workshops the first exercise is to ask attendees: "What percent of people you have hired and promoted in recent years have turned out to be the high performers you hoped for, expected, and paid for and the only other category is a mis-hire?" Again: 25% success hiring, pre-Topgrading.
- **Survey of Topgrading professionals.** I sent out a questionnaire to consultants at ghSMART and the Topgrading professionals at Smart & Associates, aggregating our combined experience of over 300 years and with over 2,000 companies. The results:

Topgrading Professionals' Estimates of Managerial
Hiring (without Topgrading Methods)

A Players/A Potentials	25%
B Players/without A Potentials	50%
C Players/without A Potentials	25%

In other words, based on our having professionally assessed talent in thousands of companies, our collective opinion is that 75% of managers hired externally (*without* Topgrading methods) are mistakes, underperformers, mis-hires. It's not that these people are total failures; it's just that Topgrading professionals believe better performers were available, but the client hiring methods prior to Topgrading simply did not let them in the door.

- **Survey of top Human Resources executives.** I met with just the #1 Human Resources professionals at just Global 100 companies, the largest 100 in the world. They said only 20% of managers hired turned out to be the expected high performers, meaning that 80% or their management hires are disappointments, mistakes, mis-hires!

- **Case study results.** Dozens of case studies reported in this and other Topgrading books report having more than tripled their success hiring high performers, A Players, using Topgrading methods. You'll see these stats throughout this book: the average improvement in high performers hired/promoted for the 40 case studies was from 26% to 85%.
- **Survey of search firm results.** When search firms are paid to recruit talent, do they deliver? Some outstanding search professionals embrace the A Player standard, but most don't. (If your search executive sent you this book, chances are they embrace Topgrading methods.) We surveyed over 500 senior managers, who reported that when they paid for retained searches, only 32% of those searches produced a candidate who was hired. They reported that in only 21% of searches an A Player was hired.

Combining these various studies, it seems that a consensus among highly informed people is that no more than about 25% of managers hired turn out to meet the A Player, the high performer, standard. The cold reality is that the average company suffers a 75% failure rate hiring people.

ONLY 25% OF PEOPLE PROMOTED IN MOST COMPANIES TURN OUT TO BE A PLAYERS

Most large companies emphasize promoting from within. Human Resources processes measure performance and provide annual assessments, and since most large companies have extensive 360-degree surveys, feedback, coaching, training, and development processes, they should be terrific at selecting someone they know for promotion, right? Wrong! All those observations of managers do *not* assure that those promoted will function as A Players. Here are major sources of data on promotion success:

- **The McKinsey "War for Talent" studies.** Those studies have shown that most managers, even in high-performing companies, believe top executives don't really know who are the As, Bs, or Cs. A lot of what we all do professionally is assess candidates for hire and promotion because clients know our recommendations result in far greater success picking people.
- **Our surveys of top executives and Topgrading professionals.** The following chart shows negative results when companies promote people.

Estimates of the Quality of Managers in Fortune 500 Companies Promoted from Within

	200 CEOs/Presidents' Estimates	Topgrading Professionals' Estimates
After Promoted, are Judged A Player/A Potential	25%	20%
After Promoted, are Judged B Player (without A Potential)	52%	56%
After Promoted, are Judged C Player (without A Potential)	23%	24%

Respondents in these studies were asked about results when Topgrading methods were not used.

- **Case studies in this book.** The average promotion success prior to Topgrading is about 25%.
- **Surveys of workshop attendees.** The same 25% promotion success comes from our surveys of workshop attendees and the (workshop) survey I did of Global 100 Human Resources executives.
- **My 65,000 oral case studies.** For decades I asked interviewees what their success was not just hiring, but promoting, and the average success my interviewees claimed was only about 25%.

AVERAGE COMPANIES HAVE 25% TO 40% A PLAYERS IN MANAGEMENT, WHILE TOPGRADERS ACHIEVE 75% TO 90% A PLAYERS

If typical companies (not benefiting from Topgrading) experience only 25% success rate in hiring and promoting managers and individual performers, it stands to reason that they have a talent mix including only a minority of high performers. They "pick away" at chronic low performers, but as has been demonstrated, if the replacements turn out to be one-fourth As, one-half Bs, and one-fourth just Cs, progress is slow.

Why is the initial baseline estimate of internal talent (prior to Topgrading) so broad—"25% to 40% A Players"? Because some companies do achieve 40% As without Topgrading. Also, we Topgrading professionals are asked to assess the top team prior to any replacements, and we typically identify a *lot* more As and A Potentials than CEOs think they have. We find talented people in the wrong job ("square peg in a round hole") and we find formerly talented people beaten down by a C Player boss. Finally, using the coaching methods explained in this book, many B and occasionally a few C Players actually move into the A Player category. It's obviously a lot less disruptive to an organization if only 10% of people are replaced, rather than significantly more. But we find that when we ask large groups for their estimates of talent, it's lower than what we personally find among clients.

For example, we asked 100 CEOs and presidents to estimate the percent A, B, and C managers in U.S. companies and they reported as follows:

23% A Players and A Potentials

52% B Players without A Potential

25% C Players without A Potential

Why Companies Claim They Have 75% Good Managers

Are you getting overwhelmed with all of these numbers? We're almost done! But please bear with me for this final point in this chapter: for talent-oriented managers, "good" is not good enough.

In speeches I sometimes ask the audience of business owners to write on a card how many managers they have who are good or better than good. The results are tallied and it usually comes out to be about 75%. But then I ask them, "How many of you would hire someone who, in performance appraisals in the last decade on a scale of Excellent, Very Good, Good, Only Fair, and Poor received only *Good* ratings. No hands go up, because that means the candidate received zero Very Good or Excellent ratings in the past 10 years. Let me restate that: how would you view a candidate who said, "In the past I have had four bosses and, let me think . . . not one would rate my overall performance Excellent . . . and hmmm, nope, I don't think any would rate my performance Very Good . . . and hmmm, yep, I'm pretty sure all would rate my performce Good." Does this sound like an A Player?

Bottom line, to talent-oriented managers, "good" is not good enough.

Returning to all our stats, if A Players are Excellent/Very Good and B Players are Good, then most companies have 75% managers who are Good or better. But when you become a Topgrader, and you realize you can hire A Players 75% of the time, and soon 85% of the time of the time, someone who is a B Player—"Good"—is no longer good enough. Topgrading is all about increasing the percentage of high performers, A Players, and not being satisfied with people (Bs) who never are worthy of a Very Good or Excellent rating.

How Dramatically Can Topgrading Improve Talent?

The average company today hires only 25% A Players, promotes only 25% A Players, and has 25% to 40% A Players in management. Topgraded companies, including those you'll read about in chapter 5 ("Topgrading Innovations: Case Studies"), have much better results.

The Topgrading Advantage

	Typical Company Results	Topgraded Company Results
Percent Hired Who Turn Out to Be A Players	25%	75%+
Percent Promoted Who Turn Out to Be A Players	25%	75%+
Percent A Players in Management	25%–40%	75%+

The case studies in this book have somewhat better results overall; the average improvement hiring and promoting people is 26% to 85%. Details of the case study statistics are reported in chapter 5.

SUMMARY

Most companies know they have too few A Players, but they've given up and accepted their mediocrity. Managers with a 25% hiring and promoting success rate often conclude, "It's so costly and disruptive to hire four people, fire three, and get an A, I won't bother trying to get all A Players." Topgrading companies hire 75%+ As.

Every manager, from supervisor to CEO, is charged with the awesome responsibility of improving company performance. Topgrading provides *the* most powerful lever to achieve success. You can ask yourself if you now have a team consisting of the top 10% of the talent available, and if not, "Why am I paying for A Players and not getting them?" You can measure your hiring success, and if only 25% or 40% of those you hire turn out to be high performers, you can ask, "Shouldn't I start using the most effective selection methods available to screen people and at least . . . *at least* . . . double my success?" You can ask why so many B/C Players are causing you problems when, for the same salaries, A Players can prevent and fix problems, making you and the company more successful. If you are the decision maker, the function or business head, or the CEO, what more important decision can you make than choosing how you pick talent?

Enough statistics and enough questions! Let's move on to the practical steps you can take to improve your results picking high performers.

Chapter 3

12 TOPGRADING STEPS TO HIRING 90% HIGH PERFORMERS

Those who build great companies understand that the ultimate throttle on growth for any great company is not the markets, or technology, or competition, or products. It is one thing above all others: the ability to get and keep enough of the right people.
—Jim Collins, *Good to Great*

This chapter is the culmination of decades of refinement of Topgrading methods. There are 12 Topgrading Hiring Steps, which are only slightly different for promoting. Master and implement each and every one and you'll be most likely to achieve 90% high performers. Each step that is skipped results in avoidable, costly mis-hires. If you tried Topgrading Lite and love your improved results, no doubt you'll want to improve on those results, and this chapter teaches you how.

These 12 Topgrading Hiring Steps are the basic building blocks of Topgrading. But before learning them, let's lay a bit more of a foundation—the Topgrading Vision and the Topgrading truth serum, or TORC Technique.

TOPGRADING VISION

Let's start with the big picture—what the 12 Topgrading Hiring Steps are, what problems they solve, what Topgrading skills you can learn, and if you apply them, what results you will achieve. Please read all of this in two pages in Appendix C: Topgrading Vision, page 289. This is your road map.

THE TORC TECHNIQUE "TRUTH SERUM"

A key concept that makes the 12 steps work is the TORC Technique. I've briefly mentioned it, but this is such a powerful hiring technique that it merits elaboration. It costs you nothing to implement it and you can begin using it successfully after reading the next few pages.

You know that one of the most serious problems in hiring is dishonesty: weaker candidates fake their résumés and sanitize their interviews with hype, omissions, and deliberate falsehoods, and they get away with it because hiring companies rarely conduct reference calls with former bosses of candidates.

For decades Topgraders have enjoyed a wonderful luxury—talking with candidates who are honest and sharp. How? They simply administer the Topgrading truth serum, the TORC (Threat of Reference Check) Technique.

If you aren't familiar with the TORC Technique, you're in for a treat—it will assure you fewer costly mis-hires. That's the good news. The bad news is that I've taught people the TORC Technique and found that quite a few didn't adopt it because they had some questions that weren't answered. So more good news—I'll first explain the TORC Technique, and then answer many common questions.

What Is the TORC Technique?

It's the Threat of Reference Check (TORC) Technique which lets candidates know, at every step in the hiring process, that a final step in the hiring process is for *them* to arrange personal reference calls with former bosses and others their interviewers (that would include *you*) want to talk with.

This "threat of reference check" scares C Players away—good! C Players can't get their former bosses to talk to you and C Players wouldn't want you to talk with them anyway. Decades of experience confirm that high performers *do* get their former bosses to talk and are happy to make the arrangements.

How and When Do You Tell Candidates About TORC?

Tell candidates at every step in your hiring process. Even before you begin the 12 Topgrading Hiring Steps, include it in the Careers section of your Web site.

The TORC Technique should be in your application form. Topgrading Hiring Step #3 is using the Topgrading Career History Form as your application form (tailored to your company) because it requests a *lot* more useful information about a candidate than any preselection tool on the planet. "Tailoring" the Topgrading Career History Form means making it look like a clone of your existing form and adding unique questions specific to your company or industry, translating it into any language, and modifying instructions to include TORC. Most companies choose a short explanation of TORC in the Career History Form instructions, but some prefer a longer explanation.

Short explanation: A final step in the hiring process is for candidates to arrange personal reference calls with former supervisors as well as others we may choose.

Long explanation: A final step in the hiring process is for candidates to arrange personal reference calls with former supervisors and others we may choose. There are three reasons for this:

(a) *Your development.* Candid insights of managers and others can be used to help you move smoothly into your next job and can help you create a powerful Individual Development Plan.

(b) *Verification.* Discussions with former managers and others will add credibility to the information you have provided throughout the hiring process.

(c) *Ease.* It's difficult for us to get former supervisors and others to talk with us, but high performers can arrange for those personal discussions.

After prescreening candidates from their completed Topgrading Career History Form and Topgrading Snapshot (mentioned already, but explained in Hiring Step #4), candidates are screened on the telephone. In the first minutes of that call, you again tell candidates that a final step in hiring is for *them* to arrange personal reference calls with former bosses, and "is that okay with you?" Weak candidates cut the call short, thinking, "My résumé is full of hype, former bosses might dispute my listed accomplishments, and . . . well . . . I probably can't get former bosses to talk with this prospective employer anyway, so I'm outta here." Good! You didn't want to waste time with them anyway. Conversely, A Players are eager to arrange those calls.

In Topgrading Hiring Step #6, a series of Competency Interviews, candidates are reminded of TORC in the first Competency Interview. And at the beginning of Step #7, the famous tandem Topgrading Interview . . . you get the picture, again there is the TORC reminder. In the Topgrading Interview Guide there are the TORC Questions—asking candidates what bosses will likely say.

What Are the TORC Questions in the Topgrading Interview Guide?

There are powerful TORC questions in the Topgrading Interview Guide. These are the questions that ask what the former boss is like and how that boss will assess the candidate. The questions look like this:

Supervisor's Name: _____ Title: _____
Where is that person now? _____
Would you be willing to arrange for us to talk with him or her?
_____

What were that supervisor's strengths? _____

What were that supervisor's weaker points? _____

What is your best guess as to what he/she really felt at that time were your strengths and weaker points:
Strengths: _____
_____
_____

Weaker points: _____
_____
_____

How would he/she rate your overall performance? _____

If someone balks at guessing what a former boss might say, you might provide a stimulus for them to answer the questions honestly by saying,

"Keep in mind that a final step in our hiring process is to ask you to arrange calls with former bosses."

How Did the TORC Technique Come About?

Early in my career I was frustrated when interviewing candidates for hire because I sensed that some of them, the weakest candidates, were fudging the truth. They would hype accomplishments, hide mistakes, and claim bosses would give them high ratings, but I didn't believe them. Then and now most companies don't permit managers to take reference calls, for fear managers might say negative things about former employees, who might sue the company for preventing them from getting a job. I knew that if I could get the truth clients would suffer fewer mis-hires, more of the candidates I recommended for hire would succeed, and my reputation would be better than if candidates continued to hide the truth.

One day a particularly talented candidate offered, out of the blue, to arrange reference calls with former bosses. I said, "Thanks, but most companies don't permit managers to take reference calls, do they?" The response was a huge epiphany: "No, but my former bosses *will* talk to you because I will ask them to, and they will talk because they know there is zero risk that I would ever sue them if they said something negative about me and I didn't get this job."

Curious and eager to solve one of the biggest problems in hiring (blatant and rampant dishonesty, particularly by weak candidates), I took the fellow up on his offer. And sure enough, he got back to me in a day with the phone numbers and availability of six former bosses. I talked to all of them, and they not only had nice things to say about this sharp candidate, but also trusted me enough to talk about the fellow's weaker points. This was incredibly helpful, for my opinions were confirmed, and more importantly, I learned details of weaker points that were helpful to my client in how best to manage this A Player.

Do candidates ask former bosses to be generous with praise? Over the years we've learned—no! A Players would be embarrassed to try to manipulate their former bosses. And when you perform the reference checks using Topgrading methods (learned in this chapter), you'll hear former bosses so openly talking about the candidate's weaker points that you will conclude that you're getting the truth!

Like a reformed smoker, I became messianic, imploring clients to use this new truth serum. Topgrading professionals would much rather interview two very strong candidates and help clients pick the better one than interview a C Player . . . then a B Player . . . then another C Player, and then implore the client not to be so desperate they hire the B, but continue searching for an A.

The TORC Technique opened the door to solving the other major hiring problems, such as lack of complete information. Hey—if candidates are motivated to be totally honest, why not ask them a *lot* of questions about everything they've done in their career? Thus the TORC Technique led to the 12 Topgrading Hiring Steps and thousands of managers tripling their hiring success. And the results, if and when the tipping point for Topgrading comes, might just be what my dream became as soon as the TORC Technique proved successful: more successful managerial careers, more successful companies, and greater economic success for the world!

By the way, clients ask Smart & Associates to conduct Topgrading Interviews with finalists for top jobs, and we are happy to do it. But when they ask us to conduct the reference calls, we decline because the hiring manager, who is one of the tandem interviewers, will learn so much more about the candidate and how to manage the person by conducting those reference calls.

Can Candidates Really Get Their Former Bosses to Talk?

Yes. Since about 1990, thousands of managers have reported that candidates arrange the interviews and 90%+ of the references are actually willing to talk. High performers usually get back to the interviewers within a day, saying, "All seven would like to talk with you, and here are their available times and mobile numbers." Easy—they do all the work and you don't play telephone tag.

The TORC Technique is no idle threat. The two Topgrading interviewers divvy up the calls, conduct them, compare notes, and decide if they want to offer the person a job. Actually, TORC is misnamed; it's not a "threat" to A Players. It should be Promise of Reference Check (PORC?), because high performers are eager to arrange the calls, knowing their former bosses and others will sing their praises.

TORC works, and when a company gets a reputation for requiring candidates to arrange the reference calls, C Players stay away, A Players are attracted to the company, and all candidates are honest in the interviews, knowing you will be talking with people who best know their work behavior.

But . . . Won't Some Former Bosses in Companies That Prohibit Managers from Taking Reference Calls Refuse to Take the Reference Call, Even if the Candidate Was an A Player?

Yes, but not many. Big companies, fearing that 50-year-old Charlie would sue them if he heard that his former manager bad-mouthed him, have standard policies: prospective employers must contact Human Resources, and HR will confirm employment dates and little else. But managers of former A Players ignore the policy.

That said, I encourage you to prohibit *your* managers from taking reference calls, unless they will be giving a reference on an A Player. For reference calls regarding people who were not A Players, ask the caller to contact Human Resources, who should give very limited information. It's *prudent* for companies to have that policy because if a manager would say something negative about ol' Charlie, who was fired for failing to do the job, maybe Charlie *would* sue (because he's in a protected class like people over forty), and maybe he'd win.

One complication is this: if a former employee committed a heinous crime, such as rape, the company must disclose that or be held liable if the former employee commits rape at the company that requested the reference. Check with your attorney on whether you might be obligated to disclose negatives about a former employer or risk losing a lawsuit when a future employer of the fired person did something similarly terrible in that company.

What Are the Risks Using TORC?

So far, none. TORC has been used for decades, with hundreds of thousands of reference calls arranged by candidates, and there has not been one negative consequence we've heard of.

With hundreds of thousands of reference calls arranged by candidates, there has not been one negative consequence we've heard of.

We're not aware that any former boss got into trouble for violating the company policy, and we have not heard that any reference-checked candidate has even complained, let alone sued a company for saying negative things about their performance. It has been used for decades and with tens of thousands of candidates.

The main point is that sharp candidates get their former bosses to talk. Managers of former high producers, hoping maybe to rehire them in the future, or just wanting to help an outstanding former employee, accept those reference calls.

Is a Business Reference Different from a Personal Reference?

Note that we refer to it as a *"personal* reference call," not a business reference call. You don't know the difference? Neither do I, but in case a manager is criticized for violating company policy, the response can be, "Our company policy prohibits taking *business* reference calls, and my former employee asked me if I'd take a *personal* reference call, which is different." Although we've never heard of a former boss being reprimanded or even asked, "Why did you accept that reference call," this could be the reason given, if asked.

But . . . Aren't We Hypocrites If We Ask Candidates to Arrange the Calls and Yet Our Policy Is to Prohibit Managers from Taking Them?

Yes, but no one seems to care. And if you still feel like a hypocrite, blame the lawyers, make up a new lawyer joke, and hope maybe our society will become less litigious in the future.

But . . . How Do You Reference Check Candidates with Their Current Employer?

If you pursue A Players who are happy in their job and not looking for a different job, they typically don't want their boss to know they are looking, and won't agree to reference calls with their current employer. A solution is to determine *who has left the company* that would be worth your talking with and see if the candidate trusts those former associates enough to arrange the call(s). High performers can almost always arrange a couple of calls.

Summary: How to Use the TORC Technique Effectively

1. **Announce TORC.** Let candidates know about TORC at every step in your hiring process. TORC can be stated on your Web site, in your job ads, in the introduction to Telephone Screening Interviews,

during Competency Interviews, and during the tandem Topgrading Interview.

2. **Tandem interviewers choose the references, after the Topgrading Interview.** Weak candidates submit lists of references, including golfing buddies, people they know at their church, and their insurance agent. I'm exaggerating to make the point: C Players tend to not want you to talk with their former managers. It's a good sign when a candidate submits a list of references including all managers in the past decade.

    The TORC Technique simply assures that you will talk with the people who can provide the most meaningful insights, and those include bosses the candidate reported to in the past decade. As you already know, the Topgrading Interview Guide asks, for every job, ratings of boss and best guess as to what the boss felt were the candidate's strengths, weaker points, and overall performance. But while exploring successes and failures, probe about people the candidate worked with—subordinates, peers, customers, or anyone else who would have good insights. For managerial candidates, most Topgraders will ask the candidate to arrange personal reference calls with three or four bosses in the past decade, two peers, and two subordinates. You and your tandem interview partner can divvy up the list of references and each take half.

3. **Call the references.** Use the Topgrading Reference Check Guide (see page 168). The aura around the call is sort of like this: picture your having interviewed a sharp candidate yesterday, and the candidate agreed to arrange a personal reference call with Pat Smith, the boss from five to seven years ago. You build rapport, ask all your questions, and Pat sincerely gives you useful feedback on your candidate. Sure, she probably is being a little generous in her appraisal with her former A Player, but you can sense it and ask appropriate follow-up questions to get her to tell you the negatives, too. Pat and you are probably peers, a former and a soon-to-be boss of the candidate, and you share a common mind-set. You both are slugging it out in life, love it when you have high producers, and so Pat is leveling with you. And even if you were 98% certain all references would be positive and you'd hire the person, the subtle insights into how you can best manage the person are extremely valuable.

4. **Compare notes.** Share your reference-check notes with your tandem interviewer, and use the information to finalize your Executive Summary.

Okay, now that you understand two important foundations for Top-grading, the Topgrading Vision and the TORC Technique, it's time to learn those 12 Topgrading Hiring Steps that have enabled one-third of the case studies you'll read to achieve not just 50% or 75%, but 90%+ high performers hired and/or promoted.

TOPGRADING HIRING STEP #1: MEASURE YOUR BASELINE SUCCESS HIRING AND PROMOTING PEOPLE AND YOUR COSTS OF MIS-HIRES

Historically, we measured nearly everything. Yet, until we embraced the Topgrading philosophy and tools, we never measured how well we hired. Now, it features as a core measure of executive success—and we see the results on the bottom-line.

—Paul Idzik, CEO, DTZ (former)

What problem does this measurement step solve? Managers who are not Topgraders almost always lack an understanding of how successful (or unsuccessful) their hiring and promoting methods are, and they don't have a clue as to how much their mis-hires cost them. So it's the elephant in the living room—most companies are in denial, fretting over bad hires but not even measuring them to see if a major improvement is warranted. I believe they don't seriously measure their success hiring for two reasons—they know the results will be bad, and they do not know a better way to hire (Topgrading). But when they do the measurements and learn about Top-grading, the negative results enhance their motivation to Topgrade. As they Topgrade, seeing the negative results plummet as their percent high performers increases only strengthens their commitment to Topgrading.

Shouldn't we be as rigorous in hiring as we are in capital spending? For a piece of equipment costing $500,000 we're disciplined in calculating ROIs, doing comparative shopping, and planning installation. Up front we have a meticulous process to justify and specify the type and amount of equipment we need and the expected outcomes, to be sure we are paying for precisely what we need to do the job. After the equipment is installed we debug it and then we systematically review the purchase to be sure it met our expectations. Did we get the capabilities we projected? The measured results? Companies nail down these numbers.

But are companies as rigorous in hiring as they are in capital spending, even if the cost of a mis-hire is $500,000? Nope. Most companies wing it on the front end without creating a clear Job Scorecard and without specifying nearly enough competencies (in Topgrading there are 50 competencies for any management job). And they wing it in the hiring process conducting easily faked Competency Interviews, and they conduct worthless reference calls or none at all. Unfortunately, most managers never go back to calculate benefits of good hires or costs of mis-hires, and never systematically consider how to do better next time. Doesn't it make sense to apply as much rigor in hiring as we do in capital spending?

Everyone knows that in business if something is important it has to be measured or the results will never be achieved and sustained. But most companies do not measure one of the most important things that can be measured in any business—success hiring and promoting people. Company vision statements commonly say, "Our people are our most valued asset," yet they do not measure their success picking people. I was Special Adviser to American Productivity and Quality Center, the not-for-profit that helped start the Malcolm Baldrige National Quality Award, and for years we researched dozens of famous companies with respect to their hiring practices and results achieved. Global 500 companies were studied but the only ones that stood out for rigorously measuring quality of hire were Topgrading companies that more than tripled their hiring success hiring and promoting high performers.

Many famous companies (except for Topgraders) only measure time to fill jobs and cost to fill them, but don't have a clue as to whether their cheap, fast hiring results in good hires or mostly mis-hires. Let me repeat that—

Some companies I know of have two main measurements of hiring success—how *fast* they hire people and how *cheaply* they do it . . . but they don't know if their fast, cheap hiring produces superior or mediocre hires.

A year after hiring or promoting people, companies only fret about their terrible choices, those whose performance appraisal says "Does Not Meet Performance Expectations." They put the terrible performers on Performance

Improvement Plans and fire those who do not improve enough, but they don't measure the costs of the mis-hire, investigate where in the hiring process they "blew it," and only rarely go out to find better hiring methods.

Some companies claim hiring success but hardly do more than find out if new hires have a pulse. Do you think I'm kidding? The head of Human Resources at a global medical supply company, in a conference call with APQC, said they achieved 97.5% success hiring. I asked how they measured success hiring and he said they send a one-item e-mail question to the hiring manager 30 days after the person started work, asking, "Does the person you hired 30 days ago have skills to do the job?"

The question doesn't even ask if the person has *excellent* skills or *all* the skills to be a high performer, and the question is asked before the new hire has figured out where the restrooms are. Of course hiring managers respond favorably almost all the time! So I asked the head of HR, "What percent of managers hired in recent years turned out to be the high performers you expected and felt you were paying for, and the only other category is mis-hire?" He said, "Only about 20% of the managers we hire turn out to be high performers." What's wrong with this picture—the reported hiring success is 97.5% when, if the standard is "high performer," it's no better than 20%?

FOUR TOPGRADING CALCULATORS

There are four useful Topgrading Calculators we've devised so that it's simple to perform the calculations that will anchor your talent perspective in reality. All of these calculators (except the first) are made even more simple at www.TopgradingCalculators.com, where you can enter your information and get the results immediately.

1. **Baseline Hiring Success Calculator.** Calculate your pre-Topgrading percentage of high performers hired and promoted.
2. **Topgrading Talent Projection Calculator.** Calculate how many people you'll have to hire and fire in order to achieve 90% As hired, given your present success rate.

3. **Topgrading Cost of Mis-Hires Calculator.** Calculate your typical costs of mis-hires, and your typical number of wasted hours sweeping up after a mis-hire. This calculator makes filling out the Cost of Mis-Hires Form (Appendix D) a breeze.
4. **Topgrading Organizational Cost of Mis-Hires Calculator.** Calculate how much it will cost you, given your cost estimates of mis-hires, to "live with" underperformers, to replace underperformers with your current methods, and to replace underperformers with Topgrading methods.

Baseline Hiring Success Calculator

Write the names of the people you have hired in the past three years, rate them a year after they were hired, either a high performer (what you expected, what you paid for) or a mis-hire, and fill in:

% high performers: _____

% mis-hires: _____

Staggering, isn't it? At the risk of repeating myself, Smart & Associates has asked 10,000 senior managers that question in workshops, I have conducted 65,000 oral case studies including that question, and I asked the #1 Human Resources executives at the world's largest 100 companies that question—and the average success rate across all of these groups is what you've now read several times: only 25%.

Now do the same exercise, but only do it for the people you've promoted. Although you'd think companies would be better at promoting than hiring people, our extensive research shows the same statistic: 25% success promoting people. Why aren't companies better at promoting? Three reasons:

1. They rely way too much on the present boss's opinion of a subordinate's promotability, when bosses generally only think about a person's current performance.
2. The promotability analysis is superficial—typically the boss takes only a few seconds to rate a subordinate's promotability.
3. When someone is considered for a promotion to a different area, say from Finance to Marketing, a lot of times the boss has very little insight into the other area, so a "promotability" rating is almost worthless.

In this book you'll learn the Topgrading methods that solve all of these problems.

Organizations that Topgrade establish pre-Topgrading baselines with a more extensive version of this exercise. They first establish baselines (percent who turn out to be As before Topgrading) for all of management or all in a certain key job (store manager, data entry clerk, accountant, or whatever). Topgraders, including case studies in this book, go back several years and note all of the people hired and promoted and then see how they turned out at least a year after they are hired. Sometimes this is impossible, such as in the case of a start-up or when there are simply no records. With the percent high performers hired/promoted pre-Topgrading, senior management can decide if Topgrading is needed. Of course it always is!

Not one Topgrading professional has ever heard of a non-Topgrading company with 90% hiring/promoting success. When the baseline measurement is made, senior managers are appalled, are more motivated to improve, and are more motivated to implement Topgrading. And when the company begins Topgrading, they can measure their results annually (Step #12) to track their progress.

This is like a weight reduction program: you measure your weight to begin with (that's your baseline), you implement the program, and you take your weight again and again to track your progress. In a weight reduction program you might also learn about the horrible costs to your health of being obese. You know—heart disease, stroke, diabetes. Faced with the facts, the pain experienced becomes a motivator to stick with the program.

With Topgrading, using the measurements to project future success and costs is very painful unless there is improvement. How do you make those future projections? Next use the Topgrading Talent Projection Calculator.

Topgrading Talent Projection Calculator

The Topgrading Talent Projection Calculator (Figure 3.1, page 67) helps overcome talent self-delusion. Talent projections, until now, have been shams, with managers assuming the people hired and promoted will be "good enough." Since the publication of the first edition of *Topgrading* we have helped clients calculate percent As in management, percent As hired/promoted using old methods, and percent As hired/promoted using Topgrading methods. Now we connect the dots *projecting* talent levels based on your estimate of your actual success in choosing talent.

The Topgrading Talent Projection Calculator will tell you how many people you'll have to hire (and fire) in order to achieve 90% success, given your present success rate (is it 25%?) and what your future success rates will be with Topgrading as you improve to 50%, 75%, and 90%.

For example, if want to hire an A Player and your success rate is 25%, you need to hire four people and replace three because you will experience three mis-hires for every A Player you hire. If and when your success rate is 100%, you need only hire one person (who will be an A) to replace the one underperformer. Topgrading promises to improve your success rate from 25% to 75%, and that's just for starters. In the meantime, to learn how many people you will have to hire, total, to finally have 90% A Players:

- Estimate Your Current Number of People to Be Replaced.
- Estimate Your Hiring/Promoting Success Rate . . . your percent As and A Potentials after hiring and promoting people. Use the Topgrading Talent Projection Calculator (Figure 3.1, or www.TopgradingCalculators .com) to show the total number of people you must hire or promote in order to end up with at least 90% As, after replacing all those who turn out *not* to be As. You'll quickly see how many people you will mis-hire (and fire?) in order to end up with 90% As.

Figure 3.1
Topgrading Talent Projection Calculator
Total Number of Replacements to Achieve 90% A Players

Number of Underperformers to Be Replaced*	Your Current Success in Hiring/Promoting			
	25%	50%	75%	90%
10	36	18	12	10
20	72	36	24	20
40	144	72	48	40
100	360†	180	120	100

* For numbers less than 10, rounding errors are significant, but you can calculate averages from the 10 row. For example, replacing one person with a 25% success rate will necessitate 10% of 36, or 3.6 replacements on average. Round 3.6 up to 4 replacements.

† You may wonder why, if your company replaced 100 people with a 25% success rate, requiring three mis-hires to get one A, it doesn't mean hiring a total of 4 x 100 = 400. Hiring 4 to get 1 A achieves 100% As, and the Calculator is for 90%. The Calculator numbers come from spreadsheet calculations, rounding upward, since humans don't like to be dissected.

The implications of the Topgrading Talent Projection Calculator are profound. Look at the table and envison your situation with different scenarios. Here's a pleasant one: If you wish to replace 10 underperformers, you hire or promote 10 using the Topgrading methods, and end up with nine or more A Players. The right column of the Calculator is the Topgrading goal, the achievable goal. That's your column for Topgraders, who lead a charmed life.

Success short of 90% success is spelled out in the Calculator and it spells pain. With a typical 25% success, for example, replacing 40 people to achieve 90% As would require hiring 144 replacements—and replacing 104 of them.* No company could survive with such a revolving door. And, by the way, what A Player would want to join a massacre-prone company?

What would you do if you want to replace 10 underperformers and find that you have to replace the first, second, and third replacements before you end up with one A Player? As the Topgrading Talent Projection Calculator shows, you'd have to replace 36 people to end up with nine As. In reality you would only replace the worst C Players, because it's just too painful to slash, slash, slash—to hire 36 people and replace 27 of them, to end up with nine A Players. These simple statistics truly explain why so many companies give up, and perhaps why almost all of the largest companies no longer exist after 100 years.

Many managers inch into Topgrading, replacing Cs but retaining Bs. The Topgrading Talent Projection Calculator shows this approach will get you an upgraded team, but just replacing Cs on a large scale logically *cannot* yield a team of 90% As, ever, with a 25% success rate. Suppose you had an unusually talented organization of 100, including 60 A/A Potentials, 20

Replacing 40 Bs and Cs, with Only 25% Success = Agony!

	Start	After Round #1	After Round #2
A/A Potential	60	50	53
B + C	40	30	27

---

* Replace 40, leaving 30 mis-hired underperformers after Round 1 of hiring replacements, 27 underperformers after Round 2 of hiring replacements, etc., etc., until the total number replaced is 144.

Bs, and 20 Cs. And suppose your hiring/promoting methods produced a typical 25% As, 50% Bs, and 25% Cs. You can replace all 20 Cs, but with 20 Bs, you cannot exceed 80% As. Use the Calculator to see how many people would be replaced with only a 25% success rate. That's a lot of disruption. Pity the upgrader if his competition Topgrades, replacing underperformers efficiently with 90% As.

An average company, using typical interviewing methods that select only 25% A/A Potentials while replacing C Players, can NEVER achieve more than two-thirds A Players.

Another important consideration is *how long* it would take you to replace people. Topgrading managers with 30 people on the team can usually replace 10 people in one year, and expect that nine will be As. But as was shown, the manager with a 25% success rate has to hire 31 people, removing 22 underperformers to end up with nine A Players. That revolving door could easily take three years. It's so disruptive, painful, and costly that, again, managers with 25% success should logically "live with" a mixture of As, Bs, and Cs, retaining Bs and only occasionally redeploying the weakest of Cs.

To decide how fast or slowly to Topgrade, you can make your own projections, year by year, and see if your Topgrading speed will be fast enough for you to succeed as an organization. Some companies initially proceed slowly, so as to minimize disruption. A global financial services company is in its 11th year rolling out Topgrading, adding new regions each year. Many entrepreneurs and CEOs of fast-growth companies Topgrade their entire company in a year or two—that is very doable when only about 20% of the team consists of B/C Players and the manager is a Topgrader with 90% success hiring. Whether fast or slow, Topgrading rollouts include:

- announcing Topgrading as a positive initiative in which managers learn better hiring, promoting, and coaching methods, with no threatening message about identifying low performers and firing them;
- learning Topgrading methods;
- using Topgrading to hire and promote people;
- measuring results annually to see their former 25% success rate improve steadily to 50%, and then 75%, and higher;

- using the Topgrading Talent Projection Calculator to realistically project the success and pain of replacing people; and
- setting the bar higher, so that only A Player performance is acceptable, when they know that the vast majority of the people they hire and promote will turn out to be high performers.

Topgrading Cost of Mis-Hires Calculator

It's time to convert a theoretical discussion of mis-hires to something real, something that will hit you in your gut. Start by completing the Cost of Mis-Hires Form found in Appendix D (page 291). You can also do this online at www.TopgradingCalculators.com. But please take a few minutes to estimate the costs associated with one of your mis-hires.

You can do this exercise right now, by yourself, although the results are more compelling if you do this as a team composed of members who all know the hire being discussed. But let me warn you: the more time you spend talking about the costs of hiring good 'ol Charlie, the higher the cost estimates will be.

Just get consensus on the costs, add them up as the exercise asks (line 8), subtract contributions (line 9), and you'll have the net cost of mishiring Charlie (line 10). Ugh! Good ol' Charlie cost you a bundle, far more than any of you would have guessed half an hour ago, before using the Cost of Mis-Hires Form.

Don't forget that last little item on the form—how many hours you and the team "wasted" sweeping up after the mis-hire. "Waste" is in quotation marks because if a C Player sales rep almost loses you your best customer and the team spends 100 hours salvaging that customer, those hours were not wasted, but were necessary additional hours invested for a good business reason. You get the distinction. Our research shows that mis-hires cause an average of 300 additional hours worked. Double ugh! And we've found that if we add more time for teams to do this exercise, the estimate of "wasted hours" shoots up, because members of the team think of more and more hours spent by more and more people dealing with the mis-hire. Doing that exercise once usually results in the team saying, "Mis-hires are far more costly and waste far more time than we assumed, and so mastering Topgrading is even more important than we thought!"

When companies launch Topgrading, this exercise is done more extensively. When a lot of people hold the same job (store manager, accountant in an accounting firm, etc.), teams assemble and work through the Cost of Mis-Hires Form. Top executives meet and estimate the costs of three or four familiar managerial mis-hires. Aggregated, all of these cost of mis-hire estimates are both credible to the organization (since they produced the numbers) and powerful motivators to fix the hiring problem.

Topgrading Organizational Cost of Mis-Hires Calculator

It is now possible to calculate, with reasonable accuracy, costs of mis-hires across your organization—specifically how much it costs you to:

- "live with" underperformers,
- replace B/Cs using your typical assessment techniques, and
- replace your B/Cs using Topgrading techniques.

Suppose you have 10 B/Cs (chronic underperformers without the potential to become high performers). And suppose you estimate the average cost of a mis-hire for managers in the group to be $500,000. (If you run a small company and can relate easier to $50,000 as a sample cost of mis-hire, you know what to do—divide by 10.) Let's "run the numbers."

Replacing all 10 with high performers (As), using a typical 25% successful assessment approach, would involve three mis-hires for every good hire. You would have to hire 40 people, mis-hiring 30, to end up with 10 A Players. The 30 mis-hires would each cost you $500,000, for a total of $15 million.

Using Topgrading, 90% or nine of your replacements are As, and chances are the one mis-hire (costing $500,000) would soon be replaced by an A, because the Topgrader has that much confidence in the system. Topgraders don't hesitate to replace all their underperformers, knowing that disruption and costs will be minor because in this example, only one person is mis-hired.

The spreadsheet calculations have been done for you in Figure 3.2 (and you can enter your stats at www.TopgradingCalculators.com). Note that in replacing 20 underperformers with a 90% A Player goal, the Topgrading approach still involves $1 million in mis-hires (two at $500,000), but with a common assessment approach, with 25% As hired, the cost is $25 million. Wow—Topgrading saves $24 million, preventing 96% of mis-hire costs.

Or if you estimate the cost of a mis-hire to be $50,000 for a manager, your cost to replace 20 people is $2.5 million if your success rate is an average 25%, but only $100,000 if your success rate is 90%.

Figure 3.2
Topgrading Organizational Cost of Mis-Hires Calculator
Total Costs of Mis-Hires to Achieve 90% As*
(average cost of mis-hire: $500,000)

	Your Current Hiring Success Rate			
Number of Underperformers to Be Replaced	**25% As Hired**	**50% As Hired**	**75% As Hired**	**90% As Hired**
1	$1.3 m	$470 k	$150 k	$50 k[†]
2	$2.6 m	$900 k	$300 k	$100 k
4	$5.3 m	$1.8 m	$600 k	$200 k
10	$11 m	$4 m	$1 m	$500 k
20	$25 m	$8.6 m	$3 m	$1 m
40	$53 m	$18 m	$6 m	$2 m
100	$134 m	$45 m	$15 m	$5 m

* The matrix is equally applicable for mis-hires and mis-promotions.

[†] $150 k is 10% of the $1.5 million cost of replacing 10 underperformers with 9 As, 1 mis-hire ($1.5 million). If you replaced one B/C you'd have a 90% chance of hiring an A, with zero mis-hire costs, but a 10% chance your one hire would be a mis-hire, costing you $1.5 million. So, $150,000 is an average cost. A different calculation would say that with 10 to replace and a mis-hire rate of 25%, you will mis-hire 3 X $500,000 = $1.5 million in mis-hires to achieve 90% As.

The costs of mis-hires using typical hiring can be 24 times the costs when Topgrading.

Figure 3.2 expands this logic across a broad range of scenarios.

When you enter a new job and find underperformers, and if you want to estimate the costs of Topgrading, *do not* include the mis-hire costs for these B/Cs you inherited. Blame your predecessor. Separately calculate the costs of not replacing them, because you should be held accountable for their continuing costs to the organization. But when you quickly replace B/Cs, the estimated costs of mis-hires should begin with *your* hires, or more specifically, with the people *you* mis-hire.

We can debate the validity of various assumptions, and you can make whatever assumptions you choose regarding your success in hiring, costs of mis-hires, and how many people you need to replace.

No matter how conservative your assumptions, failing to embrace a practice that selects 75% to 90% As is unnecessarily costly and disruptive.

MIS-HIRES AT THE TOP

Chief Executive published an article entitled "The Costs of CEO Failure." The author quotes me and uses the Topgrading Cost of Mis-Hires Form, juicing up the numbers for CEO mis-hires. Bottom line, the average costs the authors calculated were $52.5 million for large companies, $22.1 million for midsize companies, and $12.6 million for small companies. An October 2001 article in *Fortune* said, "The mean tenure of a *Fortune* 500 CEO has fallen from 9.5 years to 3.5 years over the past decade." Staggering, isn't it— huge costs and huge rate of failure at the CEO level.

To hire a CEO of a public company, typically a committee of the board considers internal candidates and hires a search firm; the search executive performs interviews on internal and external candidates and performs reference checks, with board members performing only perfunctory interviews. Many board members are CEOs, yet in chapter 1 we cited research showing CEOs and presidents believe that four out of five executive searches result in mis-hires. Recently boards of Topgrading companies have been taking their CEO selection responsibilities more seriously, and relying on more thorough assessment approaches, including Topgrading. It sounds self-serving, but if boards do not themselves conduct Topgrading steps on candidates for CEO and other C-suite positions, the companies would be far more profitable if they would use Topgrading professionals to assess candidates, for they would make far fewer mis-hires, and shareholders would reap huge benefits. That is precisely what some major private equity companies do.

How Do Your Cost of Mis-Hire Statistics Compare with Others?

Intuitively you no doubt know that mis-hires/mis-promotions are costly, but we won't even attempt to measure the costs of:

- your own career stalling because you failed to Topgrade and your team's performance was mediocre;
- unhappiness of mis-hired people;
- your diminished fun, increased pressure, and excessive work hours because of your low performers' deficiencies; and
- strains in your family life because of those unnecessarily long hours.

Published research on costs of mis-hires is sparse. A computer search of over 200 studies and articles produced a hodgepodge of single-company results, with costs of mis-hiring factory workers to be $1,500 in one company, salespeople $6,000 in another.* Governmental studies have placed the costs of mis-hiring programmers at two to three times their annual compensation.†

Those numbers appear low and too sterile. I know that many managers in my sample of 6,500 interviewees have *been* a mis-hire in at least one job. I've heard thousands of accounts of the pain involved in making a major career decision that goes awry, of being a mis-hire, an underperformer, who is eventually fired. As Topgrading consultants, we are sometimes asked to help correct an insidious corporate "death spiral" in which poor executive hires result in lower-level A Players quitting, leaving B/C Players who hire and promote more B/C Players. The shareholders are left bleeding and wounded, and the company may become moribund. Mis-hires can kill companies, individual careers, and real people whose stress causes heart failure.

Over the years Smart & Associates has probably done more studies of costs of mis-hires than any other organization. For various books and other publications we have interviewed hundreds of managers, taking them through that Cost of Mis-Hires Form. I once Googled "cost of mis-hire," and 9 million results popped up, with two-thirds of the first 10 pages referring to our publications. In hundreds of workshops we have an exercise (the one starting on page 291) and post the results—the costs of the mis-hires/ mis-promotions and the wasted hours because the person was an underperformer.

---

* "Retaining Top Salespeople: How to Motivate Star Performers," *Small Business Report* 13, no. 2 (February 1988): 23–27.
† F. L. Schmidt, J. E. Hunter, and K. Pearlman, "Assessing the Economic Impact of Personnel Programs on Workforce Productivity," *Personnel Psychology* 35 (1982): 333–47.

Distilling *all these sources* of information, here is a chart summarizing estimated costs in terms of time and money. The costs are stated in terms of how large the costs are in relation to salary (2 x base salary, 10 x base salary, or whatever).

Cost of Mis-Hire Research

Level	Costs vs. Base Salary
Supervisor	4 x base salary
Sales Rep	6 x base salary
Mid-Manager	8 x base salary
Vice President	15 x base salary
Executive	27 x base salary

Interpretation: The average cost of mis-hired sales reps is about 6 times their base salary.

In the 2008 publication of *Topgrading for Sales*, co-author Greg Alexander performed a study of sales rep mis-hires, with the results shown below, indicating the total cost of an average mis-hire, for $100,000 base compensation for sales reps, is $565,000.

Mis-Hire Costs for Sales Reps

- Compensation 28%
- Maintenance 3%
- Opportunity Cost 46%
- Disruption Costs 19%
- Hiring Costs 4%

About one hundred clients supplied data on their costs of mis-hires, in interviews with Chris Mursau, Vice President of Smart & Associates, Inc. This yielded the data below, supplemented with Wasted Time estimates from about 100 Topgrading Workshops. Chris asked respondents to generate estimates on a *typical mis-hire*, not the most costly, not the least, and include mostly B Player mis-hires, not more costly C Player mis-hires.

Figure 3.3
Cost of Mis-Hire Study Results
MANAGERIAL MIS-HIRES

	Average (mean) Statistics
Number of Years in Job	1.6
Base Compensation	$102,692
1. Cost in Hiring	$31,643
2. Compensation (All Years)	$255,452
3. Cost of Maintaining Person in Job	$67,653
4. Severance	$33,962
5. Cost of Mistakes, Failures; Wasted and Missed Business Opportunities	$1,232,092
6. Cost of Disruption	$242,356
7. Sum of Costs (#1–#6)	$1,863,158
Value of Contribution	$360,721
Net Average Cost of Mis-Hire	$1,502,436 (14.6 times base compensation)
"Wasted time" of hiring manager and others	278 hours

Note that the $1.5 million mis-hire cost is the "bottom line," since costs were offset by contributions the person made.

The $1.5 million in costs for a single mis-hire is a lot of waste. We consider the numbers a bit inflated, because in hundreds of workshops the costs for mis-hiring $100,000 per year managers averages $800,000; respondents were encouraged to be conservative in their estimates, but perhaps because they were interviewed by a Topgrading professional they (unconsciously?) wanted to show that they realized mis-hires are costly.

The single biggest *estimated* cost in mis-hiring is the wasted or missed business opportunity. For decades I have witnessed multi-million-dollar fiascoes that clearly could have been avoided had an A Player been hired instead of a B/C Player. Gross neglect by a B/C Player salesperson resulted in the loss of the #1 customer in one client company. In another, incompetent information technology consultants were hired. Why? Because they were friends of a B/C Player CIO. The losses in information technology bankrupted the company. In companies that Topgrade sales departments, the sales of new A Players are sometimes twice that of the replaced Non-As; the "wasted or missed business opportunities" are easily estimated in sales organizations.

Using the Topgrading Cost of Mis-Hires Form is an eye-opener when done at the beginning of Topgrading, and it motivates the team to embrace Topgrading. You'll see in Hiring Step #12, using the form every time there is a mis-hire provides a reminder to not cut Topgrading corners, which is usually the reason for a mis-hire.

Topgrading Hiring Step #1 might appear on the surface to be "just an exercise" to a top executive who knows, "I must improve my success hiring people." But please perform the quick versions of the exercises and use www.TopgradingCalculators.com to powerfully drive home to your team how painful it will be to continue to hire and promote with such limited success.

TOPGRADING HIRING STEP #2: CREATE A CLEAR JOB SCORECARD (NOT A VAGUE JOB DESCRIPTION)

Creating scorecards has made a huge difference in hiring and keeping the best people because everyone now knows what A Player performance looks like. In the past, performances were vague. Now we are all on the same page and we are getting A Player performance month in and month out.

—Travis Isaacson, Senior Director
of Organizational Development, Access Development

With your key Topgrading measurements done, the prospect of joining Topgraders who enjoy a 90% hiring/promoting success rate has perhaps turboboosted your commitment to learn Topgrading methods.

The next step is to write a Job Scorecard. Why? One of the problems

Topgrading solves is that job descriptions are so vague that hiring managers and others who will be affected aren't really clear about what they are hiring someone to do and candidates are equally confused, hoping to figure it out once they're on the job, so avoidable, costly mis-hires are the result. Appendix A (page 277) is a sample Job Scorecard, but hold on, please don't read it yet because it's a loooong document, and it might blow you away. Let me make the case for why this one "bureaucratic" Topgrading step is important, and then I'll again say where the sample can be found.

Approximately three dozen Topgrading professionals have interviewed tens of thousands of candidates for hire or promotion, and clients routinely have sent job descriptions to us, which are so vague that we always have to get on the phone to get clarity. After all, our reputations are at stake and if we don't know what a high performer will have to achieve, how can we evaluate candidates? We're very familiar with exit interview results, and know that fired managers frequently blame the company: "They just didn't tell me I'd have to . . ."

- "cut my staff";
- "travel 75% of the time";
- "achieve an unrealistic X level of profitability"; or
- "sell those new but lousy-quality products."

Too often we regard the failed person as a lousy performer, making excuses. But most job descriptions are typically so vague that *most* low performers can perform the stated responsibilities and still be judged a mis-hire. When C Player performance can result in achieving all the accountabilities, the job description is partly to blame.

I recommend that you do what I do and every Topgrading professional does: nail down the first-year measurable accountabilities, the numbers to be achieved, including the ratings to be achieved on competencies, for the new hire to be considered a high performer.

Nail down the first-year measurable accountabilities, the numbers to be achieved, including the ratings to be achieved on competencies, for the new hire to be considered a high performer.

The good news is that Topgrading companies write Job Scorecards, making life easier for us, but more importantly easier for themselves, because the step lessens costly mis-hires. Here's an abbreviated example of a typical, vague job description:

JOB DESCRIPTION: VICE PRESIDENT, SALES

Responsibilities:

1. Boost global and domestic sales.
2. Launch some new products.
3. Achieve profitability goals.

Budget: (whatever)

Competencies:

1. Leadership
2. Integrity
3. Excellence
4. Team Player
5. Communication

The VP Sales job description might be four pages long but essentially says the job is to boost global and domestic sales, launch some new products, and achieve profitability goals, while exhibiting some common competencies.

This is a vague job description. The president really is most interested in boosting global sales because their #1 global competitor is vulnerable and declining, the VP Manufacturing wants only to keep the domestic plants closer to full capacity, the VP Marketing was hired because patents are running out and the company has *no* future without new product launches, and of course the VP Finance wants profitable sales. Perhaps no mortal could possibly achieve all of the expectations, but because the goals were never converted into actual numeric accountabilities, no one realized how vague it was, or how high and mutually exclusive the various components were.

A year later the new VP Sales could be frustrated, having been jerked in many different directions and at best ended up satisfying one of the executives who had a real stake in the job. Perhaps the new VP Sales would have been fired for having emphasized global sales (after all, the boss is the president, who required it over the other responsibilities), but the other three VPs complained loudly that the VP Sales had failed to achieve "most" of the job responsibilities. Oh, and by the way, maybe the VP Sales had always been strong in *all* of the key competencies, but after being jerked in four different directions, he would be criticized by the three peers for not Achieving Excellence, not being a good Team Player, and not Communicating well. You get the picture.

A Job Scorecard would have nailed down measurable accountabilities with actual numeric goals such as boosting global sales 10%, increasing domestic sales 15%, launching three new products on time/on budget, and maintaining profit margins of 7% . . . or whatever. And maybe the measurable accountabilities would include an average rating of 7 on a 10-point scale when rated by the team in an e-mail 360 survey on the key competencies. High performers might accept the offer and perform, and weak candidates might drop out because maybe that Job Scorecard is ridiculously unrealistic.

But without measurable accountabilities the executive team and the new hire would all be unclear as to what the job really was, and of course the chances of a costly mis-hire are higher due to that vagueness.

START WITH A JOB ANALYSIS

In large companies in which there might be hundreds of employees in the same job, Human Resources professionals need to be involved to be sure all the right steps are taken, not "just" for the clarity to avoid mis-hires but to be sure that legal requirements are met.

But for small companies and "one-off" jobs in larger companies, you can do exactly what Topgrading professionals do every day and what hundreds of Topgrading companies do as well: write your own Job Scorecard. For management jobs you need to know the company mission and strategy—is the company growing? Is there a mission statement, and if so, how does the job advance it? Then get key stakeholders (you—the hiring manager, peers, HR, others) together to nail down first-year numbers to be achieved, for operating results and competencies, such that if the new hire achieves them, *by definition* that person is a high performer, a great hire, an A Player. It is *not* a good Job Scorecard if the new hire achieves all the numbers but is deemed a low performer because some accountability "we didn't think of" was not achieved, or the person didn't exhibit some competency that wasn't written or measured.

SCORECARD COMPONENTS

1. **Identify Mission and Strategy.**
2. **Identify Measurable Job Accountabilities ("what").**
3. **Identify Competencies ("how"), linked to accountabilities.**

KEYS

1. **All stakeholders *agree* on <u>measurement</u> that will <u>differentiate</u> <u>A/B/C Players.</u>**
2. **Be sure Competencies spell out the fit for the specific job.**
3. **Competencies are measured.**

Do all the people who have a real stake in the success of the new hire have to agree on the accountabilities, including competencies? Yes, and if not, work it out or there will be conflict and confusion later.

COMPETENCIES *ARE* MEASUREABLE ACCOUNTABILITIES

How many times have you seen people achieve "the numbers" but are such lousy leaders or mediocre team players that they are fired? Unfortunately, how people perform with respect to competencies is typically not measured systematically, and new hires are given vague feedback until they are let go. It's unfair to candidates and new hires, and it results in costly mis-hires.

How to Include Competencies in a Job Scorecard

1. **Hold people accountable for up to 50 competencies for management jobs.**

   Most companies have 5 to 10 competencies for most jobs, but I learned decades ago that for any management job, there are at least 50 competencies, and every one is important, meaning if a new hire is only Fair or Poor on even one, that new hire is apt to be considered a mis-hire. Given that reality, no candidate is hired who is demonstrably Fair or Poor on those competencies.

   "Fifty competencies?" you wail, "I can't keep track of *five* competencies when I interview people." Oh yes you can! In every Topgrading Workshop almost every attendee says they can't do it, and on the second day of the workshop they do it well—they interview someone and accurately rate 50 competencies. In the section on the Topgrading Interview I'll explain how to do it and why you can do the seemingly impossible.

Sorry, but I'll now sound bureaucratic: you must write precise definitions of each competency for the job. The definition of Energy for a warehouse worker is quite different from Energy for a financial analyst. Team Player for a caregiver is quite different from that for a business unit head of a global company. Full definitions are available in the Topgrading Workbook, and sample Job Scorecards and templates are available with the Topgrading Toolkit (see Topgrading Resources, Appendix H, page 331).

For now, just glance through the following brief list of 50 competencies. Note that, of course, Topgrading is a key competency (broken out into Selecting A Players and Redeploying B/C Players).

Ease of Changing Competencies

Relatively Easy to Change	Hard, but Doable	Very Difficult to Change
Risk Taking	Judgment/Decision Making	Intelligence
Leading Edge	Strategic Skills	Analysis Skills
Education	Pragmatism	Creativity
Experience	Track Record	Conceptual Ability
Organization/Planning	Resourcefulness/Initiative	Integrity
Self-Awareness/Feedback	Excellence Standards	Assertiveness
Training/Development/Coaching	Change Leadership	Vision
Empowerment	Conflict Management	Inspiring Followership
Team Player	Compatibility of Needs	Energy/Drive
Communications—Oral	Independence	Enthusiasm/Passion
Communications—Written	Stress Management	Ambition
First Impression	Adaptability	Tenacity
Customer Focus	Likability	

Political Savvy	Listening
Selecting A Players	Balance in Life
Redeploying B/C Players	Negotiation Skills
Coaching/Training	Persuasiveness
Goal Setting	Team Builder
Diversity	
Running Meetings	

2. **In the Job Scorecard, list the Minimum Acceptable Rating a candidate must achieve on all competencies, after all Topgrading steps, to be hired, and color code them.**

   The color coding is simple: Green is for Relatively Easy to change, through coaching, training, and experience. Red means Very Difficult to Change, and yellow means Hard but Doable. Two dozen Topgrading professionals provided the color ratings based on our experience coaching tens of thousands of people. The color coding is just a quick reminder—even though, after all the Topgrading Hiring Steps, a candidate appears to meet almost all the Minimum Acceptable Ratings for, say, 45 out of 50 competencies, you'd be foolish to offer a candidate the job if there is a low rating for Integrity, Energy, or any other red competency.

   Now please go to Appendix A (page 277) to see a very thorough example of a Job Scorecard, with very clear accountabilities and color-coded Competencies, 50 of them. The Job Scorecard happens to be for Chief Talent Officer.

3. **Measure the new hire on competencies.**

   How can you measure an employee on Team Player and other competencies? Simple—conduct an e-mail 360 survey.* There are

---

* An "e-mail 360-degree survey"—shortened by some companies to "e-mail 360 survey," shortened by others to "e-mail survey"—is simply a survey taken by people online; "360 degree" simply means the respondents are usually subordinates, peers, and bosses—all around the person rated.

dozens of inexpensive versions (just Google "online employee surveys"). Most of our clients limit surveys to about 25 items (so respondents are not overwhelmed), and for managers there are two separate groups of respondents—subordinates and boss/peers.

Topgrading companies generally hold a person accountable for achieving a minimum rating of 7 on a 10-point scale, when rated by high performers who are peers, subordinates, and those at a higher level. For some competencies such as Integrity, Track Record (achieving accountabilities), and Topgrading, the Minimum Expected Rating is usually a 9.

I helped Jack Welch design a model in which managers are rated as achieving Results (or not) and showing GE Values (or not). Those who fall short are given a second chance, but if someone achieves Results and continues to fall short on GE Values, that person will typically quit (knowing a termination is forthcoming). The reason for this was that some autocrats were squeezing people for short-term results but driving even high performers to quit. Topgrading coaching converted some autocrats to managers with acceptable Emotional Intelligence and they achieved *even better* operating results, so Jack insisted on a minimum rating on Emotional Intelligence competencies (which are called "GE Values").

In our experience, too many companies list too few competencies, rarely define or measure them, and then fire someone for not exhibiting a competency. You have competencies to help reinforce your culture and the performance, but if they are gobbledygook, they don't help drive performance and they are unfair to individuals. Fortunately, there is a practical solution—define the competencies, measure them with e-mail surveys, and hold people accountable to achieving the minimum standard.

USE THE JOB SCORECARD AS
THE BASIS OF PERFORMANCE MANAGEMENT

It's amazing—no, tragic—that in most companies job descriptions are vague, and it is only *after* the person is hired that the hiring manager and Human Resources figure out the accountabilities—what the person has to do to Meet or Exceed Performance Expectations and, for managers, get a bonus. An annual performance appraisal is done, and because it has little relationship to the vague job description, the new hire too often is frustrated and the hiring manager dreads providing negative feedback. If you're going to fire someone for not achieving 7,000 widgets or for not exhibiting a competency, it's smart to figure out all the numeric accountabilities for the job and for the competencies to be exhibited *before* the person is hired. And needless to say, candidates should be fully informed of the complete Job Scorecard before they accept a job offer.

If you're going to fire someone for not achieving 7,000 widgets or for not exhibiting a competency, it's smart to figure out all the numeric accountabilities for the job and for the competencies to be exhibited *before* the person is hired.

With a Job Scorecard, the annual review is a much simpler scenario. A year into the job the new hire does self-ratings and you agree or disagree on what might be excuses, but you rarely disagree about accountabilities. Your new hire, Joe, agreed that selling 7,000 widgets, with 10% margins, and receiving at least a 7 rating by peers on Team Player would be necessary for a Meets Performance Expectations rating. If he made the numbers, Joe gets the promised rating. But if you didn't think of it when writing the Job Scorecard, but salvaging customer Z should have been an accountability, and Z was lost, the annual review will be pretty intense if Joe is given a Failed to Meet Performance Expectations rating for something that was not clearly described as an accountability.

Do You Have to Anticipate Every Conceivable Accountability?

No, but as new or different ones become apparent, rewrite the Job Scorecard accordingly. In the example above, if maintaining current customers is crucial, spell it out, and maybe include minimum customer service ratings in the Job Scorecard. An economic downturn can change everyone's Job Scorecard. An especially successful product launch can, too. That's okay, so change the Job Scorecards. The last thing you want is your A Player sales reps filling domestic plants if you decide to close those plants.

TOPGRADING HIRING STEP #3:
RECRUIT FROM YOUR NETWORKS

Recruiting has become a way of life for us through Topgrading. Once we began to implement a Recruit from Networks program, hiring has been quicker and more accurate. We have learned that A Players recommend other A Players, and we've built a good network of potential candidates. We find that this is a key to our hiring strategy.

—Frank Evans, CEO, Triton Management

Now that you have a clear, thorough Job Scorecard, so you know exactly what job you are going to fill, it's time to recruit candidates. For decades in Topgrading Workshops we ask, "What's the best way to recruit?" and it's clear that everyone knows the answer—recruit from your Networks of high performers and others you personally know. We've heard it a thousand times: "We get our best performers from referrals—referrals from our best performers."

And then we hear, "We just don't get as many referrals from our people as we want." A Players want to work with A Players and are happy to refer the A Players from their Networks, but it just doesn't happen often enough. Why? The answer is usually, "Because everyone is too busy to stay in touch with their A Player former associates." In this section, you'll learn some solutions.

Case studies in chapter 5 include companies that are very successful recruiting from Networks. K&N Management and DPT Laboratories estimate 40% of their hires come from Networks, and Red Door Interactive estimates 75%. And you read, in the quote above, how vital Frank Evans of Triton feels recruiting from Networks is.

Granted, every manager is busy, and so building and maintaining your Networks is difficult because it's time-consuming. But the advantage of recruiting from your Networks is that it is *faster* (pick up the phone, use e-mail, use your social media), *better* (because you know the people to be high performers), and *cheaper* than running ads or using recruiters (no fees). It's no coincidence that over a dozen billionaires interviewed by Geoff Smart (of ghSMART) said that their principal method of recruiting talent is through their, you guessed it, Networks.

Networks is plural because Topgraders have at least two—A Players they've worked with and Connectors, people who know A Players they can refer. We recommend that every manager build and maintain lists of 20+ A Players and 10+ "Connectors," people who are not suitable for your company, but who know a lot of high performers you might hire. And it's useful to use a form (below) that enables people to jot down sources of Networks.

Suppose you have a job opening for Software Programmer. You pick up the phone and call three A Player software programmers you worked with at other companies, and you locate and hire a terrific person in a couple of weeks. Perfect—that's the essence of recruiting from your Networks. It's quick, effective, and inexpensive.

So, one group within your Networks is composed of high performers you've worked with in the past. This Network can also include high performers you know through professional associations, your neighborhood, or other places.

The other component of your Networks is Connectors, people who know a heck of a lot of high performers you might hire and whose judgment you trust. So if you can't hire a high performer you worked with in the past, next contact your Connectors to see if they can produce excellent candidates. This Connector group can include retirees who stay in touch with lots of talented people, vendors with an eye for talent, professional associates, and former peers who know lots of As. If your Networks don't produce your A Player candidates, it's time to beef up your social media, hire a recruiter, or run ads on Monster.com (or wherever).

To put recruitment in perspective—in my 65,000 oral case studies of total job experiences, I always asked the standard Topgrading Interview question about talent—"In that job how many A, B, and C Players did you inherit, how many As, Bs, and Cs did you end up with, and what happened in between—training, coaching, hiring, firing, etc.?" The managers who said they ended up with mostly A Players almost all had recruited from their Networks. How can you and your team build your Networks?

Exercise: Create Your Networks Lists

List 20+ A Players you know and who might possibly go to work for you, and 10+ Connectors who might refer A Players to you. Add a "Sources" category, a reminder of their professional associations and clubs they will think about as possible sources of candidates and Connectors.

20+ A Players You Know		10+ Connectors
1 _____	11 _____	1 _____
2 _____	12 _____	2 _____
3 _____	13 _____	3 _____
4 _____	14 _____	4 _____
5 _____	15 _____	5 _____
6 _____	16 _____	6 _____
7 _____	17 _____	7 _____
8 _____	18 _____	8 _____
9 _____	19 _____	9 _____
10 _____	20 _____	10 _____

Future Sources of Network of A Players and Connectors

1 _____

2 _____

3 _____

4 _____

HOW COMPANIES BOOST HIRING SUCCESS THROUGH NETWORKS

Topgrading companies understand how to actually get busy, sharp high performers to allocate time to stay in touch with the A Players and Connectors. Their strategies include the following:

1. **Make recruiting through Networks a Job Scorecard accountability.**
   - At a minimum, ask people to go through their BlackBerry and Address Book and identify high performers to include in their Networks of A Players, Connectors, and Sources.

- Require your team to submit annual updates—profiles of each person in their Networks. Managers and key individual contributors either maintain active and productive Networks or sacrifice their annual bonus.
- Require managers to discuss their Networks with their subordinates quarterly, to be sure subordinate Networks are being maintained, and to report the results.
- Require managers to recommend at least one person per year who is hired and who turns out to be an A Player a year later. (Be careful—you don't want someone thinking they won't get an annual bonus unless they refer someone and unconsciously lower the bar and offer marginal candidates.)

2. **Pay bonuses (sometimes called "bounties") for referrals.** The amounts used to be token—$500 for referring someone for a $50,000 per year job, but recently companies have offered a lot more. One client offers $25,000, and ghSMART offers $100,000 to their consultants who refer people who are hired as consultants and who turn out to be high performers. Geoff Smart tried $15,000, but his consultants were too busy working to allocate the extra time to call people, connect using social media, or whatever. The $100,000 means giving up billable time to network. At ghSMART and other companies, part of the bonus is awarded when the referred person is hired, and the rest is awarded on the next few anniversaries. That way the maximum award only is given when someone turns out to be a multiyear high performer.

Singapore-based QuEST has shown, in a creative referral process, that lucrative bounties are *not* always necessary, and might even be counterproductive in their situation. In a blitz to hire a lot of engineers in a single month, the entire company was challenged to generate referrals. The bounty was only $500 for an individual when an engineer was hired. Eight teams of about fifty engineers designed their own name and logo, and created their own ways to motivate people to contact talented engineers who might join the company. The team submitting the most referrals received $50 apiece for dinners—enough to stimulate team competition, but hardly enough to pay for a fancy dinner. Marketing distributed posters and management had constant communications praising people for referring people. The result: 350 referrals and 100 offers in only one month.

The QuEST experience suggests there is a big opportunity for every company to leverage teamwork to generate referrals. Years ago

I designed ten programs in which employees were put into groups (with no supervisors), trained for four hours in teamwork, and given generous incentives to go out and get new customers (six programs) or cut unnecessary costs (four programs). All were successful. Teams met on their own time off-site, huge increases in customers and dramatic reductions in costs were documented, awards were distributed on Friday afternoons ("those new golf clubs will be used tomorrow"), people who had never led had risen to lead groups and were elected Team Supervisor and did so well they were admitted to management training programs, and the ROIs were very high. I predict that in the next decade there will be many case studies in which creative use of informal teams produce terrific referrals at very little cost.

3. **Encourage high performers to use social networks (Facebook, Linked-In, etc.).** A CEO for a $300 million company recently told me how he was hiring an executive. He has over 100 high performers in a personal Facebook group. He first sent the Job Scorecard to his Networks in this group, they made referrals, he spoke with connections on the phone to get additional information, personally contacted six who seemed to be in the ballpark (because not one was looking for a job), and went through the Topgrading Steps to hire someone he's sure will turn out to be a high performer. Remember—recruiting through Networks is better, faster, cheaper than alternative recruitment strategies.

For anyone not using social media to nurture and refresh their Networks, may I suggest that you ask a younger A Player to help you? A 30-year-old recently showed me her Networks, consisting of A Players she has worked with, "Probable" A Players highly recommended by people she respects, and Connectors in various community groups. In her world (and the emerging world for all of us) updated profiles are shared all the time. She says that probably 10 times each week someone in her group of—not 30 or 40 but 150—sends out an updated profile saying they got a promotion, completed an educational program, or whatever. So it's easy for her to send a "congratulations" note, and if someone seems to be more likely to be available to go to work for her or her employer, she might call them. So, for those of us (I'm one!) who are not about to get tweets saying someone's cat died, maybe we should ask someone to help us avoid costly mis-hires by using social media to better use our Networks.

Smart & Associates is trying to help, and at www.Topgrading .com you'll see if we've been successful or not. As of this writing there is a LinkedIn Topgrading Group for anyone who signs up, and 1,200 are members, asking questions, offering Topgrading insights, and . . . networking to hire or get hired. We've created a Topgrading CEO Network group, and a Topgrading Human Resources Network group for heads of HR. Why? The more Topgraders interact with Topgraders, the more they reinforce each other to stick with the Topgrading disciplines, because cutting corners leads to costly mis-hires.

4. **Ask new hires for their Network lists.** Specifically, ask every new hire to write profiles of A Players and Connectors in their Networks, and to update those profiles periodically.

    When you are a Topgrader, getting newly hired managers to do this is easy, because in the Topgrading Interview they gave you some names of As. In Topgrading Hiring Step #7, you'll learn that for the most recent two jobs, you will ask your candidate for profiles of all the subordinates they inherited, and profiles of all their subordinates when the candidate left the job—that's strengths and weaker points of maybe 20 people. Ask your new hire to build a Network including the high performers in these profiles. This isn't a complete Networks list but it's a good starting point for your new team member.

5. **Make a point of encouraging networking, at least weekly.** CEO Ann Drake put it succinctly: *"We recruit all day, every day, with everyone we meet."* In her firm, DSC Logistics, it's embarrassing to *not* hire from Networks. Her managers pump A Players for names of A Players; they ask vendors who's the best (fill in the blank) people they've worked with.

    Be a cheerleader for hiring through Networks. Teams that hire through Networks 80% of the time have leaders who reinforce use of Networks almost every day, praising people for making referrals. Encourage everyone to allocate one hour per week to staying in touch with Networks.

6. **Don't rely solely on e-mail; use the telephone, Skype, and any method to have live, personal communications.** Encourage the use of the good ole telephone. E-mailing people is fine and social networks are a modern way to

network, but we all know that live communications are best for building and maintaining meaningful relationships.

7. **Attract A Players by having exciting Web pages, Careers sections, and job ads.** A lot of companies use their Web sites to sell products, not to attract A Players. The two goals are not mutually exclusive. You only get one chance to make a first impression and you should know now that A Players are already visiting your company Web site.

In chapter 5 you will read about how building the recruitment brand of companies helped recruit A Players. Mega companies such as Apple have huge recruitment budgets to attract As, but even small companies can do a lot. Some companies build their recruitment brand through community service. Several case study companies earned awards such as "Best Company" to work for in the area. With more and more people using social media to judge whether they would want to work for a company, those Best Company awards are accompanied by positive employee testimonials. Here is an example of what we took directly from a Web site:

A BEST PLACE TO WORK

Having a career at Red Door Interactive means you are on a team that helps each other win. You will have the opportunity to work with people who inspire, share, evolve, exceed, and are 100% jerk-free.

Benefits of a Career at Red Door We offer a benefits program that reflects our values of sharing and evolving together, and benefits are effective on the first day of the month following hire. Red Door Interactive pays the full cost of some benefits for employees. For other benefits, our employees share the cost with the company. Programs include health-care coverage, life and long term disability insurance, 401k retirement plan with employer match, variable compensation bonus plan, flexible schedules, professional development, including tuition reimbursement, paid parking, and vacation time that increases with tenure.

Stay in Touch Keep up to date on career opportunities at Red Door by following @reddoor on Twitter and sign up for Red Door Buzz, our e-mail newsletter.

"Nationally recognized by AdAge as a Best Place to Work, voted a Best Place to Work by San Diego Business Journal, recognized for our

Workplace Excellence by San Diego's Society of Human Resource Management, and recognized as a winner of the Top Small Company Workplaces by Inc. Magazine & Winning Workplaces."

—San Diego's Best Places to Work 2011, 2010, 2009, 2008, 2007

When you are a Topgrader, say so. Los Niños won a Best Place to Work in Utah award in part because an independent survey showed that one of the things employees like most about the company is Topgrading. Put "We are Topgraders" in your Careers section of your Web site, with a link (get our permission please) to www.Topgrading.com.

When visitors to your Careers section learn what Topgrading is all about, C Players will get the message and stay away, and high performers, wanting to join a company with other high performers ("Birds of a feather . . .") will be more apt to apply. Don't be shy—boast that you are a Topgrading company. For example:

As a Topgrading company our hiring processes are unusually thorough. There are Competency Interviews but also a chronological Topgrading Interview in which we ask about your entire career—all your successes, mistakes, key decisions, and key relationships. And finalists are asked to arrange personal reference calls with former managers. The benefits to high performers who apply are many: (a) you'll join our family with almost all high performers, (b) career opportunities with Acme are unusually good because so many high performers continue to grow the company, (c) 90% of people who join us are happy on the job a year later and are rated High Performer, and (d) within a couple weeks of joining us you will receive comprehensive coaching to help you assimilate smoothly into Acme, perform very well quickly, and begin formulating your Individual Development Plan to help you grow.

I've thrown a zillion ideas out for building Networks, so here's a thought to make it all simpler: Next time you have a need to hire a lot of people for a common job, assign an A Player in that area to read this section, especially the QuEST approach, and design a program to boost referrals.

But What Should We Do to Get Candidates When Networks Don't Produce Enough (Which Is Most of the Time)?

Don't despair, Topgrading has practical suggestions—not as quick, effective, and inexpensive as hiring A Players you've worked with, but better than just running ads and screening ads, which produce résumés that are too often deceptive. No doubt you have used contingency recruiters to find candidates for some jobs and search firms to find candidates for executive jobs.

Get your money's worth from contingency recruiters. Contingency recruitment firms are paid only when a job is filled (hence, "contingency"), and typically when a company has an opening they contact several firms and say, "Send over your best résumés." No screening is expected, since competitors are all trying to fill jobs, and believe that if they actually interview candidates, they might lose out, since a competitor will send résumés right away and the job could be filled within a day or two. Contingency recruiters rarely use their own name as the company name, since, sorry to say, the industry has a very bad image, frequently explained as, "All they do is throw stuff against the wall to see what sticks." Recruiters are accused of helping C Players pack their résumés with lies, coaching candidates to lie in interviews, and manufacturing false references.

Recently some contingency recruiters have told me they are adopting Topgrading methods, producing better candidates for their clients, and have jumped way ahead of their competitors. I hope so!

In the meantime, here's how you can get your money's worth:

- Reference check the recruiter. Even if they give you their closest buddies, five positive references from real companies should be good enough.
- Require them to conduct at least a two-hour Topgrading Interview and submit at least a three-page report, including real weaker points and failures, not just the positives.
- Give them an exclusive. It's only fair—if they will take more time to interview candidates, they should not be preempted by a competitor who doesn't.

Get the best results from executive search firms. An executive search firm is typically paid about one-third of the anticipated starting pay, regardless of whether they find a candidate you hire. When search firms are paid to recruit talent, do they deliver? Some outstanding search professionals embrace the high performer standard and use Topgrading methods, but most don't. In chapter 2 I reported on a study we conducted of search firm success. We asked CEOs and other senior executives in 1998, 2004, and 2011, with a total sample of over 500, to report on their experiences. In about one-third of searches, the search firm got paid but did not deliver a candidate who was hired; in 79% of the searches, the executives reported that they did not get their money's worth from the search engagement.

When challenged with the dismal statistics on searches, A Player search executives often fire back:

- "B/C Player hiring managers say they want A Players but won't hire one that threatens their status. This search firm shouldn't be blamed."
- "We produce A Player candidates who have other job offers and need to meet our client now, but the client is too disorganized to schedule a visit and loses good candidates."
- "Many times I have tried to put the client through the paces of job analysis and construction of meaningful competencies, but the client is lazy. It's clear they haven't really thought through the job requirements, and when I try to pin them down, they become evasive and defensive."
- "We in the search industry have done a poor job of instructing clients on how they can get the best results."

I believe that some excellent search executives accept assignments only where they are very confident they will succeed. To get A Player search executives to serve you:

- Favor boutique firms of fewer than 10 professionals. Large search firms have some excellent professionals, but if they can't invade their premier clients to attract high performers for you, their value is diminished. Be wary of firms specializing in an industry (computer software), because many top companies might be their clients and therefore locked out of your search.
- Require a written list of companies they cannot penetrate—their

"lockout" list—before you or HR signs a contract. Be sure they can penetrate the companies with the most A Players.

- Check references of the key search executive before signing a contract. Accept nothing less than rave reviews on the consultant you hire, and be sure he/she does 75% (or more) of the work, and is not mostly a salesperson who delegates the work to low-paid "associates." When Larry Bossidy was CEO of Honeywell, he collapsed 44 search firms into four that were outstanding and that promised to use Topgrading methods (and they did, so Honeywell got super service).
- Sign a fixed-fee contract that removes the incentive for the search firm to find more expensive candidates, and requires the professionals you want to do the work (and not delegate it to underlings you haven't met or approved).
- Require thorough Job Scorecards plus several dozen competencies, written after a minimum of two full days of on-premise meetings with hiring managers and key team members.
- Require weekly updates—names and discussions of prospects, not just statistics ("We screened 100 people").
- Insist that they conduct Topgrading Interviews of all finalists, with written reports citing mistakes and failures, not just accomplishments. Tell the search executive, "If you cannot motivate candidates to disclose failures and shortcomings, you're not the right professional for us."
- Be reasonable—don't punish search firms when they present candidates with shortcomings. After all, there is no perfect candidate.
- Require candidate reports to disclose at least six real weak points—everyone has at least that many.
- Require reference-check summaries that disclose negatives, not just positives. Repeat reference calls with all bosses in the past decade after you and the Topgrading professional conduct Topgrading Interviews.
- Sign a contract requiring the search firm to not steal your company's employees for three years. Make your entire company off-limits, not just your division.
- Evaluate some résumés, Career History Forms, and Topgrading Snapshots, and review some Telephone Screening Interview notes early on to be sure you're "on the same page" with the search firm.
- Be very accessible to meet with candidates and to meet with search people to do job analyses, etc. Return their calls promptly.

Topgrading professionals have a love-hate relationship with most search professionals. After all, our Topgrading Interviews are the "second opinion" that really second-guesses their work. When our reports disclose negatives and clients consider the search report a whitewash, the search executives are fired.

Mediocre search people hate Topgrading because the clients require so much from them, but the true high performers love Topgrading. There are a couple of leading search firms that are getting trained in Topgrading methods and telling clients they are different—they probe for negatives and they disclose negatives, not just positives. Good for them! I periodically receive a box of *Topgrading* books FedExed from a search executive, asking me to autograph them so they can distribute them to their clients. An article in *Recruiter Magazine Online* said that nudging clients to Topgrade is one of very few powerful actions recruiters and search executives can take to build business. One put it succinctly: "*Topgrading* makes the most compelling case to replace B/Cs with As, and when clients Topgrade, they hire us to find those A Players."

Run ads! Obviously I've saved the most common recruitment method for last. Most companies fill most jobs through ads and through the Careers section of their Web site. The result is a frustrating experience you know all too well—screening résumés, which too often are deceptive, and hiring too many disappointing performers who got away with deceiving you in their résumé and your interviews because they knew they could get away with it. You already know Topgrading has solved the dishonesty problem with the TORC Technique and candidate-arranged reference calls with former bosses.

Topgrading Hiring Step #4 has powerful additional tools, but before we get to them, do you want to know what the big guys do, the biggest, most powerful companies in the world?

When recruiting from Networks is too overwhelming, particularly when large companies have thousands of jobs to fill and only 5% of hires come from Networks, they use an Applicant Tracking Systems (ATS) to sort through zillions of résumés. They buy HR software that has modules for recruitment, compensation, EEOC, succession planning, etc., and the ATS "scrapes" résumés to make it easier for staffing people to have a small group to actually screen. So, if a staffing manager needs to fill a sales rep job, she can enter into the ATS the region, industry experience, technical expertise, education, or whatever, and the system presents her with a small group of résumés—that's right, résumés, including deceptive résumés of C Players. ATSs serve a useful function—culling the universe of résumés to a much smaller, and more narrowly qualified, group of candidates. But darn—within that smaller group are always candidates who hyped their résumé and are well prepared to deceive you in interviews.

The solution for big and small companies is to accept résumés but to immediately ask for more complete, verifiable, and honest information through the Topgrading Career History Form, which produces the Topgrading Snapshot, the "instant" screening tool.

TOPGRADING HIRING STEP #4: SCREEN CANDIDATES WITH THE TOPGRADING CAREER HISTORY FORM AND TOPGRADING SNAPSHOT

Résumés are too often vague and include a lot of fluff, so it is difficult to differentiate between A Player candidates and Non-As. The Topgrading Career History Form gets a lot of important information that isn't in a résumé, so at K&N we don't waste time with candidates who will not be a good fit for our company. Subsequently, the interviews we conduct are more effective and efficient because we have the details about a person's career like salary history and boss's performance ratings, so we can discuss important topics with candidates like accomplishments and mistakes in interviews. And I love the Topgrading Snapshot because it summarizes the Career History Form information in a picture, enabling us to screen candidates in—or out—in seconds.

—Danielle Robinson, Topgrading Director, K&N Management

Thank you, Danielle, for a succinct summary of how Topgraders use the Topgrading Career History Form to get honest and complete information, and then how they can instantly understand a candidate's total career by looking at their Topgrading Snapshot.

If you have not been using these crucial Topgrading tools, please read this section of the book carefully, because combined, the Topgrading Career History Form and Topgrading Snapshot solve the major hiring problems of *dishonesty* (in résumés), *incomplete information* (in résumés and application forms), *verifiability* of what candidates say (the TORC Technique is embedded), and *speed* to sort through candidate information (would you believe 10 seconds?).

Screening from Résumés Is "Garbage In, Garbage Out"

> *The closest anyone ever comes to perfection is how they represent themselves in their résumé.*
>
> —Stanley J. Randall, author and philosopher

CEOs of two companies that vet résumés told me that more than 50% of the hundreds of thousands of résumés they'd checked out had "deliberate falsehoods." Go to the Careers section of any bookstore and you'll find that every book—not most books but *every* book—on how to get a job encourages job hunters to lard their résumé with mistruths; a book I bought is on my desk and the title of chapter 3 is "It's Okay to Lie on Your Résumé."

Companies mis-hire *far* too many people because popular culture, not just in the United States but throughout most of the world, considers it okay to fake résumés and interviews. And because Applicant Tracking Systems don't sort deceptive from accurate résumés, it's "garbage in, garbage out."

About a zillion years ago, when I began my career interviewing candidates for executive jobs, all clients sent me candidate résumés, and all the résumés looked great. My job was to probe in Topgrading Interviews and sort the As from the Non-As. Wow, that was hard work! It's not that I hate taking client money, but it drove me nuts to interview some candidates clients should *never* have sent me. The chronic C Players had résumés that hyped the positives and conveniently omitted the negatives. To help clients screen people better I created the TORC Technique to get the truth. And since it worked so well, I created the Topgrading Career History Form so clients would get more thorough and valuable information and better screen candidates, *before* they interviewed anyone.

Today hundreds of companies use the Topgrading Career History Form, which, when tailored (with our approval, to be sure no improper questions are included), *is their application form*, with their logo, their special questions, and translations. Following is the online version of the Topgrading Career History Form (shortened a bit to fit the page in the book).

candidate career center

How to interview, hire & promote ONLY top performers

Job History

Candidate Overview	Contact Information	Job History	Military & Education	Qualifications & Goals	Review & Submit	Snapshot & Interview Guides

Do not combine jobs - fill out a *complete* section of this form for *every* job where job title changed (every full time job you have held in your career, and every part time job you have held in the last 6 years).

Jobs may be entered in any order.

EMPLOYER & POSITION

* **Company Name:**

* Address:

* City:

* Country: United States

* State: Select State

* Zip Code:

* Phone:

* **Position Title:**

* **Start Date:** Jan / 2012

* **End Date:** Jan / 2012 ⊙ Still employed in this position
We will not contact any current employer without your expressed premission

COMPENSATION

* Salary Starting: USD ($) ⊙ Hourly ⊙ Weekly ⊙ Monthly ⊙ Annually

* Salary Final: USD ($) ⊙ Hourly ⊙ Weekly ⊙ Monthly ⊙ Annually

MANAGER AND PERFORMANCE INFORMATION

* Manager Name: ⊙ Manager name unclear or n/a

* Manager Title:

* What is your best guess as to how this manager would rate your overall performance?

⊙ Excellent ⊙ Very Good ⊙ Good ⊙ Fair ⊙ Poor ⊙ Impossible to Provide

OTHER INFORMATION

* What do (did) you like most about your job?

* What do (did) you least enjoy?

* If you are leaving (or have already left) this position, what was the reason for leaving...

⊙ 100% Mine ⊙ Mutual ⊙ 100% Employer's (terminated) ⊙ Not Leaving the Company ⊙ Other Circumstances

Reason(s) for leaving:

* Please be aware that prior to a job offer, you may be required to arrange an interview with your previous boss/supervisor. May we contact your employer?

⊙ Yes ⊙ Not at this time ⊙ Never

SAVE THIS JOB   SAVE THIS JOB AND POST ANOTHER JOB   DELETE THIS JOB

The Topgrading Career History Form is far more than an application form with TORC in the instructions. As you can see, it requests all the information you and I wish résumés routinely included, but don't, such as full compensation history, true reasons for leaving jobs, likes and dislikes in jobs, honest estimates of boss ratings of overall performance, honest self-ratings of competencies, a self-appraisal, and more. It is, quite simply, the best preselection tool available, because it produces honest, thorough, verifiable information. And there's another advantage: C Players realize, after reading the instructions:

- "Omygosh, they'll ask me to arrange reference calls with former bosses."
- "My hyped résumé won't cut it because my, uh, untruths will be uncovered."
- "There's no way my former bosses will speak highly of me."
- "There's no way I'll ever get my former bosses to agree to doing a reference call on me."

So *bam!* C Players drop out. And A Players will eagerly complete the Form and look forward to interviews and arranging reference calls. Beautiful! But let's back up to how you get the Topgrading Career History Form information. As mentioned in the previous chapter, Applicant Tracking Systems are useful in reducing a zillion résumés to people who meet the criteria you set—geographic residence, education, experience (shown in job titles), years of experience (shown in job dates), and more.

Applicant Tracking Systems (ATSs) can scrape 1,000 résumés and leave your staffing person with 100 résumés, but how can she tell which of the 100 are honest A Player résumés and which are fictitious C Player résumés? She can't. So she tweaks the ATSs some more, submitting more criteria to cut the 100 to maybe 25 by reducing the geographic area in which a person lives, adding more education requirements, or whatever. But it's still garbage in, garbage out, and when she cuts the stack to five and begins the interviewing process, she feels she's at a disadvantage. She is, because the candidates, even the C Players, totally control what she sees and hears.

The smart "one-two" punch is to use ATSs to cut the number of résumés, but then to use the Topgrading Career History Form to cut the stack to only sharp, honest candidates.

HOW COMPANIES USE THE TOPGRADING CAREER HISTORY FORM AND THE TOPGRADING SNAPSHOT

Allow me to first explain how companies used the Topgrading Career History Form for decades, and how they recently have added usage of the picture of the candidate's career, the Topgrading Snapshot.

Topgrading companies for decades have not talked with any candidate without having their completed Career History Form in hand. If recruiters or executive search firms are used, they send you the candidate's résumé *and* completed Career History Form. You need not waste your time studying fictitious résumés; you'll only review résumés of candidates with impressive, revealing, and honest Career History Forms, because the instructions to the Topgrading Career History Form include the TORC Technique.

When candidates go to the Careers section of your Web site, they are invited to complete the Career History Form (which, as mentioned, for most companies becomes their application form) online. When candidates respond to ads by sending their résumés, most Topgrading companies routinely send all candidates the following e-mail:

"Thank you for responding to our ad for [job]. We take pride in hiring the best. To move to the next step in the hiring process, please complete our application form by clicking [here]."

Some larger companies have a computer simply send the above e-mail to everyone who submits a résumé, or they provide a link on their Careers section to go fill out the online Career History Form.

To summarize, for decades hundreds of companies have used the Topgrading Career History Form to screen candidates because it convinces weak candidates to drop out and screens in the best candidates by providing their full career, with rich, full, relevant, *honest* information.

TOPGRADING SNAPSHOT: INSTANT INSIGHT INTO CANDIDATES

Brad . . . I don't like the new Topgrading Snapshot. I LOVE it! It's clean, clear, simple to understand, and provides a wealth of information that is "at your fingertips." Short of your book and the Topgrading Interview Guide, I believe the Topgrading Snapshot is the best Topgrading tool yet.

—Dr. Ray Bowman, VP Team Development, MarineMax

The Topgrading hiring process gets even better, with an innovation released in 2011, the Topgrading Snapshot. Although the Topgrading Career History Form (converted to a company application form) scares C Players away and attracts A Players, and it enables you to only interview the best candidates, there is one problem clients have asked us to solve, and the Topgrading Snapshot solves it.

The problem is this: time! The Topgrading Career History Form is *sooo* revealing that a hiring manager or HR person can study one completed Form for 15 minutes, and if there are 30 candidates and their 30 completed Forms to read, that's 30 x 15 minutes = 450 minutes, or omygosh—7.5 hours! Spending almost a day to screen candidates for a job is time well spent because interviewing a bunch of B/C Players will waste a *lot more* time. And screening candiates from Career History Firms is a heck of a lot more productive that spending hours studying questionably accurate résumés. However, everyone is so busy that no one seems to have a full day to screen résumés/Career History Forms for one job. For years clients have said it would be great if we could devise some way to screen completed Career History Forms faster, but not do it superficially.

Would you believe cutting the 7.5 hours to half an hour, saving most of a day? We created the Topgrading Snapshot, the picture ("snapshot," if you will) of the most important and revealing parts of the Career History Form, and with it you can honestly, accurately, and validly screen candidates in and out in only seconds. That is a super time-saver!

The Topgrading Snapshot is a one-page picture (actually a graphic image) of the most vital data elements from the completed Career History Form, which as you know gets truthful, complete, verifiable information. Now, with the addition of the Topgrading Snapshot that distills the really essential information in the Career History Form into a one-page summary graphic, you'll save a huge amount of screening time.

How the Topgrading Snapshot Works: If you recruited from your Networks, when your candidate agrees to spend a day interviewing at your company, that is the time to ask them to complete your application form (the Career History Form). Just say, "By taking the time to complete this, you'll give our interviewers a lot of valuable information about you, so all of the interviews will go smoother and your time will be more productive."

If you are using a contingency recruiter or executive search consultant, just say you will only meet with candidates when they have the completed the Career History Form (which produces the Topgrading Snapshot).

But most hiring is not from Networks (yet!) or from screening by recruiters. So in these instances when a candidate e-mails you their résumé in response to an opening in your company or to advertising for a position, you will then respond by using the Topgrading Snapshot's automated mailing feature to send them a preformatted e-mail inviting them to fill out your application form, the tailored Career History Form, complete with the TORC "truth serum" and all the powerful questions about boss ratings, compensation, etc.

Allow me to personalize this. I ran an ad for a Topgrading Professional and received 30 résumés. My office manager, using the Snapshot's automated mailer, sent an e-mail to all 30:

> *Thank you for responding to our ad for Topgrading professional. Smart & Associates has exciting opportunities for talented professionals to run their own consultancy and yet be part of a growing team of global Topgraders. As the next step in the hiring process, please complete our online Career History Form.*

The truth serum no doubt scared away 10 candidates—the weakest ones—and 20 others completed the online Topgrading Career History Form. As soon as candidates clicked Submit, we received both the 20 completed multipage Topgrading Career History Forms as well as their Topgrading Snapshots.

And here is the value: in just 15 minutes of looking at the 20 Topgrading Snapshots, I cut the 20 candidates to 3. What a time-saver! And of course I then studied the Career History Forms of the 3, and decided to pick up the phone for a phone interview with 2. With just a little experience with Topgrading Snapshots, you too can literally zoom through Snapshots in seconds and decide which you want to talk with.

Let's look at two real Topgrading Snapshots (with names changed) to see how just the most important information you need is shown. What you see next is pretty illegible—one small black-and-white version. Please study it, because I've inserted arrows to teach you how to interpret it. But then see two real (names changed) full-page, multicolor Topgrading Snapshots in Appendix B, pages 287–288.

Note that the years go across the bottom and Erik Dorsman had only two employers—A (when he was a teacher) and B (his present employer, where he has enjoyed promotions). He has been with his current employer since 1997. This shows solid longevity—Erik is no job hopper.

Compensation is on the vertical axis, and shows Erik's comp moving

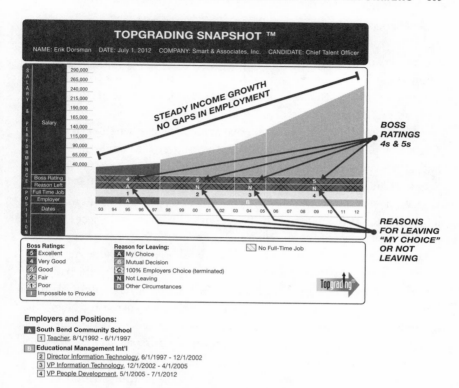

Employers and Positions:

A **South Bend Community School**
  [1] Teacher, 8/1/1992 - 6/1/1997

B **Educational Management Int'l**
  [2] Director Information Technology, 6/1/1997 - 12/1/2002
  [3] VP Information Technology, 12/1/2002 - 4/1/2005
  [4] VP People Development, 5/1/2005 - 7/1/2012

higher across his career. He has steadily earned more and more money—one mark of a high performer. We can see from his current compensation whether Erik is in about the right compensation range for the job being filled. If he is way too high or too low, he might be an A Player, but just not a good candidate for *this* job.

The Topgrading Snapshot also shows you the reasons why a candidate left an employer. Erik's chart indicates that he has left two employers, and both are shown as an A—100% his choice, which is more often the case for A Players than C Players. (N means Not Leaving—he got two promotions.)

Finally, the Topgrading Career History Form requests boss ratings, and Erik says that his first boss (school principal) would give him a Very Good overall performance rating but all three bosses in the past 15 years would rate his performance Excellent—an indication that he is probably an A Player in his present job.

Now here's a little game you can play, but with a serious purpose. Please go to Appendix B (page 287) to see two Topgrading Snapshots (again—real people, names changed) as the Snapshots appear in real life—bigger and in color, without arrows explaining things you will "get" with a little experience. Glance at the color version of Erik Dorsman, which you just studied, but then study John Doe's Topgrading Snapshot and see how long it takes you to make a decision to pursue or reject him. Ready? Go! All you need to know about Doe is that he applied for a job as President of a company with 800 employees, and that the CEO was looking for someone to run the company at least eight years.

How long did it take you to arrive at a conclusion whether to consider Doe worth pursuing as a candidate? I've shown over 100 people the Dorsman Snapshot to explain what's in it, and then asked them to study the John Doe Snapshot and tell me what they see. Everyone "gets it," immediately saying Doe was a job hopper, with weak boss ratings and dubious reasons for leaving jobs. I'll bet it took you less than 30 seconds to be *sure* you'd reject Doe.

And with experience studying just a few more Snapshots, your average time to accept or reject candidates will be even shorter. Companies report that they first look to see if the person's current compensation is "in the ballpark," and if not, rejection takes a couple of seconds. Then they look for dark green boss ratings and reasons for leaving—and if they see a lot of red and blue, that's not indicative of a top candidate. Green boss ratings are Very Good and Excellent, and green for Reasons for Leaving means the person's leaving was 100% their initiative (they were not fired and it was not "mutual").

Although the main reason for creating the Topgrading Snapshot was to save users of the Topgrading Career History Form time, the more important value is to choose only the very best candidates for interviews. Earlier I said I truly believe that the Topgrading Career History Form is the best prescreening tool because of the truth serum and valuable information (comp, boss ratings, etc.). The Topgrading Snapshot just makes it even more valuable by saving time and by having this picture of the candidate's career when conducting all the different interviews.

And later in this chapter you'll read that along with the Topgrading Snapshot, Topgrading interviewers can get all of the Telephone Screening Interview Guide, the Topgrading Interview Guide, and the Topgrading Reference Check Guide, *with all the Career History Form data already in them*, making it extremely easy to just ask the questions and not have to transfer any information from the Career History Form to a Guide.

So, where do the superior Career History Form and Topgrading Snapshot hiring tools fit in with Applicant Tracking Systems (ATSs)? Simply take the résumés the ATS produces and then ask those candidates to complete the Career History Form, which produces the Topgrading Snapshot.

In short, the wave of the future is for the ATS to produce a reduced number of résumés, followed by the Career History Form and Topgrading Snapshot to accurately identify only the best candidates to interview.

TOPGRADING HIRING STEP #5: CONDUCT TELEPHONE SCREENING INTERVIEWS

The Telephone Screening Interview, incorporating the Career History Form information, keeps the interviewer on point and produces valuable applicant insights. It eliminates most weak candidates, so when we meet in person, it's with only the best candidates.

—John Dickey, Senior Vice President, Corporate Support Services, Hill-Rom

In a hypothetical effort to fill a job with a high performer following the 12 Topgrading Hiring Steps, you've measured hiring success and mis-hire costs, created the Job Scorecard, and let's pretend that because you're new at Topgrading, your efforts to recruit from your Networks failed, so you ran ads. You received 50 résumés (using an Applicant Tracking System or not), sent 30 candidates Career History Forms, got 20 back along with their Topgrading Snapshots; you analyzed them, and in fifteen minutes of reviewing the Snapshots, you cut the 20 to 5 candidates who had Career History Forms that looked as though they could be high performers. So you studied their Career History Forms and rejected 2 more, leaving maybe 3 excellent-appearing candidates you want to pursue.

What's next? Are there any potential problems we face?

If you invite the three candidates in for face-to-face interviews, you could spend hours with poor candidates who could have been screened out in a few minutes on the phone. So most Topgrading companies find that to save time it's usually preferable to screen candidates on the phone next. Here's a caveat: if you are desperate and have very few candidates but they are local (no travel cost), or if you are screening for an entry job in which professional appearance is crucial, it probably is best to go ahead and conduct face-to-face interviews, even if you waste more time with poor candidates than you would with phone screens.

So the skill to learn is how to conduct Telephone Screening Interviews, where you really do screen out weak candidates and invite only the best in for face-to-face interviews. All the different interview guides used in *Top-grading* are online, prepopulated with Career History Form information, and are available when the Topgrading Snapshot is used. This book gives you the essence of each. To conduct an effective Telephone Screening Interview, do the following:

1. Prior to the phone call, review the completed Topgrading Career History Form and Topgrading Snapshot.
2. Tell the candidate:
   "Thanks for completing the Topgrading Career History Form. In this phone call, I'd like to tell you a bit more about the company and job, and answer your questions. And, I'd like to ask you questions about your background and goals. Ultimately, before a job offer, we'll ask you to arrange personal reference calls with bosses. Okay?"
3. Describe the company and position to the candidate.
4. Invite the candidate to ask questions about the job.
5. Review the following for the most recent two jobs (start with second to last job and then ask about current or most recent job):
   Successes
   Failures
   Boss's appraisal of your strengths, weaker points, and overall performance
   Reasons for leaving
6. Add two questions each from three competencies.
7. If you and the candidate want to move to the next step, it's time to explain Topgrading . . .

As a Topgrading company, our hiring processes at Acme are un-usually thorough. There are Competency Interviews but also a chrono-logical Topgrading Interview in which we ask about your entire career—all your successes, mistakes, key decisions, and key relation-ships. And finalists are asked to arrange personal reference calls with former managers and others. The benefits to high performers who apply are many: (a) if you're hired, you'll go to work in a company with almost all high performers, (b) career opportunities with Acme are un-usually good because so many high performers grow the company, (c) 90% of people who join us are happy on the job a year later and are rated High Performer, and (d) within a couple of weeks of joining us you will receive comprehensive coaching to help you assimilate smoothly into the company, perform very well quickly, and begin formulating your Individual Development Plan to help you grow.

After this Telephone Screening Interview you can go to the Job Scorecard and enter tentative ratings (using the 5-point scale, 5 being high), which are far from final ratings. Ratings of candidates are all "best-guess" ratings, but after analyzing the Career History Form and Topgrading Snapshot you entered an early set of "best guess" ratings. Now, after conducting the Telephone Screening Interview, you'll no doubt change some ratings, because this is how the total hiring process works: after each of the Topgrading steps go to the Job Scorecard and revise your ratings. As you get more and more revealing information, your ratings will be closer and closer to reality. As long as your ratings exceed the Minimum Acceptable Rating, you of course will continue going through the Topgrading steps. To the extent that your ratings fall below that Minimum Acceptable Rating, you could choose to no longer pursue the candidate.

In our book *Topgrading for Sales*, my co-author Greg Alexander suggested supplemental questions for sales reps:

1. *Please describe your territory.* (Is the sales rep selling based on geography, product line, or names of accounts? Is he/she really on top of the territory?)
2. *Please describe the quota system.* (Is the candidate measured on revenue, gross profit, unit sales, new accounts, etc.? How well does the candidate explain the keys to success?)
3. *Please describe your production.* (Nail down performance vs. targets. How engaged is the person? Make excuses? Get answers to #1–#3 for more than the present job, perhaps the last three jobs, to perform a more thorough screen.)
4. *Please describe your compensation plan.* (Is there understanding of how sales rep success drives company success? Is the person motivated?)
5. *Please describe your company's value proposition.* (This should be an "elevator pitch," 30 seconds.)
6. *Please describe your major competitor's value proposition.* (The differences between #5 and #6 should be very clear.)
7. *Please explain the top three objections you must overcome to close sales, and how you overcome them.* (Does the candidate beat the competition?)
8. *Please describe your typical day and week.* (Does the person work hard and work smart, doing administrative work after hours?)

9. *What do you like most and least about your job?* (A complainer? Would things be different in your company?)
10. *Please describe what you like and dislike about your last two bosses, and give your best guess as to what they would tell me, in reference interviews you would arrange, are your strengths, weaker points, and overall performance.* (Do you fit the profile of what the candidate likes in a boss? Does he/she come from a competitive culture? Is the person honest or doing a whitewash?)

To summarize, use the Telephone Screening Interview Guide with candidates who truly look as though they could be high performers from your analyses of the Topgrading Career History Forms and Topgrading Snapshots, and only invite the ones who really appear to be A Players in for face-to-face interviews. These tools work, and they help you save time and only meet candidates who are pretty good or better.

TOPGRADING HIRING STEP #6: CONDUCT COMPETENCY INTERVIEWS

Although the one-hour competency or behavioral interviews are not nearly as good as the tandem Topgrading Interview in giving us insights into candidates, we include several Competency Interviews because candidates want to talk to more people than just the tandem Topgrading interviewers. Also, in those Competency Interviews, the candidates get plenty of time to ask the interviewers tough questions about what it's like working here.

—Ann Smith, Regional Sales Director for the Northeast Region at PharmaSales (fictitious name of manager and company; company is anonymous so as to not alert competitors to the value of Topgrading)

You're now ready to interview candidates face-to-face. It may surprise you that of the 12 Topgrading Hiring Steps this first face-to-face interview is the weakest. You've just read two reasons for including this step, but if they aren't convincing, eliminate it and your hiring success will probably not be affected.

What are Competency Interviews? They are interviews in which different interviewers spend an hour (including a short break) with a candidate, asking questions about one or more of the key competencies that were identified and listed in the Job Scorecard.

Disadvantages of Competency Interviews

Decades ago the business world flocked to so-called competency (or "behavioral") interviews, because they were clearly better than "tell me about yourself" chats. Trouble is, Competency Interviews are weak predictors of job performance when compared with the Topgrading Interview. Competency Interviews are *still* the main hiring method that #1 Human Resources executives of Global 100 companies said produce 80% of their mis-hired managers. As the former CEO of UBS (Mark Sutton) once said, "How can one-hour Competency Interviews, in which the candidate selectively shares information, reveal as much as a four-hour Topgrading Interview that scrutinizes 100% of successes and failures?"

The Competency Interview model sounds good—analyze the job, write a list of competencies necessary for success in the job, and prepare a list of behaviorally anchored questions that require disclosure of not just successes, but failures. It's a structured process, with standardized questions, note taking, and face-validity (meaning the questions all sound reasonable to candidates). EEOC likes all those features.

Unfortunately, Competency Interviews generate maybe 100 data points to address maybe six competencies, whereas the Topgrading Interview (Step #7) generates thousands of data points to address dozens of competencies. Competency Interviews fail because a typical competency question is, "Pat, can you give me an example of when you had a lot of passion for your work?" *Of course* anyone can come up with an example and anyone can claim more passion than exists.

Competency Interviews overlook too much. Typical competencies for management jobs are Team Player, Passion for Excellence, Integrity, Organization, Leadership, and Judgment. Most competency questions are like the Passion example above—"Give me an example of . . ."—and the competency was shown or not shown in the response. Another example: "Pat, can you give me an example of a time you were an effective Team Player, and a time you weren't so good?" The candidate is in total control of the responses, and it's simple to . . . *um* . . . put one's "best foot forward."

A senior manager of one of the larger recruiting firms told me, "I can coach a candidate to successfully fake his way through any Competency Interview." I replied, "You coach them to lie?" and he responded, "No, no, no . . . just selectively disclose the truth." Uh-huh. An outplacement counselor I met flat-out told me he creates fictitious résumés and coaches people to lie in interviews, and when challenged on the ethics, he said, "Everybody lies to get a job and I just help people lie better."

So, Why Include Competency Interviews?

Despite the inability of Competency Interviews to result in hiring success, we do recommend this step because, as mentioned in Ann Smith's opening quote, (1) sharp candidates want to talk with a lot more people than just the Topgrading interviewers, and (2) we add letting candidates ask questions for 15 minutes of each interview. Here's a third reason: companies like the "inertia" of keeping this step. So Topgraders oftentimes include this step, and rather than interviewers "winging it" in unstructured interviews, they create structured interview guides. Topgrading licensees use our catalog of hundreds of competency questions to create the guides.

As you have probably noticed, there are caveats and exceptions to a lot of the principles and steps recommended in this book. So here's another: some of the case study companies eliminate this step, finding that the Competency Interviews add nothing beyond what the tandem Topgrading Interview discloses, and in fact the Competency Interviews resulted in some strong but totally inaccurate conclusions about candidates. Out went the Competency Interviews. But A Players do want to ask more people than the Topgrading interviewers questions about company/boss/decision making/ etc., so they just arrange additional interviews for that purpose.

Create Competency Interview Guides

Every time Topgrading professionals hear that round-robin Competency ("behavioral") Interviews are *not* structured, and the interviewers do not use interview guides and "wing it," we ask, "How many years do you want to spend in a minimum-security prison?" It's a smart-aleck question designed to get their attention with this fact: EEOC favors structured interview guides to minimize discrimination, and they want all candidates to be asked the same basic questions (it's okay to have unique follow-up questions). Before EEOC existed I favored what EEOC expects—job analysis, job scorecard, and structured interviews (in which all the interviewers ask all the candidates all the same basic questions). When interviewers "wing it" by asking any question that pops into their head, candidates obviously are *not* all asked the same questions, and to EEOC that is suspect. If a rejected candidate raises an issue with EEOC, and if you had to produce data on hiring steps, it would get serious if the six (or whatever) competency interviews were shown to systematically reject a protected group (race, age, gender, etc.). And it would be even more damning if the competency interviewers all asked different questions.

You will read more about this in chapter 4, the section on legalities in hiring (pages 189–195), but for now here's the bottom line: I have not heard of one legal challenge for any aspect of Topgrading, let alone a successful one—a successful lawsuit or a settlement. Let's keep it that way—use structured competency interview guides (and in Hiring Step #7, of course use the structured Starter and later full Topgrading Interview Guides).

You can buy competency guides. Or create your own from our catalog of competency questions.* Or you can just make them up yourself.

Here's How to Create a Competency Interview Guide

1. **Pick key competencies.** Most jobs have five or six "key competencies," though as mentioned previously, all management jobs should be assessed and rated on all 50 competencies. In workshops we always ask attendees to help us out and reduce the list of 50. We ask, *"If you would hire someone who is Poor or Very Poor on a competency, then it's not important enough to be in the list of 50, so which ones can we eliminate?"* After hundreds of workshops the answer is . . . you guessed it . . . not one of the 50!

2. **Write four questions about each competency** (or at least two questions if you will be asking questions about several competencies as in the example below). Two of the questions can ask the candidate to describe situations in which the competency was demonstrated, and the other two ask the candidate to describe situations in which the competency was not shown.

3. **Write as many culture-fit questions as there are interviewers.** Every competency interviewer will focus on one or more competencies *plus* ask at least one question to try to determine how the person will fit with the organizational culture. For example, if it is a job requiring

---

* Available in the Topgrading Shop at www.Topgrading.com.

communicating with peers many times every day, questions should focus not just on communications in general, but frequency of communications with various groups.

4. **Create the competency interview guide,** with the questions and spaces for responses. An example is below and there are hard copy or online versions available in the Topgrading Shop at www.Topgrading .com.

5. **Choose the competency interviewers** (typically four to six for a management job). Typically the competency interviewers will include peers of the hiring manager and a couple of people at the candidate's level in the organization. The hiring manager is *not* one of the interviewers for competency interviews, but instead will be one of the tandem Topgrading interviewers. The hiring manager sometimes greets the candidate at the beginning of the day, to essentially be the host for the day.

Here is a sample in which a company had 12 key competencies, so each of four competency interviewers asked questions about three competencies, plus culture fit.

COMPETENCY INTERVIEW GUIDE:

Job: Chief Talent Officer
Date: June 1, 2012

Candidate's Name: Erik Dorsman

Interviewer's Name: Brad Smart

Competencies Discussed:

Change Leadership

Selecting A Players

Resourcefulness

Culture Fit

Questions

Competency	Question
Change Leadership	1. *In what specific ways have you changed an **organization** the most (in terms of direction, results, policies)?* Candidate's Answer:
Change Leadership	2. *What is an example in which you think you could have done a better job of change management? (Look for communicating like mad!)* Candidate's Answer:
Selecting A Players	3. *What have your most **recent two teams** looked like (how many A, B, C Players) and what changes were made?* Candidate's Answer:
Selecting A Players	4. *Explain your **selection process** in terms of job analysis, job description, behavioral competencies, amount of structure to interviews; if there is an in-depth chronological interview, how are reference checks done?* Candidate's Answer:
Resourcefulness/Initiative	5. *What actions would you take in the **first weeks,** should you join our organization?* Candidate's Answer:
Resourcefulness/Initiative	6. *What sorts of obstacles have you faced in your present/most recent job, and what did you do? (Look for passion and effectiveness in figuring how to surmount barriers to success.)* Candidate's Answer:

(Continued)

| Culture Fit | 7. *As you have read in the Job Scorecard, the Chief Talent Officer is expected to travel 50% of the time. Have you ever traveled that much for a job, and if so, how did it work out in terms of getting the job done?* |
| | Candidate's Answer: |

| Culture Fit | 8. *We're undergoing some financial pressures and recently all of our budgets were cut. Please describe a situation, if there has been one, in which you had your budget drastically cut.* |
| | Candidate's Answer: |

| Culture Fit | (Invite the candidate to ask questions about anything they want—organizational culture, decision making, etc.) |

Overall Conclusions:

Would you Recommend Hiring, or Not Hiring:

What happens after the Competency Interviews? Someone might take the candidate to lunch, but then it's decision time—do you want to continue to pursue the candidate, and if so, does the candidate still want the job? The hiring manager meets with the competency interviewers at end of the day to hear the interviewers' opinions, including whether or not they recommend moving forward with the candidate. The hiring manager decides whether to ask the candidate in for the Topgrading Interview.

Usually the Competency Interviews are done before the tandem Topgrading Interview, so that the hiring manager doesn't waste time on candidates that are eliminated (or drop out themselves) at this stage, but some companies prefer the reverse order so that the time of competency interviewers is not wasted on candidates screened out in the Topgrading Interview.

TOPGRADING HIRING STEP #7:
CONDUCT TANDEM TOPGRADING INTERVIEWS

The Tandem Topgrading Interview, using the Topgrading Interview Guide, has become critical to our staffing process. It is set up in a logical and systematic way, and permits the interviewers to hear a thorough review of all the previous jobs that got the person to where they are today— the events, motivations, accomplishments, and failures. It's really opened our eyes to important things that we otherwise would have missed.

—Rick Steinberg,
Vice President of Human Resources,
Columbus McKinnon

There is no surprise that the intensive Topgrading Interview provides much better hiring, focusing on not only "what" was done but also "how" things were done.

—Paul Idzik, CEO, DTZ (former)

The tandem Topgrading Interview is the most powerful hiring tool. It contributes more to improved hiring and promoting than all the other 11 Topgrading Hiring Steps combined. As stated in Step #6, the hiring world is chugging along on the equivalent of a 10-minute shallow, superficial online insurance physical exam, relying on Competency Interviews that are easy to fake; Topgraders generally include this flawed Competency Interview step because they make it more useful by permitting candidates to ask the questions about the job. A Players insist on getting answers! However, the Topgrading Interview is like a Mayo Clinic five-day executive physical exam—identifying everything that is important. The Topgrading Interview "made" my career, enabling me to earn a reputation that 90%+ of the candidates I recommended turned out to be high performers. And since the mid-1990s managers like you have learned how to conduct Topgrading Interviews, and enjoy 70%, 80%, and even 90%+ success picking high performers.

If you were to read only one part of this book very carefully (not skim it), make this the section. It will do the most to help you hire better.

What Is the Topgrading Interview?

It's a chronological interview starting with school years and progressing through many questions about every job starting with the first job and moving forward to the present. Then there are additional questions—Plans and Goals, Self Appraisal, and a few final Competency Questions. Unlike the Competency ("behavioral") Interviews in Step #6, in which candidates are asked very few questions about very few competencies, the Topgrading Interview delves into every success, failure, important decision, and important relationship—particularly all boss relationships and boss ratings—for every job. And there are many additional questions.

This is the world's best, most thorough, most proven interview, and no other interview has one one-hundredth of the proven success for hiring and promoting people. In this chapter you'll learn a simplified version of it, but enough that you will be able to try it out and then want to learn more. And when you are ready, a (free) online course will train you to conduct the full Topgrading Interview.

What Is the *Tandem* Topgrading Interview?

It's simply using two interviewers. Two heads are a *lot* better than one.

I'll explain more about the tandem approach later, but for now just figure on picking a tandem partner for your Topgrading Interviews, when you are interviewing candidates for managerial or professional positions (scientist, engineer, teacher, sales representative). Experienced Topgrading interviewers can usually "go solo" when interviewing for lower-level jobs (clerk, stocker), but only if their "solo" hiring results are 75%+ high performers hired.

LEARN TO WALK BEFORE YOU RUN: THE TWO-PHASE TOPGRADING INTERVIEW LEARNING PROGRAM

Previous editions of this book went into so much detail about the 30-page Topgrading Interview Guide that readers got "lost in the weeds." That was my fault—I overwhelmed readers with too much information. So I'm teaching you the Topgrading Interview in phases, sort of like a beginning skier learning to ski green runs before blue runs.

A lot of Topgrading steps are straightforward and easy to implement, but the most important step, the Topgrading Interview, is difficult to do well. As previously mentioned, in our workshops, on Day 1 we survey attendees, and typically no one—*no one*—believes they will be able to conduct four-hour interviews of managerial candidates smoothly and professionally, and arrive at valid conclusions on 50 competencies. Day 2 is pairing off to conduct a full tandem Topgrading Interview, coached by Topgrading professionals. After conducting the coached interview, managers write an Executive Summary, and then provide feedback and coaching to their interviewee, just as they would do in "real life." And they pull it off. They *finally* believe they can conduct this long, complicated interview only when they've done it and done it well. There is no way to teach the full Topgrading Interview in any book—sorry—so I suggest two learning phases, with your practicing with a simple version first.

Phase 1: Try the Starter Topgrading Interview Guide

In chapter 1 (page 13) you read about Topgrading Lite, and now let's make those steps operational, expanding on your conducting the Topgrading Interview:

- **Use the Topgrading "Truth Serum," the TORC Technique.** As you know, *TORC* stands for "Threat of Reference Check." At every step in the hiring process let candidates know that just prior to a job offer *they* will have to arrange personal reference calls with supervisors and others you choose.
- **Ask candidates to complete the Topgrading Career History Form**, which produces the Topgrading Snapshot. For our readers we are providing a free trial use of the snapshot. (For how to get and use these, see Topgrading Resources, pages 331–333.)
  - Before you try the Starter Topgrading Interview Guide you need to decide on who will be your first interviewee(s). Are you confident enough to interview a real candidate for a crucial job? If you are not very experienced in any type of interview, interview a lower-level candidate or interview someone who works for you. You can make mistakes and not feel awkward, work the bugs out and decide if you want more practice interviews or to "go live" with real candidates.
- **Ask a sharp person to be your tandem interviewer** because two heads are much better than one; you'll be more comfortable than if you go solo, and frankly you will do a much better job.
- **The two of you just ask all the questions in the Starter Topgrading Interview Guide** (Appendix E), probe with follow-up questions, and take a lot of notes.

- **Ask the candidate to arrange reference calls.** After the interview, if you and your tandem partner decide you want to proceed with the candidate (assuming of course that your interviewee is a candidate), ask the candidate to arrange personal reference calls with former supervisors and others *you* choose. The TORC Technique is not an idle threat; you absolutely should talk with supervisors and others, but ask the candidates to do the work of arranging the calls. After you have gotten descriptions of all supervisors (and others) during the Topgrading Interview, you choose which people you'd like to talk with. Chances are you want to talk with all supervisors in the past 10 years (if the candidate doesn't want you to talk with the current supervisor, okay, but ask the candidate to arrange a call with someone at the supervisor's level who left the company).
- **Make the reference calls.** You and your tandem partner divvy the calls up and you each make half of them. Then you compare notes and decide what to do—make a job offer, offer the job to another candidate, or whatever.

Almost certainly your tandem partner and you will believe that this is the best, the most revealing interview you've conducted. So after only a couple of times using the Starter Topgrading Interview Guide you'll want to progress to the full guide.

Phase 2: Learn and Conduct the Full Topgrading Interview, Using the Full Topgrading Interview Guide

When you are comfortable using the Starter Interview Guide, it will be time for you to master use of the full 30-page Topgrading Interview Guide. To do this, first watch a free 47-minute video, *How to Use the Topgrading Interview Guide*. Go to Topgrading Resources (page 331) for specifics.

Although you will initially use the Starter Topgrading Interview Guide, with just a few questions about every job, just so you know what to look forward to, the image opposite shows one job covered in the Topgrading Guide, shortened a bit to fit the page of this book.

You can see that candidate information is inserted in this sample. How did that happen? When the Topgrading Career History Form produces the Topgrading Snapshot, if after the Telephone Screening Interview you decide to invite the candidate in for Competency Interviews and then the Topgrading Interview, you can print out the Topgrading Interview Guide

Prepopulated Topgrading Interview Guide

EMPLOYER & POSITION

Company: **Educational Management Int'l**

Title: **Director Information Technology**

Start/End Dates: **June 1997 - December 2002**

Type of Business: **Education Management**

Address: **444 Main St. Bingham, Ohio 23456**

Phone: **666-666-6666**

Can you tell me about the company's revenues, products, services, and number of employees?

SALARY

Starting Salary: **50,000 (Annually)**
Base: **40000**
Bonus: **4000**

Ending Salary: **104,000 (Annually)**
Base: **68000**
Bonus: **16800**

RESPONSIBILITIES & PERFORMANCE

What were your expecations for the job?

What were your responsibilities and accountabilities?

What did you find when you arrived? What shape was the job in (talent, resources, performance problems)? What major challenges did you face?

What results were achieved in terms of successes and accomplishments? How were they achieved? (As time permits, get specifics, such as individual vs. shared accomplishments, barriers overcome, bottom line results, and impact on career-bonus, promotability, performance review.)

We all make mistakes - what would you say were mistakes or failures experienced in this job? If you could wind the clock back, what would you do differently? (As time permits, get specifics.)

All jobs seem to have their pluses and minuses; what were the most enjoyable or rewarding aspects of this job? **Opportunity to develop an infrastructure and build a team from scratch.**

What were the least enjoyable aspects of the job? **Early resistance to leveraging technology as an accelerator; dysfunction at the management level.**

TALENT

(For management jobs) What sort of talent did you inherit (how many As, Bs, Cs)? What changes did you make, how, and how many As, Bs, and Cs did you end up with?

SUPERVISOR

Supervisor's Name: **Paul Andrews**

Title: **President & CEO**

Where is that person now?

Would you be willing to arrange for us to talk with him or her? **Yes**
(Say you will want to talk with all supervisors in the past ten years.)

What were your supervisor's strengths?

What were your supervisor's shortcomings?

What is your best guess as to what that supervisor really felt at that time were your strengths and weaker points?

STRENGTHS	WEAKER POINTS

How would that supervisor rate your overall performance? **Excellent**

OTHER

Are there any important decisions or relationships that we have not discussed?

What circumstances contributed to your leaving? (Always probe for initially unstated reasons.) **Not Leaving the Company** with—get this—100% of all the valuable information the candidate provided in the Topgrading Career History Form. The benefit is huge—you don't have to transfer that information by hand from the Career History Form to the Topgrading Interview Guide. What a time-saver!

As you know, interviewing isn't easy, even with a time-tested interview guide to follow. In any given moment during an interview, you naturally want to *listen* carefully to the response to a question, and in doing so you might wonder if further clarification is necessary. If so, you might want to compose an original, probing question, so you need to figure out the wording to it ("try to make it open-ended, don't bias the response," and so forth). You perform a quick *memory scan*, to see if the current response possibly contradicts a previous response. You are trying to tune in to your gut feelings in order to develop the intuitive sense that can only be valid if anchored in facts. All the while you are also trying to maintain adequate eye contact and a high level of rapport while taking copious notes and, by the way, carefully observing the candidate's body language. Some people are very perceptive, accurately reading nuances in verbal and nonverbal communications, but that talent can make interviewing more complicated because such people generate more hunches to check out in follow-up questions. The opposite— someone who is interpersonally dense—has the challenge of trying to connect dots that just don't connect. *Phew!* Interviewing is difficult! This is enough to do, and you don't want to have to manually transfer the huge amount of information in the Career History Form to the Topgrading Interview Guide; so voilà, it's automatically done for you.

So, both the Starter and full versions of the Topgrading Interview Guide simplify this highly complex intellectual exercise called interviewing by providing a clear, logical sequence of questions and using two interviewers who cover for each other. Just ask each and every question in order, take a lot of notes, follow up with questions to get clarification, and turn the page when all the questions have been asked. The wording, fine-tuned for decades, is presented, and there is space to take notes. If there is a blank after a question, this is a visual signal for you to ask the question (unless there is a good reason not to). By mechanizing the interview just enough, but not too much, you can look and feel professional and devote your energies to analyzing the candidate.

Marshall McLuhan, creator of the notion of the global village, proclaimed, "The medium is the message," and so it is with interviewing. Thoroughness and honesty is the message, the passageway to truth. It's thoroughness and honesty that show you revealing patterns, patterns for how the candidate evolved to today, for not just a few but literally dozens of competencies.

The only disadvantage of using the Topgrading Interview is that it takes longer than other interviews, and on top of that there are two interviewers when interviewing managerial candidates. With your improved hiring "batting average," however, in the long run you save an enormous amount of time, not only in the entire selection process but in managing A Players rather than B/C Players.

If you used the Topgrading Talent Projection Calculator (page 67), you know that as soon as you improve your hiring and promoting success, you save not only a fortune in mis-hire costs, but hundreds of hours you no longer have to allocate to "manage" low performers. Managers who say, "I don't have three hours for a Topgrading Interview" should finish the sentence with, "so I will waste hundreds of hours and I'll mis-hire three out of four people, at a cost of $300,000, plus 750 wasted hours." Some logic! The Topgrading Interview Guide, infused with all of what the candidate entered on your application form, makes interviewing amazingly . . . easy!

Managers who say, "I don't have three hours for a Topgrading Interview" should finish the sentence with, "so I will waste hundreds of hours and I'll mis-hire three out of four people, at a cost of $100,000 (or whatever) × 3 = $300,000 plus 3 × 250 = 750 wasted hours."

HISTORY AND ADVANTAGES OF TWO INTERVIEWERS (THE TANDEM TOPGRADING INTERVIEW)

Using two interviewers of managerial candidates (not entry-level candidates) turbocharges hiring success. I began using two interviewers in Topgrading workshops in the 1980s. The Topgrading Interview was so complicated and difficult that we had to use two interviewers rather than one. Somewhat feebly I'd say toward the end of workshops, "You just experienced the use of a tandem interviewer and you all love it, because it makes the interview and decisions about the candidate a heck of a lot easier. So please do it in real life." And maybe 5% took the advice.

Enter Jack Welch. I had been consulting with General Electric for a couple of years, and CEO Welch saw that GE's success picking A Players was much improved thanks to use of the Career History Form and Interview Guide. However, initially GE used solo interviews. Jack asked me how GE managers could do even better at picking high performers. He hoped that they would become as successful as Topgrading professionals. I said, "Jack, for years I've used two interviewers in workshops and I know the tag team will improve success for GE managers." He didn't hesitate a second—done! Flash forward many years and in fact GE managers dramatically improved success picking high performers with the tandem approach.

Thousands of managers love the tandem model because they have a backup—a tag team with someone else to help ask questions, to probe deeper, to offer insights from a different point of view, to tone down biases, to help analyze notes after the interview, to give each other feedback on interviewing technique, and to help provide feedback and coaching for new hires. With GE's success with the tandem approach, in workshops I became quite emphatic with all Smart & Associates clients: "To achieve anything better than 50% A Players hired you *must* use the tandem Topgrading Interview." A year after our two-day Topgrading Workshops, almost all attendees report that they conduct—you got it—*tandem* Topgrading Interviews. And in the dozens of case studies in this book, you'll read the tandem Topgrading Interview is, indeed, the most powerful hiring method.

Jack Welch was the first CEO to accept my advice to have two interviewers. As GE achieved prominence as one of the most respected companies in the world and Welch *the* most admired CEO, companies copied GE, and the tandem Topgrading Interview has been the model embraced by Topgrading clients achieving that 90% hiring success rate. If Jack had not approved the tandem model, you would probably not be as interested in Topgrading . . . because few managers seem capable of achieving even 50% A Players hired when they "go solo" (except for entry, nonprofessional jobs).

If Jack had not approved the tandem model, you would probably not be as interested in Topgrading.

How Are Tandem Interviewers Best Matched?

To be truly effective with your tandem partner (usually called "tandems" in companies) pick an A Player for a tandem, ideally someone trained in Topgrading. Pick someone who is not your clone—if the job is in marketing management and you are a whiz in management but not a whiz at marketing, pick a marketing expert as your tandem. Joe is kind of cold, so he chooses a warm tandem. Pat is technically weak, so she chooses a tandem who is a techie. Every day Jon works closely with Susan, so he wants her to be his tandem. Senior managers, who sometimes have little experience conducting Topgrading Interviews, frequently pick a Human Resources professional, if that person has conducted dozens or hundreds of tandem Topgrading Interviews.

There is one more decision: who will be the primary interviewer who asks most of the questions and takes a few notes, and who will be the secondary interviewer who will probably ask 25% of the questions but take copious notes. Fortunately the tandem interview is a very robust process, so that different modes all seem to work. You can decide someone will be the primary interviewer the first half and then switch or just be a tag team, alternating jobs, or change your mind partway into the interview. It doesn't seem to matter if the personalities are similar or different. It just works. At least one of the tandems must be higher in the organization than the interviewee, to maintain control. And one of the interviewers should be an experienced Topgrading interviewer; the Human Resources manager serving many hiring managers is usually the most experienced interviewer and is most often asked to be the tandem partner.

How Do Tandem Interviewers Structure the Interview?

Tandems review the candidate's résumé and Career History Form and Topgrading Snapshot, and then they talk about how they want to structure the interview. Generally the hiring manager introduces the process and the tandem partner takes over as the principal interviewer for the first half (with the hiring manager taking most of the notes but chiming in with a question or comment periodically). There is a break (drinks, washroom) at about the midpoint. Then the hiring manager becomes the primary interviewer for the more recent (and relevant) half of the chronology, with the tandem taking more voluminous notes and periodically injecting rapport-building comments or asking questions. Finally both ask a few competency questions.

About one-quarter of interview teams plow ahead with no one as the primary interviewer. This truly evokes the tag team image, and we see it work just fine in Topgrading Workshops. Both know the Topgrading Interview sequence of questions, both take notes, and it's a free-flowing two-on-one.

It's less organized but more spontaneous to not have a designated primary interviewer.

After the interview both tandems review all notes and reach consensus on rating all competencies (this post–Topgrading Interview process is elaborated on later in this chapter).

WHAT A TOPGRADING INTERVIEW IS LIKE

Would you like me to walk you through a typical Topgrading Interview to give you a feel for how it goes and explain some of the most important principles? In this section you will recognize some topics already discussed, but I'll pull it all together and add some further clarification.

Let's assume that you will enter the Topgrading Interview having gone through the various preparatory steps you have read about: Steps #1 through #6. You measured your hiring/promoting success and cost of a typical mishire (Step #1). A thorough job analysis has been done, and a Job Scorecard has been written (Step #2) that includes first-year accountabilities. In the Job Scorecard, extensive competencies have been spelled out, written in behavioral terms, and assigned a Minimum Acceptable Rating (which can be measured with e-mail surveys). For most technical or staff positions, approximately 15 competencies should suffice, and 50 competencies are necessary for managers.

Suppose you are going to conduct your first Topgrading Interview, using the Starter Interview Guide. You have decided to interview a subordinate or a candidate below a level that would be typical for you, just so you have a psychological advantage and won't feel you have to apologize for possible lack of smoothness. Let's say you have recruited that person (Step #3) through running ads. You've taken advantage of the offer (Appendix H) to get free Topgrading Snapshots, and your candidate has completed the online Topgrading Career History Form (Step #4), which produced the Topgrading Snapshot.

You personally conducted a Telephone Screening Interview (Step #5). You are the hiring manager, so you partnered nicely with Human Resources, and HR coordinated six Competency Interviewers to conduct those interviews (Step #6) last week. After the Competency Interviews you met with those interviewers to get their opinions, they all entered (in the Job Scorecard) tentative ratings for the various competencies, with those ratings to be refined after each Topgrading Hiring Step. You decided to continue to pursue the candidate, so the Topgrading Interview (Step #7) was scheduled a week later.

How to Prepare for a Topgrading Interview

A couple of days prior to the Topgrading Interview you and your tandem interviewer review the Job Scorecard, the individual's résumé, application form (Career History Form), and Topgrading Snapshot, and the notes from the Telephone Screening Interview and all the Competency Interviews.

How to allocate time. First-time Topgrading interviewers sometimes find so much revealing information in early positions or the education years that they run out of interview time. Literally. They start at 8:00 AM and the candidate has lunch scheduled at noon, but . . . at 11:45 AM they haven't gotten to the most recent three jobs.

As interesting and job-relevant as an experience 15 years ago might be, it is not sensible to spend 20 minutes talking about it, leaving almost too little time for your discussion of the most recent jobs. Sit with your tandem and the candidate's Career History Form, and write on the Interview Guide a schedule for when to start each section. Estimate that with half the time remaining—say, two hours—plan to be discussing a job within the most recent decade. Here are additional guidelines:

With half the time remaining—say, two hours— plan to discuss a job within the most recent decade.

	45-Minute Entry-Level Interview	2-Hour Individual Performer Interview	4-Hour Management Interview
Opening "Chitchat"	4 minutes	5 minutes	10 minutes
Education	4 minutes	7 minutes	20 minutes
Work History	20 minutes	70 minutes	155 minutes
Plans and Goals	4 minutes	8 minutes	10 minutes
Self-Appraisal	4 minutes	10 minutes	15 minutes
Competency Questions	9 minutes	20 minutes	30 minutes

Arrange seating. Some interviewers make a big point of sitting side by side with the interviewee rather than behind a desk because they had been taught, "Physical barriers create psychological barriers." Bunk! Indeed, interviewees *like* a physical barrier. If they want to cross their legs, or scratch their knee, the desk provides a little privacy. Twenty-five books on interviewing say you will have to go to detention if you interview from behind a desk, but those authors never asked interviewees their preference. Most interviewers *and interviewees* like to use a small conference room with a small table to sit at and a separate table for water, coffee, and soft drinks.

People ask me what my interviewing setup is. When I had an office in Chicago, I initially interviewed behind a desk and later sat on a chair, the interviewee sat on a couch, and the coffee table had drinks. Twenty years ago I got smart and began working out of my home. My office has a desk, couch, and chair, but it's claustrophobic, so interviews are conducted in a sunroom, at the end of a hallway. With French doors, the room is separated from the rest of the house. The sunroom overlooks a pond and the neighbor's 150 farming acres, so during breaks we walk out on a deck and get some fresh air. Around a coffee table are a couch and two chairs; I take my favorite chair and offer the candidate to choose the chair or couch.

Adopt a mind-set that you are a professional, in control of the interview. Hiring, including the Topgrading Interview, is like a mating dance. Whether you are recruiting from your Networks or from ads, you initially spark the person's interest, then get information, return to intriguing the individual with the opportunity, then get some more information. You give information to the candidate, get some, and it's really a two-way street. However, it's important to prepare the individual for the Topgrading Interview, because during the Topgrading Interview, *you* get to ask the questions. A four-hour interview of a candidate with 15 years of experience is fast paced—you must move it along, and not go off on a sales pitch for more than a brief moment, and not let the interviewee take control, avoid questions, or take you off on tangents. Try to schedule time *after the interview* for the interviewee to ask you questions.

Use a padfolio for note taking. We're just about to the moment when you begin the Topgrading Interview, so let's deal with note taking. Many books on interviewing suggest that taking notes will impair eye contact, destroying rapport. Nonsense! Ask interviewees, and they say they very much *appreciate* your taking notes, particularly when they see you recording their accomplishments and interests. Don't ask permission! Taking notes shows you are conscientious and thorough. Momentarily losing eye contact to record the details of an accomplishment will give the interviewee time to scratch that knee. Note taking, done with a little finesse, is definitely a rapport builder.

Note taking, done with a little finesse, is definitely a rapport builder.

All the managers we train do what we Topgrading professionals do— use a padfolio, a leather- or vinyl-bound portfolio with an 8 ½ × 11 ruled pad on the right, and a flap on the left to hold the résumé, Topgrading Career History Form (which will become your application form), Topgrading Snapshot, and Job Scorecard. (When you graduate to using the full Topgrading Interview Guide, you won't need to have the Career History Form in the padfolio because all of that information will have been inserted automatically in the Topgrading Interview Guide.)

This arrangement permits you to take notes unobtrusively. Laying any interview guide down on a desk and taking notes makes it obtrusive; as soon as you write anything the slightest bit negative, the interviewee's eyes will be drawn to the paper. Simply put the padfolio on your lap, leaning it against the table, and make no attempt to hide note taking.

The Topgrading Interview Guide (Starter or full version) is easily placed on the open padfolio. You write on the Guide, and the padfolio provides a firm backing. If any questions require more elaboration than the Guide has room for, simply make the notes on the 8 ½ × 11 tablet. When you go out for a break, you close the notebook and hide the Guide without making a big point of it.

When you use the Guide you ask all the questions (unless there is an obvious reason not to; for example, you wouldn't ask a candidate questions about leadership examples if the person was in an individual contributor job). Don't go to the next section until there is something jotted after *every one* of the questions. You'll naturally spend more time on the more recent jobs, so there will be more notes following each question on each page. These days some clients go paperless and take notes on their laptops. Good for them!

As previously mentioned, one of the main advantages of a tandem interview is that the principal interviewer is focusing on asking the right questions and maintaining rapport, while jotting a *few* notes, while the tandem interviewer is conscientiously taking *voluminous* notes.

Are the tandems essentially "court reporters," recording every word? No, they are more than that . . . and less. As a tandem interviewer you scribble in your own shorthand the essence of responses, but the only verbatim notes are cryptic phrases that, when read later, will enable you to recall a longer conversation. For example, you might jot "Pain in the neck policies" and later you'll easily recall what three policies the candidate called the "pain in the neck." So, you write much less than a transcript. But you also write more, in a sense because you jot down hunches about what was unsaid, body language ("voice suddenly quiet"), questions to maybe ask toward the end of the interview, and conclusions if you think you "connected the dots" with deeper insights than the simple words convey.

One more example of note taking: suppose the candidate says, "I averaged 70 hours per week that year, you know, getting up at 5:00 AM, working out, rushing through breakfast, catching the train, going through e-mails the first hour, and then, you know, and then I'll review correspondence for any customer presentations. I always prepare three days in advance, rehearse the day before, and take one more pass through my presentation the day I'll meet with the customer because that impresses them, they say so, and that's one reason I was #1 of 50 reps that year. . . ." Suppose that goes on and on and you get a full account of someone who in that job was supremely organized. Record cryptic notes that enable you to later recall the essential points. In this case I'd scribble: *"70 hrs, 3-day prep, customers like, #1 of 50."*

Record cryptic notes that enable you to later recall the essential points.

Here's a note of caution: although no Topgrading company has experienced any discrimination lawsuit we are aware of, and although EEOC loves note taking, don't write (or type) anything that might be incriminating. See pages 191–195 for legal advice.

Let the Starter Topgrading Interview Begin!

Our Topgrading Toolkit has seven hours of Topgrading Interview demonstration videos, but this walk-through will be more like a run-through, quickly giving you a feel for some of the essential principles that will make even your first Topgrading Interview successful in every way. This tour through a Topgrading Interview corresponds to the Starter Topgrading Interview Guide, although I'll make some references to what you'll want to know when you graduate to using the full Topgrading Interview Guide.

Starter Topgrading Interview Guide

As you know, this Guide is for beginning Topgrading interviewers, and the full Topgrading Interview Guide will be introduced later. So feel free to photocopy Appendix E (pages 293–294) and keep it handy as I walk you through each section of it.

You're eager to get started, so build rapport but also take copious notes on a padfolio, and of course you have a tandem interviewer. If you arranged for a conference room for the interview, have all the paperwork and the padfolio handy and drinks available. And put yourself in the right mindset—you're the professional—friendly, but in charge.

How to get the interview started. Greet the candidate warmly, shake hands, and offer something to drink. In this interview, the interviewee does most of the talking, and a dry mouth is inevitable. Add a little bit of nervousness for the candidate, and maybe you, too, and dryness is exacerbated. If the interviewee or you would like a moment to collect some thoughts, taking a sip of something provides a welcome crutch. Chat about the flight in, the weather, the accommodations the candidate used, sports, or something else light, just to build rapport. Two or three minutes of rapport building is enough; the three of you are there for an interview and it's time to get down to business. Exception: if the Chicago Cubs win a World Series, that's worth marveling about for an hour. (Apologies to non-Americans—dumb humor about perennial losers.)

Memorize your opening "script" or have a cheat sheet of bullet points to cover. Before beginning the actual interview questions, provide an introduction that reminds the candidate of the time frame, purposes, TORC Technique, advantages of participating in such a thorough process. And in this opening script come across as a solid professional, in charge of what will be a fast-paced interview:

> *Pat* (tandem interviewer) *and I appreciate your time today to review your background, interests, and goals to see if there is a good fit here at Acme Corporation. During the telephone interview I explained the Topgrading hiring methods we use, but I'd like to say again that Topgrading is a very thorough process, including the Topgrading Interview we're doing today, which could take four hours. This is in your best interest. If we offer you a job and you accept it, this interview and subsequent reference checks you arrange will help us figure out how to help you enjoy a smooth assimilation here. Also, by getting to know your strengths and areas for improvement, we'll be able to work*

with you better to help construct a developmental plan right away to help you be very productive as soon as possible. And because you are ambitious and we want to hire someone who is promotable, the Individual Development Plan you write can include some actions you and we can take to help you grow into the next job. This is a two-way street, of course, so after we have interviewed you, you get to ask us all the questions you want, either today or in the very near future. We both need to perform our due diligence, to see if working together makes sense. How does that sound?

"Terrific!" is the response of most interviewees. High performers like the thoroughness and professionalism of the Topgrading Interview. If you are a little nervous, you might add

I've studied the Topgrading Interview method but this is my first one, so bear with me and my tandem interviewer if we push the Pause button to ask each other something about the process.

Education Years

The first questions have to do with education. In order to fully understand how the acorn became the oak tree with its strong parts and weak parts, you want to begin early, with the acorn taking root, and then you will come forward chronologically.

Although we will spend most of this time on your career, and specifically your most recent jobs, this is a chronological interview, starting with your education years and coming forward to the present.
Please describe:
The schools attended (and dates), starting with your first school

Grades

Degrees awarded

High and low points

People who influenced you—your career interests, personality, and values

Meaningful work experience during school years

Note: For candidates with college experience, start with college. For those without college experience, start with high school.

Having read the Topgrading Career History Form and Topgrading Snapshot, modify the wording of questions in the Guide to show that you know some answers. For example:

> Joe, Let's start with high school. I see you attended Lincoln High School, in Lincoln, Nebraska, got good grades, were Vice President of the senior class, active in hockey, and you worked summers at a bank. Please tell us a little more about high and low points during your high school years, describe how certain people might have been influences and contributed to who you are today, and if your work experiences were meaningful, tell us a little about them.

Since the candidate took the time to complete the Topgrading Career History Form, you really must show you read it, so keep it in your padfolio to remind you what the candidate has already shared.

Most experienced Topgrading interviewers actually like to begin interviewing even 25-year veterans with a discussion of high school and then college. All Topgrading professionals do. High school days are important developmental years. But—and this is important—start with college if *you'd* be embarrassed asking about the high school years.

Start with college if *you'd* be embarrassed asking about the high school years.

A major point is this: you are asking about occurrences decades ago only to get a clearer understanding of the person *today*. I've written thousands of reports on candidates, and every report has included my professional opinion of the ways the candidate acquired permanent behavior patterns during high school years. Almost all of us get hardwired in our formative years, and some motivations, values, and behaviors are ingrained for life. In fact some psychologists (including me) feel that two-thirds of all people's careers can be accounted for in terms of living up to, or living down, one's high school reputation.

Two-thirds of all people's careers can be accounted for in terms of living up to, or living down, one's high school reputation.

That's why the questions about influential people and events are important to ask. Note that you are asking how people were influential in contributing to "who you are today." That makes the relevance clear to your interviewee. People talk about parents and teachers, and they mostly mention positive influences. But when they describe negative influences, pay attention, because there are voices in their head today from those traumatic experiences and your job is to learn how those voices affect behavior *today*. For example, a candidate told me he was the oldest of five children and his father abandoned the family when he was eight years of age. His mother struggled in every way and this child grew up fast, becoming a responsible leader in his preteens. Most of this was good from a career standpoint, but ever since he has been so intolerant of irresponsibility that he frequently overreacts to co-workers who appear to slow down for a second . . . even very recently.

Another example: Team Player might be an important competency in the Job Scorecard. In the Topgrading Toolkit, an ongoing case study features Erik Dorsman, a real person but the name has been changed. In high school and college, Erik was *not* voted co-captain of the soccer team because he constantly pushed his teammates to work harder, play harder, and party less. His parents strongly encouraged him to do his best, and it was understandable that he sought parental approval. He just went a bit too far, coming across to his peers as superior, intolerant, and not a "fun guy." Learning this about Erik's high school years alerted me and my tandem interviewer to look for his overcoming this weaker point—or not overcoming it—in college and every future job.

Actually Erik did *not* overcome his tendency to put people off with his hyperintensity until years later, when a boss told him directly that his career potentials were minimal *unless* he could win the support and trust of peers. Erik then got an executive coach, worked hard to improve, and reference calls confirm that Team Player is now a strength.

When answering questions about education years, it is common for interviewees to switch to the present tense, helping you generate hypotheses about how strong the person is today in competencies. With the person's full educational and career history to be explored, you will have multiple opportunities to confirm or disconfirm your hypotheses, and that's how you discern the revealing patterns I keep referring to. By the time you are discussing the current job, you should feel confident you have this person "pegged."

When answering questions about education years, it is common for interviewees to switch to the present tense.

Suppose, despite what I just explained, you would prefer to start the Topgrading Interview with the college years because you think your candidate would think it irrelevant to discuss high school years. Okay, it's better for you to feel comfortable and confident as you learn Topgrading, so begin with this:

> *Would you please expand on the Career History Form information and give us a brief rundown on your college years . . . particularly events that might have affected later career decisions. I see that you attended the University of Texas, got good grades, participated in the Business Club, and had two summer jobs. We'd be interested in knowing just a little about meaningful work experiences, what the school was like, what you were like back then, high and low points, and so forth. And we'd be interested in hearing about people who influenced you, people who helped you develop the personality, values, or career interests you now have.*

This "smorgasbord" question shows what you already know—the candidate's background—so that will save time. And asking for specific additional information lays out what you want, which will minimize tangents you don't need to hear. Think in terms of spending just a few minutes on education years, not half an hour!

When you ask the smorgasbord question, the interviewee reveals a lot by what is answered, in what order, what is avoided, and what relative emphases are. It makes the interview a bit more spontaneous than a series of questions. For interviewing managers, this smorgasbord question is most appropriate; for interviewing entry-level employees, asking one question at a time is usually best. And, to repeat, by reciting some of the basic information (Lincoln High School, etc.), you show that you read the Career History Form (which builds rapport) *and* you speed up the interview.

If the candidate has loaded the college section with accomplishments, this walk down memory lane will be quite a positive experience for them. If the interviewee's grades were not good and there were no stated activities of note, perhaps this was a negative part of the person's life, so don't harm rapport by spending a lot of time on it. Just ask for high points and low points, successes and failures, and influential people, nod and show understanding and don't dwell on negatives. Many A Players can empathize with this honest statement: "Teen years were messy for most people, me included!" That's enough—move on.

This is the interview sequence throughout the entire Topgrading Interview: Get successes (so the interviewee feels good and feels appreciated), then failures, and then if there is any doubt, ask about additional high points, then low points. This sequence provides the "meat" for valid assessment. If the individual attended college 20 years ago and was a goof-off, but has been very successful since and now takes full responsibility for immaturity back then, you might conclude that the candidate today is quite a mature individual. That's the whole point. The tandem Topgrading Interview is a guided tour through the candidate's complete education and career history, and as you learn what this unique individual liked and disliked, succeeded at and failed at, across dozens of different competencies and various life experiences, with lots of different challenges and people to interact with, you learn the *truth*. And understanding those valuable patterns, and later verifying your conclusions in candidate-arranged reference calls, will make it likely that you will hire only A Players.

WORK HISTORY

This is the "guts" of the Topgrading Interview. It comprises about three hours of a four-hour interview. Each job title is a different job to cover with all the questions, so for example if she had five jobs with Acme, that's not one job (Acme), but five. Here's an exception: if a person entered a large company that had job rotation consisting of four jobs in two years, and those all occurred 15 years ago, group all four together into one job. If the candidate has a 15-year work history, spend at least half of the work history time on the most recent five or six years.

Ask every question in the Work History section for every job. Even if you allocate only three minutes for a very early job, nonetheless ask every question and jot a short response. With the later jobs you will be probing more, supplementing the standard questions by asking for more clarification, challenging apparent inconsistencies, getting examples.

Start with your first full-time job and come forward to your present job. For each job, please tell us about the following:

1. *Why you took the job*
2. *Your successes and accomplishments (and how you achieved them)*
3. *Your mistakes and failures*
4. *What you liked most and least about the job*
5. *(For management job) How many A, B, and C Player direct reports did you have when you entered the job . . . and at the end? What happened to change the talent mix—hiring, firing, coaching, etc.?*
6. *Name of supervisor, and that supervisor's strengths and weaker points*
7. *In order to receive a job offer we may ask you to arrange reference calls with supervisors you've had in the past 10 years. What's your best guess as to what that supervisor would say were your strengths, weaker points, and overall performance?*
8. *What was the reason(s) you left that job?*

Experienced Topgrading interviewers begin the Work History section of the Topgrading Interview Guide with another "smorgasbord" question. The purpose is exactly as it was for starting with college: you learn more if an individual has to organize the entire career history and present it, emphasizing this, excluding that, and so on, than if you conduct an interview in rapid-fire question-answer, question-answer, question-answer. The latter format would probably take twice as long, too.

Practice the opening question, which might go something like this:

Now we would like you to tell us about your work history, and there are a lot of things we would like to know about each position. Let me tell you what these things are now, so we won't have to interrupt you so often. We already have information from your Career History Form and previous interviews. Of course, we need to know the employer, location, dates of employment, your titles, and salary history, and we have that. We would also be interested in knowing why you took each job, your successes and accomplishments, your mistakes and failures, and what you liked most and least about the job. And we need to know your appraisal of each supervisor and your best guess as to how that person would appraise your strengths, weaker points, and

*overall performance. And as you already know, a final step before a
job offer is to ask you to arrange personal reference calls with former
bosses and some others, people you've worked closely with in the past
10 or 12 years. Finally, tell us why you left each job.*

Question #5 (for management jobs) is too complex for the introductory
question, but of course will be asked for every management job.

Asking why the person took a job is revealing, because if you hire the
candidate, knowing her expectations going to work for you will be crucial.
Learn the *pattern* of why people took jobs and whether their expectations
were met and you will learn about their values, due diligence, ability to assimilate into a new job, and overall performance. A Players tend to take jobs
at a higher salary but not for the money as much as the opportunity to
learn, meet challenges, perform, earn promotions, and have fun working
with sharp people. C Players tend to take jobs just to get a paycheck.

Next ask for every major success and accomplishment, and especially
for the jobs in the past decade, dig in and ask *how* they pulled off successes.
Then ask about every significant failure and mistake. Probe to see what lessons were learned from failures, and make a mental note to learn if the
same mistakes were repeated in future jobs. Learning about successes and
failures, you'll automatically learn what was liked most and least in a job,
but if there is any doubt, ask. High performers tend to have lots of successes
and when they tell you how they succeeded, they give you specifics that
show their drive, resourcefulness, persistence, and ability to work well with
people. And they admit making mistakes . . . but they learn from them. Low
performers are vague about accomplishments, have to be asked again and
again about mistakes and failures, tend to blame others and circumstances
for those failures, and they tend to make similar mistakes in the future.

For all management jobs ask question #5—what talent was inherited
(number of As, Bs, Cs), what the breakdown was when the person left the
job, and what happened in between—coaching, hiring, firing, etc. A Players
tend to inherit a "mixed bag" of As, Bs, and Cs, and struggle mightily to
keep and grow the As, develop the Bs, and replace the Cs. Because most
managers find that only 25% of the people they replace turn out to be As, it's
smart for them—until they learn Topgrading and achieve 75%+ success—
to keep the Bs. After all, replacing a B Player will result in an A Player only
one time in four. C Player managers tend to lose their A Players and stum-
ble along with mostly Bs and Cs.

Next ask the TORC (Threat of Reference Check) questions (# 6–7), beginning with the candidate's appraisal of the boss. Later, when you review your notes, you'll pay a lot of attention to what the candidate liked or disliked in a boss, and whether it is compatible with you, the hiring manager. And realizing that arranging calls with former bosses is the last step before a job offer, the candidate will be remarkably honest in saying what bosses will say are strengths, weaker points, and overall performance.

The TORC questions, asking candidates to appraise their boss and guess how their boss will appraise them, are the most important questions for hiring A Players. To make the point I'll exaggerate: Suppose you were somehow limited to a half-hour interview (crazy in real life because we never cut corners like that!), but just suppose. Then you should (1) let candidates know about TORC, (2) ask the TORC questions for the past four jobs, and (3) conduct reference calls with people you pick, including former bosses, and have the candidate arrange the calls. The result of this Incredibly Super, Super Lite Topgrading model would definitely be better hires (need I say, but not 90% As?).

The TORC questions are the most important questions for hiring A Players.

High performers tend to get along with almost all good and not-so-good bosses well enough to be given Very Good or Excellent performance ratings. Low performers tend to not like most of their bosses and describe them as unreasonable, hypercritical, lousy coaches, and so on. By learning what the candidate liked and disliked about all bosses, and what bosses (in reference calls they might be asked to arrange) would say about them, you will naturally project yourself into the pattern and see if you're a good match. Maybe this sales rep soars when left alone but you require daily call reports; maybe your managerial candidate does well when bosses are complimentary almost on a daily basis but, hey, you just are not that warm and fuzzy. It's not that one is necessarily bad and the other good; it's a matter of fit. Topgrading absolutely nails the fit factors—not just whether the candidate will be compatible with you but also with the company as a whole.

To transition from one job to the next, do not read everything the candidate wrote in the Career History Form. Just say:

Joe, I see you next worked for Acme and your first job there was from 1999 until 2003; please tell us:

what you did,

how you did,

how you liked it, and

why you left it.

The logical last question for every job is why they left it. As you would expect, high performers tend to leave jobs because they were promoted, or if they left the employer, they generally were not looking for a job but someone they worked with in the past recruited them for a better position in their company. Weaker candidates tend to leave jobs because they were laid off, "couldn't stand" working for a boss, or were let go in a "reorganization." "Reorganization" is in quotation marks because in every economic downturn companies protect earnings by eliminating people. And a lot of times they reorganize so that the weakest performers are let go.

At the end of an interview you have a very good idea of the person's strengths and weaker points, but this is the time to slow the pace, ask the self-appraisal question, and really "digest" responses so see if they match your appraisal.

The Self-Appraisal Question Is . . .

Please list your strengths and weaker points, in detail.

First ask for the pluses, since you are a positive thinker. Get the "grocery list" of 10 or 12 strengths, and then go back and get elaboration, digging for specifics on ones that are unclear. Then ask for shortcomings, weaker points, or areas for improvement. Again, get the "grocery list" of five or six weaker points, urging the person to produce at least that many. Then go back and get the specifics. If you interrupt to get elaboration on the first weaker point, you're not likely to get many more when you ask, *"What additional weaker points do you have?"*

If the interviewee lists impatience as a shortcoming, challenge them on it. Plenty of A Players are impatient, particularly with peers and subordinates, and they will admit to being excessively impatient. But almost every book on how to pass interviews suggests that candidates say that impatience is a shortcoming, "because my standards are very high and I mostly am just impatient with myself." Fire back at the person, *"Exactly how is impatience a shortcoming, because it sounds as though it's a strength to me."*

A Players tend to list important strengths, but this might surprise you—they rarely list many. As just mentioned, A Players are usually recruited by others, so many have never created a résumé or read a book on how to get a job. When interviewed they are oftentimes humble, knowing that the person who is recruiting them will sing their praises. So draw them out—ask them to think of more strengths and to elaborate on those strengths. And A Players freely admit their weaker points and are willing to talk about how they plan to overcome them. C Players hype their strengths, as though reading from a How to Get a Job book (which they own), and they cite weaker points that are . . . sorry, basically BS . . . "I work too hard," "My expectations are too high, for myself."

Next is a look to the future. The **Future** question is . . .

What are your goals for your next job? What are your long-term career plans and goals?

Nothing should surprise you in the answers because you've already learned reasons why the candidate left every job they've ever had and what was liked and disliked about everyone.

Your tandem Topgrading Interview is over, and maybe you and your partner love the candidate and want to offer the job. Hold on! Your work is not done. Topgrading Hiring Steps #8 through #12 remain. Chances are you and your tandem interviewer figure that you have "missile lock" on the interviewee's strengths and weaker points. But Topgraders systematically give each other a couple of minutes of feedback on the other's interviewing techniques (Step #8), analyze all the information, and write a draft Executive Summary (Step #9), ask the candidate to arrange personal reference calls with former bosses and others (Step #10), and conduct those calls, all before hiring someone (and then there are two post-hiring steps after that).

More Advice to New Topgrading Interviewers

Having trained thousands of Topgrading interviewers, we at Smart & Associates know what eager learners new Topgraders are and what is most difficult for them to learn. In the workshops, all of Day 2 is practicing interviews, and we observe and give advice. Here are the most common suggestions (some are new, some you already know) to our trainees for how to make their first few Topgrading Interviews successful:

1. **Follow the Interview Guide.** Most managers have experience interviewing, competency interviewing, and in order to seem professional and confident, they sometimes abandon the Topgrading Interview Guide (Starter or full Guide) altogether and fall back on their old interviewing method—the one that produced 75% mis-hires. We go nuts when the interviewers are supposed to be discussing a job 15 years ago, and we observe, *"How do you stay organized today?"* The proven magic of Topgrading interviewing is to learn how the person evolved across the educational years and full career history, and to stop halfway through the interview and start asking for a self-appraisal (which is what Competency Interviews do) destroys the foundation of Topgrading. And, by the way, that question—*"How do you stay organized today?"*—"leads the witness," forcing the candidate, who might *not* be organized these days, to claim this as a strength.

So we tap the interviewer on the shoulder, and say, "You just jumped ahead 15 years; stick with the Interview Guide; when you get to the present job you'll see how the patterns have evolved and you'll learn how organized he is by asking about accomplishments, failures, and how the boss would rate him through his entire career."

The good news is, when people get back on track and actually complete one tandem Topgrading Interview, full or Starter, following the Interview Guide by asking every question, following up for clarification, and taking great notes, they get great insights. They conclude it has been the most revealing and valid interview of their career.

2. **Move the Topgrading Interview along faster.** Earlier you saw a chart (page 127) with suggested amounts of time to spend on each section of the interview. Please plan your time accordingly.

Topgraders are so conscientious that they want to do everything correctly as they embark on their first Topgrading Interviews. But they can literally get stuck talking about the high school years for 20 minutes, spending way too much time learning about highs and lows in soccer seasons. As explained in this chapter, Topgraders ask about the full education and career history only in order to get a good fix on the person's current competencies, but if you're not learning something about what the person is like in relation to the Job Scorecard, move the interview along.

Fortunately, there is a very clear signal that you're wasting time—you're not taking notes. When we observe the tandem interviewers listening and not writing, almost all of the time the interviewee is not revealing anything important. The solution is also simple: interrupt, saying, *"That was a terrific sports season for you, Joe, congratulations, but I'm going to have to move on because we have your full education and career history to cover this morning."*

Fortunately, there is a very clear signal that you're wasting time—you're not taking notes.

---

3. **Don't wimp out in the Topgrading Interview.** Topgraders aren't wimps, but we sometimes observe timidity in asking the tough questions in Topgrading Workshops. Probably most of that hesitancy is due to managers just beginning to learn the Topgrading methods; they do not want to risk harming rapport as they struggle to follow the Guide. The trouble is, costly mis-hires occur when interviewers fail to ask the tough questions. In full Topgrading Interview Guides, the two toughest questions are as follows:

- Question # 8:
  - *We all make mistakes—what would you say were mistakes and failures experienced in that job?*
  - Hesitant interviewers tend to reword it to, *"Could you have done something a little better in that job?"* That's weak! Interviewees sense the weakness and talk about a nice accomplishment that could have been even more successful: "Yeah, I'm sorry to report that although I exceeded the sales goal by 200%, I could have worked even harder and achieved 210%."
- (Part of) Question #15:
  - *What is your best guess as to what (supervisor's name) honestly felt were your weaker points?*
  - Timid interviewers reword it to, *"What would your manager say were your opportunities in that job?"* Too soft! The interviewee can answer honestly and say nothing negative: "In order to qualify for promotion sooner I could have taken a seminar on strategy."

Don't deny yourself crucial insights into the interviewee's shortcomings and weak points by softening or, worse yet, avoiding the tough questions. Please look the person in the eye, don't hesitate, and ask the question directly.

4. **Don't become discouraged.** Topgrading Interviewing is not a perfect science, and neither you nor I will ever be perfect at it. The tremendous saving grace of the Topgrading Interview approach is that
it is resilient and robust. You can "miss" the body language indication of a possible lie, fail to delve into the specifics as deeply as you
should have, bias responses to a question or two unintentionally, or
even blunder into harming rapport. However, because this is not a
short interview, you have time to regain your insight and rapport
with the interviewee. Since so much emphasis is put on patterns of
how competencies evolved over the years, you can flat-out miss some
important pieces in that jigsaw puzzle and still figure out if the candidate is an A Player, B Player, or C Player simply because you have so
many opportunities to look deeply into the candidate.

For example, if my tandem interviewer and I had failed to probe
whether Erik had overcome his intensity when discussing a job 10 years
ago, we'll probably find out when we discuss jobs he's had more recently.
(And have I mentioned that I've done 6,500 Topgrading Interviews? Oh,
yeah, I have . . . and I still make mistakes.) And if we really blew it and
didn't probe about his intensity in the most recent five years or so and realize this after the interview was concluded, we can pick up the phone and ask
Erik a few more questions.

The resilience of the Topgrading Interview explains, in large part, why
interviewers like it, A Player candidates like it, and shareholders benefit
from its use.

TOPGRADING HIRING STEP #8:
INTERVIEWERS GIVE EACH OTHER FEEDBACK

*About 250 of our managers have given each other constructive
suggestions for improving their interviewing technique, using the
Topgrading Interviewer Feedback Form. We can all benefit from just
a couple of minutes of feedback from another interviewer, and doing
this after the tandem Topgrading Interview makes a lot of sense.*

—Kevin Silva, Former Senior Vice President
of Global Human Resources, Argo

Step #8 helps solve a big problem, which is that, well, most interviewers are not very good at interviewing. The solution is simple—immediately following the Topgrading Interview, the interviewers give each other a couple minutes of feedback and constructive suggestions:

> *Pat, you did great at asking all the questions in the Interview Guide and you took a lot of notes, but maybe you were so conscientious, trying so hard to do a good job, that you seemed colder than the Pat I know. Specifically, you never called Joe, our interviewee, by name, and even when Joe related wonderful successes, you kind of frowned.*

Preparing for a future interview, Pat will make a note on the Interview Guide:

> *Use the candidate's name and throughout the interview, show more warmth.*

We have conducted dozens of total company employee surveys, and have surveyed over one million people; our results match what a thousand heads of Human Resources have told us: "Most interviewers are not very good—even with an interview guide to follow, they don't ask all the questions, wing it and ask leading questions, don't listen well, don't take notes, etc., etc." McGill University studies showed that most interviewers make up their mind about whether to hire someone in four minutes or less.

Managers who have attended workshops on interviewing do better than untrained interviewers, but interviewer training is not part of the management development curriculum in most companies.

In hundreds of Topgrading Workshops, most of the interviewers struggle during the first half of the interview. We warn interviewers, "Whoever volunteers to be the primary interviewer to start the interview, you'll be trying so hard you'll probably spend too much time on some things, not take enough notes, and seem less warm than you will after an hour or so. But we'll let you get started and then come around and offer some specific suggestions to help you get the right flow."

You've already read a few tips for how to conduct your first interviews. Chapter 4 is a mini course called "Advanced Interviewing Techniques." But for now let's learn some more basics—the checklist for Step #8, giving and getting feedback after Topgrading Interviews.

We have a published Topgrading Interviewer Feedback Form with 39 interviewing techniques. To give you a feel for what feedback you'd give and receive in Step #8, here are some of the 39 interviewing techniques:

- Greeting (warm, friendly, shake hands)
- Rapport Building (necessary, but for only a couple minutes)
- All Interview Guide Questions Asked
- Interviewers Took Copious Notes
- Effective Follow-Up Questions (probes reveal the "so what?")
- Warmth
- Interviewer Controlled Interview
- Interviewee Talked 90% of the Time
- Breaks Taken
- Inappropriate Humor Not Shown
- Shock Not Shown
- Points Summarized (every 15 minutes or so)
- "Connecting" with Interviewee
- Active Listening Used

In a somewhat simplified form, Step #8 is when, following the Topgrading Interview, the interviewers look at that list of interviewing techniques and ask, "How did I do on these and what couple of suggestions do you have for how I could be a better interviewer?"

The beauty of Step #8 is that clients report that their interviewers *do* improve when they regularly get and give this feedback. And no tandem interviewer should be shy about getting constructive feedback or giving it. I do both.

When I say I make mistakes, that's not false humility. You'll read about one example when I made mistakes during an interview with a convicted murderer. In our Topgrading Toolkit, with seven hours of demonstrations, I show some interviewing weaknesses. . . . I didn't intentionally make the mistakes and I didn't edit them out. You're curious—how did I specifically fail to use the best interviewing techniques? When I "connected the dots" and saw a pattern explaining a lot of the interviewee's motivations, I nervously ran my hands through my hair. Instead of calmly using follow-up probes to test my hunch, I got a bit too eager, ran my fingers through my hair again, leaned forward, and my eye contact was too intense; you can see this in the video. All of this signaled to the interviewee that I felt I was "onto something" and my intensity might have caused the interviewee to be less forthcoming . . . at least until I settled down. Later my tandem partner, following Step #8, suggested I chill out more when I have a hunch. I accepted this nondefensively and fired him for not showing proper respect. (Sorry, that was inappropriate humor by the author.)

I'm just giving you a pep talk, reinforcing the fact that a four-hour tandem Topgrading Interview is incredibly robust. You can be far from perfect, violate many of the best interviewing techniques, still get back on track, regain a high level of rapport, and complete an interview that is highly revealing.

So, make it part of your Topgrading processes, part of your organizational culture, to assume that every manager *can* improve interviewing techniques and every manager *will* get and give feedback after every tandem Topgrading Interview.

TOPGRADING HIRING STEP #9: WRITE A (DRAFT) EXECUTIVE SUMMARY

Hill-Rom views the Executive Summary as one of the most critical aspects of the selection process. The Executive Summary is a great tool for helping the interviewer to recognize a candidate's work history and behavioral themes. Experiencing the process of writing the Executive Summary requires the HR leader or hiring manager to dig deep, reflect upon the full career of the candidate, and pull out interview insights that are critical to making a next step. And when a selection is made, the Executive Summary serves as an excellent development reference and tool. We have made it part of our onboarding process.

—John Dickey, Senior Vice President,
Corporate Support Services, Hill-Rom

As each tandem Topgrading Interview is completed, you're eager to get on with reference checks, but please push the Pause button. As the John Dickey quote suggests, this step is important, but if I just listed the bullet points of how to do it, you might roll your eyes and think this is bureaucratic and not do it. Although I've written articles on how to communicate with high-powered A Player executives, and the first principle is, "State the bottom line succinctly, first, and then make your case." I'll violate that principle, making the case first and then outlining the things to do to write the draft Executive Summary. If there is a "bottom line" argument for completing this step it's this: *the value is in the careful analysis of candidate data*, and now is the time to do it; writing the draft Executive Summary is just the byproduct.

The value is in the careful analysis of candidate data, and now is the time to do it; writing the draft Executive Summary is just the byproduct.

There is an enormous amount of research showing that relying on gut feelings without systematically analyzing all available candidate data leads to bad hires. The problem is interviewers jumping to conclusions—wrong, ill-informed conclusions. Systematic analysis of the wonderful information you have about the candidate is the skill that enables you to arrive at valid, correct conclusions about all the competencies. Skipping this step will result in more bad hires; perform this step and you'll make more of the right decisions to hire, or not. So that's what this step is all about—mostly good analysis, summarized in a report, leading to good hires!

Early in my career, clients would call within an hour of when the interview was over and ask, "Brad, what do you think of (candidate)?" I've learned the hard way to explain to my client that my initial feelings are dead wrong 15% of the time, because they are intuitions not grounded in the hard facts. And I ask them to please let me earn my keep by . . . you guessed it . . . performing Step #9, writing the Executive Summary. I tell clients it's embarrassing to wing it and recommend their candidate for hire, only to call them a couple hours later and say, "I'm sorry, the candidate's winning personality snowed me, but when I went back and looked at his full career history it became clear that he would not be a good hire for you."

Of course, in the Topgrading Interview, as soon as the candidate reveals something so negative that you definitely will not offer a job, writing an extensive report is a waste of time.

However, for candidates you are still interested in pursuing, you will improve your hiring batting average if you and your tandem partner patiently analyze all the information you have so far, which is a lot. So far you have information from the:

- résumé,
- Topgrading Career History Form,
- Topgrading Snapshot,

- Telephone Screening Interview,
- Competency Interviews,
- Tandem Topgrading Interview, and
- informal interactions (lunches together, phone calls for various reasons, and so forth).

Since the Job Scorecard has all the competencies listed, and is color coded by how difficult it is for people to improve them, most hiring mangers enter their "best guess" rating after each of these data-gathering steps, essentially fine-tuning their conclusions with deeper, better, more revealing information with each step in the hiring process. There is one more step to perform before a final report can be written, and this is a very important one—reference checks that are arranged by the candidate. Why not wait on analyzing the information and writing a report until *after* the reference checks have been done? Here's why:

1. **The analysis sometimes leads to asking more questions prior to reference checks.** After analyzing all the information and making best-guess ratings of the competencies, interviewers sometimes conclude they need more questions answered. Maybe they just didn't probe *how* certain accomplishments were achieved, or maybe "taking on too many projects" was a weaker point right up until the present job and . . . they forgot to ask some specific questions about workload, boss requests, etc., to figure out if "taking on too many projects" is still a weaker point or if the candidate has learned to manage the volume. So, the interviewers can pick up the phone and talk to the candidate, getting the additional information.

2. **It sometimes requires analysis to figure out exactly which people you want the candidate to contact to arrange reference calls.** Certainly all former bosses in the past decade are likely choices, but after delving into interview notes, certain subordinates, peers, customers, and others might seem worth talking with.

3. **After systematic analysis of a seemingly good candidate, two other candidates might seem so much better that this candidate is rejected.** If those other candidates were neglected a bit because you thought you had the job filled (until the tandem Topgrading Interview), you'll want to get back in touch with those two candidates right away.

4. **By going through all the notes, the interviewers figure out exactly how to probe for specifics, particularly regarding weaker points,**

during the reference checks. When conducting the reference-checking interview the Topgrading Reference Check Guide leads the way, but it's always a good idea to review the notes on a job before talking to the boss in that job. And you don't want to be too blunt and cause the reference to clam up, so you need to design your questions.

For example, suppose you are concerned that your candidate might be too independent, and as you review your notes it appears that you'll be talking to a former boss who was criticized by the CEO for not managing Joe better. You decided to first ask, "Joe said you criticized him for sometimes making decisions without your approval; how much of an issue was it?" And if you don't learn enough from the former boss's response, you plan to follow up with: "Specifically, Joe said he verbally agreed to the Acme contract without your approval, and although he was sure you would approve it, the CEO heard Joe had done it and blasted you. Is that what happened?"

So for all these reasons, please analyze all the candidate data and write a draft report before conducting the reference calls.

KEY PRINCIPLES FOR INTERPRETING CANDIDATE INFORMATION

Before writing the draft, let's learn some key principles that Topgrading professionals use (and so can you) to validly interpret all that wonderfully detailed information you have gained. In a sense this entire book is about how to interpret information about candidates, but what follows are some of the most useful principles.

Look for Patterns

I have referred to the "magic" of the Topgrading Interview, explaining that the *patterns* revealed across an entire career, across 50 competencies, are what enable you to really, really know what the person's strengths and weaker points are today and are likely to be in the next few years. I know I must explain this, because just saying that leaves most people confused.

The patterns of responses across the chronological interview reveal Truth. How a person evolved from high school days to today is captured beautifully in the thoroughness of the Topgrading Interview (supplemented with data from the other sources). For some competencies (Integrity, Energy), it's common that the person has always been honest and energetic. By asking about highs and lows throughout the person's life and career, by delving into every success, failure, key decision, and key relationship, it will be abundantly clear that the person is solidly, deeply high in integrity and very energetic.

Use what words you will, you can never say anything but what you are.

—Ralph Waldo Emerson

Most competencies evolve, sometimes from scratch. You can ask a person about her leadership style today, which is typical of Competency Interviews, but questions like that are easy to fake. By delving into every leadership role she's held, perhaps since high school, and doing so in depth, you will see how she evolved, perhaps from naive and overly trusting, maybe into a hard-nosed autocrat, or maybe into a modern professional leader.

And it's typical for talented managers to have to constantly learn and relearn time management and personal organization, because with each promotion, they are thrust into a more complex job and their former organizational methods can be inadequate. A lot of first-time managers don't delegate well, as in the above example, thinking they can do the best job if they do it themselves; however, if they get promoted and have 20 subordinates, they must either learn to select high performers and develop them to be able to accept delegated tasks, or the poor manager will work 100 hours per week and fail anyway.

In writing an Executive Summary, which again is just a discipline for analyzing all the data and arriving at valid, accurate conclusions and decisions, you will see constant contradictions in the data because of the fact that all people are sometimes good and not so good in most competencies. Interviewees finally getting your Excellent rating in a competency are apt to be excellent almost all the time, while people getting a Good rating might be generally strong in the competency but with exceptions. One value of going through all the data and noting *patterns* is to see the *patterns* for the exceptions, finally enabling you to clearly understand how strong the competency is today, in what circumstances the person might be stronger or weaker in it, and how to *best manage* the person so that the competency is as consistently strong as possible.

As an example, let's say the competency in question is Results-Oriented, and let's compare two people you've met, sort of. Erik, the candidate that goes through all 12 Topgrading Hiring Steps in our Topgrading Toolkit, is the man whose Job Scorecard and Topgrading Snapshot you've read. And you've read John Doe's Topgrading Snapshot—remember, he's the job hopper. If John and Erik walked in the door of some business social event, in no time most people would peg John as highly results-oriented and Erik as, well, he's so calm and understated that he probably would not immediately impress people that he's highly results-oriented, certainly not like the dynamic dynamo, John Doe.

And they'd be dead wrong. In the Topgrading Interview of Erik you can see me and my tandem interviewer elicit how Erik's parents motivated him to always do his best, how he worked extremely hard to get good grades in school and perform on the soccer field, how he went on to teach and tutored some kids without pay, and how he got two promotions and *all* Excellent performance ratings in his past three jobs. The pattern is that Erik is always results-oriented to an extreme, and if he's not at any given moment, there is a good reason for it. In the Topgrading Interview we see the strong pattern of Erik being so intense in his results-orientation that he was told to work with an executive coach (he did) and tone down that intensity (he has—that's why he seems low-key today).

But we also saw that sometimes Erik would not change course quickly enough, if new information would indicate he should abandon Plan A and go to Plan B. Why? The pattern is that Erik the bulldozer has so thoroughly thought through a plan that he forges ahead with great force and it takes a lot of new information for him to reverse his high commitment to Plan A.

John Doe, on the other hand, is a world-class BSer. He has a terrific image, speaks a great game, charms the heck out of people, immediately and constantly exudes energy and drive, and he manages to get higher- and higher-paying jobs because of his image and not because he has been results-oriented on the job! Indeed, his Topgrading Snapshot shows a pattern of lousy ratings by bosses. (The Topgrading Snapshots of Erik and John tell a *lot* about patterns, don't they?) People look at Doe's Snapshot and say, "Man, maybe he should be in sales, where his image would convert to actual results!" Maybe, but if we're looking at candidates for actual leadership and achieving results, Erik has the pattern of putting points on the scoreboard and John doesn't. In a Topgrading Interview John Doe has sold himself for jobs he couldn't perform; he bluffed a lot, hoped his team would perform without his leadership, and when bosses became disappointed in his results, he'd just start looking for the next job. (How do I know so much about Doe, beyond his Topgrading Snapshot? Not gonna tell!)

The patterns in all of the data, but mostly in the tandem Topgrading Interview, will reveal that people are strong or weak in a competency, but also what might be done developmentally to help you manage them toward improvement. Erik perhaps should take a public speaking course so that his evolutionary pattern will be from hyperintense to calmly professional to inspirational leader. Maybe John Doe needs to hear that he needs to *perform, accomplish something,* and get Excellent or Very Good boss ratings to be a happy, successful A Player in some job.

No one is an A Player with Excellent ratings on all competencies; it is extremely useful to understand a person's complexity, so that you can manage people best to maximize their strengths and minimize their weaker points. And with some experience conducting tandem Topgrading Interviews, you will get better and better at noting the patterns of responses for C Players vs. A Players. Earlier in this chapter I walked you through a typical interview and pointed out how As and Cs differ in responses. Here's a summary chart that might help.

Sample A Player vs. C Player Patterns

	A Player	C Player
Employer, location, dates	Stable work history	Job hopper
Title	Job progression	Lack of progression
Compensation	Progressively increasing	Unimpressively increasing
Expectations for the job	Challenge and opportunity	"Just a job"
Responsibilities and accountabilities	Increasing	Static or decreasing
What was "found" when entered job	Obstacles that can be overcome	Insurmountable obstacles
Accomplishments	Impressive	Unimpressive
Mistakes	Few and learned from them	Many and didn't learn
Most enjoyable aspects of job	A lot	Very little
Least enjoyable aspects of job	Not much	A lot

(Continued)

Talent	Improved it	Did not improve it
Supervisor	Willing to arrange reference call	Not willing
Supervisor's strengths/shortcomings	Respects most bosses	Problems with most bosses
Supervisor's appraisal of candidate	Very positive	Not very positive
Other decisions/relationships	Impressive	Not impressive
Reasons for leaving	Candidate's initiative	Nudged out

The genius of the Topgrading Interview lies in the patterns it reveals across all of those dimensions—success patterns, failure patterns, patterns for decisions made, patterns for relating to people, patterns for motivation. Just look at the A Player column and that is what you want to see as you ask every question in the Topgrading Interview. Patterns across the candidate's entire life and career make it easy to predict exactly how the person will function in the near future.

Any interview process that asks what a person did in only the most recent job, or what would be done under hypothetical situations, misses the boat big-time, and will lead to costly mis-hires. By tracing how a person developed over an entire life and career, the patterns that emerge give 1,000 times the insight into the recent past than if you only asked about the recent past.

Another example: if you ask a candidate what she likes and dislikes about the current boss, you get "recent past behavior," and this can be valuable, though not sufficiently insightful to know what the person is really like today. If, for example, she says that she totally respects her current boss because he delegates a lot and gives her credit for accomplishments, you learned something, and if you delegate and give credit, this bodes well for your relationship. But just because she gets along with one boss for reasons relevant to your leadership style does not tell you why she might not have gotten along with previous bosses in ways that do not bode well for your relationship. By asking for appraisals of all 10 bosses she has had, you'll learn a lot more. Maybe the three previous bosses all loaded her up so much she missed deadlines, freaked out when she was held accountable, and twice quit with no notice. And maybe you tend to load up your team, and even though you delegate and give praise (she'd like that), you delegate so much you overwhelm people (and she'd quit within months). This is a hypothetical extreme, but it makes the point that only discussing the recent past can be misleading and you will definitely glean the deepest insights by getting the full chronological history.

Here is another truism: the value in understanding patterns will be reinforced with every Topgrading Interview you conduct. How can I make such a statement? Simple—*you* conduct Telephone Screening Interviews, so you hear about the current job and the one previous to it (together, the recent past), without the full education and without the full career history. And later *you* conduct the tandem Topgrading Interview. We hear all the time, "Wow, when I asked about the most recent two jobs in the phone screen, I concluded this candidate was a superstar, but at the end of the chronological Topgrading Interview I'd seen such clear patterns of poor team relationships and questionable ethics that I was able to ask probing questions and learn that, sure enough, he still picks fights with peers and is comfortable doing things our company considers unethical."

Another boss example: Suppose candidate Joe has had a difficult relationship with the current boss. Okay, almost everyone has had a boss who was an autocrat, a poor communicator, or something negative. But suppose, in going through the details of his entire career, he has nothing positive to say about even one of eight bosses? I reported to a client exactly how a candidate I interviewed described all of his bosses:

- Boss #1: "a turkey"
- Boss #2: "a jerk"
- Boss #3: "an idiot"
- Boss #4: "politically inept"
- Boss #5: "untrustworthy"
- Boss #6: "an ass-kisser"
- Boss #7: "can't be trusted"
- Boss #8: "totally disorganized"

This has happened. I have submitted reports to clients in which in the Conclusions section I started with summarizing how the candidate described every boss in negative terms, as in the above example. They realize that with such a consistent disrespect for bosses, no matter how great potential bosses might be, almost certainly they will not be respected by this candidate.

The patterns tell all. In the Topgrading Toolkit, to show the power of patterns, we take various competencies and then show short video segments from the Telephone Screening Interview, Competency Interviews, mostly the tandem Topgrading Interview, and a Reference-Check Interview with Erik's boss Jeff . . . to show the patterns of how Erik evolved into the A Player he is today.

From an interviewer's standpoint the three hours leading up to the current job in a Topgrading Interview of a manager are in a sense getting tuned into the candidate to be able to ask outstanding, revealing follow-up, probing questions. While delving into career experiences decades ago, the candidate reveals *current* competencies.

In short, only the chronological Topgrading Interview gets *all* the job-relevant information, gets the *patterns that emerge* and show how the person has succeeded (or not), and shows how the person has learned from mistakes (or not). As you see patterns emerge across all 50 competencies, across the person's entire life, you end up with such accurate insights into all competencies and how best to manage the person, so that they perform at their best and so that you can avoid those costly mis-hires.

Assume Strengths Become Weaker Points

The Topgrading Interview asks for accomplishments/successes and then failures/mistakes. Candidates naturally reveal what they are good at, and you'll note that for most people, strengths are at times overused and become weaker points.

As an example, Erik is very hardworking and disciplined, so when he plans something, it's planned out thoroughly. However, when new information suggests the plan ought to be changed, Erik struggles a bit because it requires him to rethink all sorts of assumptions that went into the original plan. He can appear indecisive.

Under pressure, we all tend to overuse our strengths, and they can become shortcomings. During interviews, entertain this hypothesis frequently. More examples:

- An ambitious person might sacrifice job performance in order to take additional classes and devote too much time to professional activities and expanding his professional network.
- A very conscientious, meticulous planner can become slow and indecisive.

- The friendly, affable customer service representative might be easily dominated by assertive customers.
- Glib salespeople who are "quick on their feet" can manipulate bosses and be "high maintenance."

Understand That Recent Past Behavior Is the Best Predictor of Near Future Behavior

I've just complicated things, explaining how recent past behavior can be misleading. Here's the resolution: *Just* getting recent past behavior leaves you with almost no patterns and it leaves you with shallow insights into the patterns you *think* you are seeing, but might be totally wrong. By conducting the full Topgrading Interview, you see much deeper patterns and are able to predict what aspects of the recent behaviors *are* likely to exist in the near future and which are not. Make sense?

Deep patterns from the full chronological interview are the Rosetta Stone.

Deep patterns from the full chronological interview are the Rosetta Stone of hiring because they reveal if someone has the same weaker point year after year after year . . . or if the person gains the self-awareness and motivation to actually change. Competencies have inertia. Success and failure patterns both persist, but sometimes change because people are not static. As you review an individual's chronological history, weigh the most recent behaviors most heavily, but only if the recent past is fully convincing. If the person was a goof-off in college but has been extremely conscientious and mature during the past five years, the previous adolescent immaturity can usually be disregarded.

On the other hand, if a person was very mature and self-disciplined 15 years ago, but underwent a midlife crisis that has resulted in four job changes in six years, watch out. Maybe the person seems stable now, but dig deep and probe to see whether that flakiness is about to rear its ugly head. Indications in this example might be, "I've been in this job for a little over a year and I've really settled down. I've achieved all my accountabilities and got an Exceeds Performance Expectations performance rating." Hey, great, maybe the midlife crisis is past. But given the past patterns, you probe and learn, "I've been getting bored and maybe it's time to get a fresh start—you know, a different city, different job, different people, just to keep the batteries charged." Do you want to hire someone who gets bored so easily?

Once, in a front-page *Wall Street Journal* article I said I recommended that a candidate be hired, even though he had been fired for dishonesty. Huh? Yes! As a stockbroker he had violated ethical principles and was fired. But that had been more than a decade ago. He told me (and it was confirmed) that he performed on himself what he called an "integrity transplant." After humiliating himself and disappointing his family and friends, he vowed to be a totally ethical person. His Topgrading Interview suggested he had succeeded and he arranged for reference calls with all bosses in the past decade; all rated him "rock solid" in integrity. He was hired, became CEO of a major financial services company, and retired with a reputation for solid character. In this case the recent past was part of a decade-long solid record of honest performance, so I bet he'd continue to be honest. "Wow, Brad, that's not exactly a risky bet," you say. But the client just knew he'd been fired for dishonesty and didn't know whether to trust him; only because of the Topgrading Interview was it so easy to bet he'd be honest.

Bottom line: understand the full pattern and rate the person based on today's performance, not that of 10 years ago.

Understand "Red Flags"

"Red flags" are warning signals to the interviewer that something has gone wrong. Rapport suddenly declines, something changes in the interview to suggest that you have touched on a raw nerve. The signals are as follows:

- Blushing
- Suddenly complex responses, when previously they were more straightforward
- Loss of eye contact that had been quite good
- A significant change in pace (speeding up or slowing down)
- A significantly higher or lower voice
- Inappropriate use of humor
- Sudden changes in voice volume, pace (faster, slower), pitch (higher or lower), or pauses (more/longer or less/shorter)

- Twitching, stammering, drumming fingers when there had been none of that behavior
- Formality in style or vocabulary, when the individual had been informal
- Inconsistency between nonverbal behavior and words (saying, "I was very happy in that job" while frowning)
- Heavy perspiring, when the person had been calm

It is the sudden change in the rhythm, style, and rapport of the interview that should tell you, "Pay attention, something is going on here." Certainly make note of it in your Topgrading Interview Guide. Then go on a "fishing expedition," using follow-up questions to get additional information. *"Could you tell me a little bit more about that?"* or *"Could you give me a specific example of what went on then?"* If it is early in the interview, don't destroy rapport by probing too aggressively. You can always come back later in the interview, after you have more information that will help you figure it out. That's what I did when interviewing the convicted murderer and when . . . you'll see . . .

BRAD'S STRANGEST INTERVIEWS: BRAD INTERVIEWS A CONVICTED MURDERER

This unusual interview contained a candidate's exhibiting lots of red flags and the interviewer (me) violating some basic interviewing principles. I was interviewing someone with a past that my client wanted to tell me about. "Nope, thanks," I said, "I don't want you to bias me. I'll do my interview and give you my opinions, and then you can give me yours." "Are you sure?" asked my client. "I . . . uh . . . guess so," I responded, wondering what I'd find.

The candidate had been a terrific interviewee up until the time his Career History Form stated he was a minister for seven years in Joliet, Illinois. Three hours into the interview, rapport was high, but it declined precipitously when Pete (not his name) suddenly clammed up, lost eye contact, and was very evasive about those years. I naturally probed and probed until he admitted he was in prison in Joliet, Illinois, for seven years . . . for killing someone. *Gulp.* My interviewee had been Gentle Ben, 6 foot 5 and 300 solid pounds, with a long scar on his right cheek. I hadn't been intimidated, but when he said, "for killing someone," and nervously raised his hands to clasp them behind his head, I momentarily thought he was threatening me.

Shock Not Shown is one of those interviewing principles on the Topgrading Interviewer Feedback Form, but I did show shock. My voice got higher. I started sweating.

"Whodja kill?" I squeaked. "My mother-in-law," he whispered.

"Yeah, yer mother-in-law," I squeaked, showing bad technique (inappropriate humor). What the heck was I doing? I had the sweetest mother-in-law in the world!

"Whydja kill her?" I timidly inquired. His response sounds made up but isn't. This was three hours into the interview and he replied, "I killed her because she asked too many questions." Now, that is a conversation stopper in a four-hour interview! I then violated about 10 interviewing techniques in the next 30 seconds.

Somehow I regained composure and got the interview back on track. I needed more specifics so I probed, and he said he accidentally bumped her and she fell down a flight of stairs. It was the second and third flights that bothered the jury (not true—I just slipped that in there for—oops—more Inappropriate Humor). I believed him and recommended him for hire. He became an A Player, and I later learned that my client (a not-for-profit) knew his criminal record before I did. I recommended him because I guessed he'd gotten abused by a racially biased judicial system in Illinois. And I trusted what he had been and done in the most recent decade—a decade of great work performance.

Bet on People Changing When They Have Changed

Interviewers are suckers, believing people who look them in the eye and say, "I've learned my lesson, and believe me, in my next job I'm going to be a lot better (organized, team player, nicer to people, etc.)." The thing is, they are usually sincere. They intend to change.

But we all know change is difficult. We can rationally understand the need to give up smoking, exercise more, be nicer to people, or whatever, but maybe we are "hardwired." Most New Year's resolutions last about a month, and people just give up and go back to what they were doing—their well-ingrained, comfortable modes of behavior.

My Topgrading advice regarding interpretation is simple—believe people will change when they have shown they have changed. Look for the pattern of their becoming self-aware, recognizing the need to change . . . resulting in a commitment and a plan to change and active follow-through which—voilà—produces real change. The example you previously read, where I recommended that my client hire a formerly unethical stockbroker, is a perfect example. Had he been fired a month before I interviewed him, I would not have "bought" his commitment to change. I might have believed he'd sincerely try to change, but I've heard such pronouncements 10,000 times with candidates who go on to describe the next job in which they— oops, too bad—just couldn't change.

We've also discussed Erik, who was self-aware, knowing he had been too intense but not changing until well into his career. But because he *had* changed, his reduced intensity was solidly ingrained. In the past few years the more mature Erik was finding it easier to work with peers and subordinates; he listened better, was gentler in encouraging them to raise the bar, and found people in general more cooperative. So, did Erik perform a "personality transplant" on himself? No. Like all A Players, he opened himself up to change, got feedback, established a plan, followed through, and found that the plan got the intended results—support by his colleagues, which made him more promotable. I can today rate him high on interpersonal skills because he's demonstrated them for years.

Now, about halfway through the book, I hope you're getting a sense that although interviewing is difficult, by following the Topgrading Interview Guide you'll arrive at brilliant insights into candidates. You will!

Which Competencies Are Easy and Hard to Change?

Tens of thousands of Topgrading Interviews by Topgrading professionals have given us terrific insights into how, when, and why people change. You've seen (on page 82) a chart listing competencies according to ease of change, and you've also reviewed 50 color-coded competencies (based on how easy competencies are to change) in Erik's Job Scorecard (Appendix A, page 277). Here's how we arrived at a consensus on this: we ask so many questions about every job that it becomes glaringly clear what people's needs are to change, exactly what they do to change, what are their motivations, and how successful they've been.

Here is a chart of all 50 competencies, not color-coded like Erik's Job Scorecard, but organized differently—into the three categories of ease of change, to help you understand the categories.

Competencies Light = Relatively easy to change Medium = Hard to change but doable Dark = Very difficult to change	Definition
Risk Taking	Takes calculated risks, with generally favorable outcomes. Does not "bet the farm."
Leading Edge	Constantly benchmarks best practices and expects others to do the same.
Education	Meets formal and informal educational requirements. Exhibits continuous learning.
Experience	Job-specific
Organization/Planning	Plans, organizes, schedules, and budgets in efficient, organized manner. Focuses on key priorities.
Self-Awareness/ Feedback	Recognizes own strengths and weaknesses. Not defensive. Does not rationalize mistakes or blame others. Uses feedback mechanisms.
First Impression	Professional in demeanor. Creates favorable first impression—body language, eye contact, posture, etc.
Customer Focus	Monitors client satisfaction (internal or external). Establishes partner relationship with clients. Visible & accessible to clients.
Team Player	Reaches out to peers. Overcomes we-they. Approachable. Leads peers to do what is best for company.
Communications—Oral	Communicates well one-on-one, in small groups, and public speaking. Fluent, quick on feet, command of language. Keeps people informed.
Communications—Written	Writes clear, precise, well-organized documents using appropriate vocabulary, grammar, and word usage.
Political Savvy	Aware of political factors and hidden agendas, and acts effectively with that awareness.
Selecting A Players	Topgrades through effective recruiting and selecting at least 90% A players.
Training/ Development/ Coaching	Actively and successfully trains people. Coaches and develops for promotion into positions where they succeed. People builder.

Competencies Light = Relatively easy to change Medium = Hard to change but doable Dark = Very difficult to change	Definition
Goal Setting	Sets fair stretch goals for self and others. Encourages individual initiative.
Empowerment	Pushes decision making down to lowest level. Provides authority and resources to subordinates.
Performance Management	Fosters high level of accountability through fair, hard hitting performance-management system. Free with deserved praise and recognition. Constructive in criticism. Provides frequent feedback.
Redeploying B/C Players	Redeploys chronic B/Cs.
Diversity	Topgrades with diversity.
Running Meetings	Demonstrates ability to organize and run effective meetings.
Change Leadership	Actively intervenes to create and energize positive change. Leads by example.
Conflict Management	Understands natural forces of conflict and acts to prevent or soften them. Effectively works through conflicts to optimize outcome. Does not suppress, ignore, or deny conflicts.
Compatibility of Needs	Needs that are consistent with opportunities in foreseeable future.
Balance in Life	Achieves sufficient balance among work, wellness, relationships, community involvement, professional associations, friendships, hobbies, and interests.
Judgment/ Decision Making	Consistent logic, rationality, and objectivity in decision making. Neither indecisive nor a hip shooter.
Strategic Skills	Determines opportunities and threats through comprehensive analysis of current and future trends. Comprehends the big picture.
Pragmatism	Generates sensible, realistic, practical solutions to problems.
Track Record	Successful career history. Generally earns performance ratings of Excellent.

(Continued)

Competencies Light = Relatively easy to change Medium = Hard to change but doable Dark = Very difficult to change	Definition
Resourcefulness/ Initiative	Passionately finds ways over, around, or through barriers to success. Achieves results despite lack of resources. Goes beyond the call of duty. Shows bias for action. A results-oriented "doer."
Excellence	Sets high stretch standards of performance for self and others. Low tolerance for mediocrity. High sense of responsibility.
Independence	Willingness to take independent stand. Not swayed by last person talked with.
Stress Management	Stable and poised under pressure.
Adaptability	Not rigid. Copes effectively with complexity and change.
Likability	Puts people at ease. Shows Emotional Intelligence. Warm, sensitive, compassionate. Not arrogant. Friendly, sense of humor, genuine.
Listening	Tunes in accurately to opinions, feelings, and needs of people. Empathetic. Patient. Lets others speak. Listens actively.
Negotiation Skills	Achieves favorable outcomes in win/win negotiations.
Persuasion	Persuasive in change efforts, selling a vision. Convincing.
Team Builder	Achieves cohesive, effective team spirit with staff. Treats staff fairly. Shares credit.
Tenacity	Consistent reward of passionately striving to achieve results. Conveys strong need to win. Reputation for not giving up.
Intelligence	Ability to acquire understanding and absorb information rapidly. A quick study.
Analysis Skills	Indentifies significant problems and opportunities. Analyzes problems and people in depth. Sorts the wheat from the chaff, determining root causes.
Conceptual Ability	Deals effectively with not just concrete, tangible issues but with abstract, conceptual matters.

(Continued)

Competencies Light = Relatively easy to change Medium = Hard to change but doable Dark = Very difficult to change	Definition
Creativity	Generates new approaches to problems or innovations to established best practices. Shows imagination.
Integrity	Ironclad. Does not ethically cut corners. Earns trust of co-workers. Puts organization above self-interest.
Assertiveness	Takes forceful stand on issues without being excessively abrasive.
Vision	Provides clear, credible vision and strategy.
Inspiring Followership	Inspires people to follow lead. Minimizes intimidation. Takes charge. Motivates by pushing appropriate hot buttons of individuals.
Energy/Drive	Exhibits energy, strong desire to achieve, high dedication level. 60 hours or more per week probably necessary for results expected.
Enthusiasm/Passion	Exhibits dynamism, excitement, and a positive can-do attitude.
Ambition	Desires to grow in responsibility and authority.

In a new job there are apt to be higher pressures, and under pressure people tend to resort to their familiar behavior style, not a new one. For example, a "top-down autocrat" might have been working on empowering people for the past year, and was doing fine. But with a promotion there were much more difficult challenges and he regressed to barking orders and making most decisions himself. So instead of people "turning over a new leaf" in a job, they usually *try* to be on their best behavior but when feeling a bit overwhelmed tend to resort to their old self.

It's prudent to assume that people are most likely to change their behaviors when the competency is relatively easy to change, when their self-awareness is high (as it is with Erik), when they are highly motivated to change, and (as you have learned) when they show a pattern of having overcome weaker points in the past.

The chart suggests that if people are lazy, it's hard to get them from Poor to Good in Energy/Drive, yet never say it's never possible. We've seen plenty of C Player managers destroy the energy of their staff, but when an A Player replacement comes in, those same people become reenergized. And the chart suggests that sleazy executives who should be in prison rarely get an Integrity transplant, but the stockbroker-to-CEO example above is the exception.

For some reason I have a lot of experience helping autocratic, top-down, heavy-handed, arrogant leaders soften their leadership styles. It's actually pretty easy. Every day they are empathetic, sensitive, positive, and good listeners with their superiors, but with subordinates they are heavy-handed, and that is where the change is needed. Such managers "manage up" well. They can be coached to use those warm and fuzzy skills more often because they have those warmer "muscles" and use them every day with their superiors.

On the other hand, the meek, unassertive manager is *never* a demanding boss, nor is he assertive in everyday life (a waiter could give him the wrong order and he will still eat it). So the autocrat merely has to be motivated, whereas the meek manager has to be motivated *and* has to learn totally new, unfamiliar behaviors.

Again—here's the point, one more time: don't bet the autocrat will change unless the autocrat has already changed, and that change can be verified in reference checks.

Weight Negatives More Heavily Than Positives

In our experience, people naturally keep developing their strengths but struggle with overcoming weaker points. I've been in hundreds of meetings in which candidates for hire or promotion are discussed, and the message is people succeed not so much because of full utilization of their strengths but because of their not having significant shortcomings.

People succeed not so much because of full utilization of their strengths but because of their not having significant shortcomings.

As you know, Topgraders scrutinize 50 or more competencies for a management job. A candidate can be strong on all but one and be appropriately rejected if that person is Poor or Very Poor on honesty, energy, resourcefulness, replacing C Players, and many other competencies. Candidates are usually quite verbal talking about their strengths, accomplishments, and successes, so Topgraders minimize costly mis-hires by, more than anything, understanding the person's weaker points. So as you sift through all the data, pay particular attention to the negatives.

With these key principles in mind, let's return to the main subject of Step #9, which is how to write a (draft) report.

How to Write a Draft Executive Summary After the Tandem Topgrading Interview, and Before the Reference Calls

Finally—here's how to do Topgrading Step #9! After taking you off on the important tangent of how to arrive at valid conclusions, here's a reminder of where we are in the 12 Topgrading Hiring Steps. The Topgrading Interview (Step #7) has been conducted, the tandem interviewers have given each other some feedback (Step #8) on their interviewing style, and if the candidate now seems like an A Player, there is a great temptation to ask the candidate to arrange reference calls. However, the whole purpose of Step #9, writing a draft Executive Summary, is for the tandem interviewers to avoid jumping to an erroneous conclusion. Below are the steps to writing a draft executive summary.

1. **Read the Sample Executive Summary, Appendix G (page 323).** Don't be shocked by how long it is; this is a combination final report of an Executive Summary *plus* a comprehensive Individual Development Plan (IDP) that the newly hired A Player, not you, creates. Your Executive Summary will consist of: the narrative summary, the list of Strengths and Weak Points, and a list of developmental suggestions. The newly hired A Player (*not* you—you've done enough work!) takes this and creates the Individual Development Plan consisting of What is to be done (that's all you suggest), Why, When, and How the results will be Measured.
2. **Write a draft Executive Summary.** After reference checks, the *final* report will be written, with the Individual Developmental Plan suggestions.
3. **You and your tandem partner review the Job Scorecard,** including your Minimal Acceptable Ratings.
4. **You and your tandem partner review all your notes two times:** once, to "get out of the weeds," to look at the overall picture: Is this an A Player? And review your notes individually again, making ratings and comments for all the competencies in the Job Scorecard.
5. **You and your tandem partner compare ratings and notes, and resolve any differences.** What if you and your partner disagree by more than a point on any of the competency ratings? Just discuss it.

Chances are one of you weighted the early career too much, when Pat was disorganized, but should have weighted her more recent career, when she became very organized.

6. **Finally, write your draft, modeled after the Sample Executive Summary, Appendix G.** Okay, writing the Executive Summary draft looks like a lot of work, but because you analyze all the data as taught in this chapter, the Summary will almost "write itself." Figure it will take an hour. If you pick tandem interviewers a bit below you on the organization chart, ask them to write the draft (heh-heh).

7. **Both tandem partners review the draft together, and agree to any changes.** Your goal is to create a draft Executive Summary that will be edited and finalized after the personal reference-check calls.

When you have completed Step #9, you will have tremendous confidence that you truly have the candidate figured out. So when you conduct reference calls, your interpretation of what those references tell you will provide no real revelations and your follow-up questions will be much more on target than if you had skipped this step.

TOPGRADING HIRING STEP #10:
CONDUCT CANDIDATE-ARRANGED REFERENCE CALLS

Having the candidate set up the reference calls after completing the Tandem Topgrading Interview has been eye-opening. Candidates know up front that they will be arranging these calls and they tend to be open and honest during the interview process because of it. We have not had any big surprises in any of the reference calls we have done.

—Larry Sheftel, Director of Human Resources for MDI Group

The Topgrading method of reference checking is powerful, easy, and fun. You already know the general approach:

• Use the TORC Technique (which is powerful).
• You and your tandem interview partner pick the people you want to talk with.
• The candidate does the work of arranging all the calls (easy).

It's frankly fun, after the huge amount of information you've gathered about your candidates, to actually talk with their past and/or current bosses and others who know them best. Why is it fun? Because you will conclude *you* know the candidate as well or better than any of them, almost all of your conclusions will be confirmed, and you will get sufficient additional insights to be able to manage your new A Player a bit better. Oh yes, and the additional insights will sometimes make the difference between offering the job to this candidate . . . or to another candidate . . . or to no current candidate at all.

You've analyzed all the information from all the Topgrading sources, including the tandem Topgrading Interview, and you've completed your draft Executive Summary, so now it's time to do reference checking, and what's the problem the Topgrading method solves? You already know—even A Players can exaggerate positives and hide negatives. The TORC Technique is the truth serum and it works, but to avoid costly mis-hires you need a solution to the third major problem in hiring—lack of verification. Candidates arrange the personal reference calls to provide you with that verification. And asking candidates to arrange personal reference calls is not a bluff; if that was true, the word would get out and TORC would become FTORC—Feeble Threat of Reference Check. And besides, when you conduct those reference checks you are gaining even deeper insights into the candidate. So please conduct these calls.

Here's how to conduct the most revealing reference calls ever:

- Conclude the tandem Topgrading Interview with, "We'll need to go through our notes to develop a list of people, mostly former bosses, we'd like you to arrange personal reference calls with. So we'll call you probably tomorrow with the list."
- Perform Step #9—analyze all the information to prepare a Draft Executive Summary, and while doing so specifically look for the people you want to talk with. For a mid-management candidate we recommend talking with
  - all former bosses in the past decade,
  - five to seven people, including former bosses, peers, subordinates, and
  - one or two people from the current place of employment—perhaps people who left the company.
- Get back to the candidate with the list of people you want to talk with. A Player candidates are eager to arrange the calls. Clients report that the sharpest candidates arrange all the calls within one day, reporting

when their contacts are available and their mobile number. And after four days if a candidate can't arrange for you to talk with the people you requested, maybe the reason is that those contacts are fearful of telling the negative truth about the candidate.

- Follow the Topgrading Reference Check Guide (abbreviated version below). Do *not* delegate this important reference checking to someone else. The tandem interviewers know the candidate best and only the two of you are sufficiently knowledgeable of the candidate, and sufficiently credible to reference sources, to conduct revealing reference calls. In the reference-check interviews, create the tone of a *trusted confidant*. Promise confidentiality and respect it.

REFERENCE CALL INTRODUCTORY COMMENTS

Hello, (name of person contacted), thank you very much for accepting my call. As (candidate) indicated, we are considering hiring her and I would very much appreciate your comments on her strengths, areas for improvement, career potentials, and how I might best manage her. Anything you tell me will be held in the strictest confidence. (Assuming concurrence . . .) Great, thank you very much. (Candidate) and I have spent _____ hours together. I have thoroughly reviewed her career history and plans for the future and I was particularly interested in her experiences when she reported to you. If you don't mind, why don't we start with a very general question.

- *What are (candidate's) strengths . . . and then weaker points.*
- *On a scale of Excellent, Very Good, Good, Fair, or Poor, how would you rate (candidate's) overall performance?*
- *Why did (candidate) leave?*
- *Let me tell you more about the job (candidate) is applying for, and our organizational culture . . .*
- *How would you think (candidate) would fit in such a job?*
- *What would be your advice to me for how I could best manage (candidate)?*

Meet with your tandem interviewer, share all your reference-check notes, decide on whether the candidate should be given an offer, and if so, take the time to finalize your Executive Summary, including the Individual

Development Plan suggestions that you'll share soon after the person starts on the job.

TOPGRADING HIRING STEP #11:
COACH YOUR NEWLY HIRED A PLAYER

Our managers now begin coaching new employees from day one. The new employees create an Individual Development Plan within 45 days of starting with us. Doing so helps them hit the ground running and adds value right out of the gates. Managers spend less time dealing with issues and more time helping them achieve and exceed goals. New employees love it and we love it.

—Travis Isaacson, Senior Director
of Organizational Development,
Access Development

Congratulations, your newly hired high performer has just arrived in the new job! It's time for coaching. What? Most new hires get their first real coaching a year after they joined the company, in their first formal performance appraisal. There are problems when coaching is delayed, and they have been well researched. The two major problems are:

1. **Without help getting adjusted to the new job, sometimes even A Players become frustrated and quit.** Companies that had been recruiting your newly hired A Player might not have given up, and when they learn that onboarding is not going so well at your company they just might pirate your A away from you.
2. **There can be delayed productivity and development.** A person is hired, the boss takes off on business travel for two months and the new hire, eager to get going, has little to do. Why wait weeks to unleash your A Player's talents? And why wait a year to start coaching if someone is high potential, eager for feedback, and eager to follow through on developmental actions? The best way to retain A Players is to offer them real challenges and active career development.

Immediate feedback and coaching allow you to keep a promise. Topgrading attracts A Players, and at each step in hiring not only should you remind candidates of the TORC Technique, but at the end of the Telephone Screening Interview and at the beginning of the Topgrading Interview you made a promise. Do you recall what it was? Here's your promise (sorry, this is so important, this is a repeated script):

> *As a Topgrading company our processes are unusually thorough. There are Competency Interviews but also a chronological Topgrading Interview in which we ask about your entire career—all your successes, mistakes, key decisions, and key relationships. And finalists are asked to arrange personal reference calls with former managers. The benefits to high performers who apply are many: (a) you'll go to work in a company with almost all high performers, (b) career opportunities with Acme are unusually good because so many high performers grow the company, (c) 90% of people who join us are happy on the job a year later and are rated High Performer, and (d) within a couple of weeks of joining us you will receive comprehensive coaching to help you assimilate smoothly into the company, perform very well quickly, and begin formulating your Individual Development Plan to help you grow.*

To keep that promise and achieve smooth onboarding, more immediate productivity, more rapid development, and more satisfied new hires (easier to retain), it will be useful to you to learn the skill of coaching your new hire.

In chapter 6, "The Art of Topgrading," you'll learn some additional coaching techniques that really do help people grow, maximize their strengths, and, yes, overcome weaker points. But for now, here's a primer . . .

YOU CAN EASILY BE SUPER COACH OF YOUR NEWLY HIRED A PLAYER

Can you picture yourself as a super coach? The bad news is that our research with over one million people shows that employees in general think their managers are not very good coaches. Managers are described as hypercritical, poor listeners, not genuinely interested in them, stingy with praise, can't be trusted (to cover for their mistakes), having unrealistically high expectations, unavailable, and . . . you get the picture.

Actually, even if your high performers consider you a great coach, your marginal and low performers don't, and they likely never will. On Friday you ask High Performer Susan about the upcoming weekend and she says, "I'll be going to the usual soccer games but I'll review my draft of the report and definitely have it on your desk at 8:00 AM Monday." You say, "Have a great weekend," and you mean it, knowing your High Performer won't let you down.

The conversation with Low Performer David didn't go that well. His answer was, "Thanks for asking—you know, I've got soccer games and parties tonight and tomorrow night." You ask about the report and he says, "Darn, I forgot, but I'll try to get to it." You become stern and say, "Don't try, *do it*, because at noon Monday I meet with the president, and so I have to have your report first thing Monday."

Monday arrives, High Performer's report is perfect and on your desk at 7:00 AM, but when you see Low Performer and ask about the report . . . you can guess the rest of the story.

Unless you are among the top 5% of managers as coaches, your low performers will never like you, trust you, or consider you a good listener— because as soon as they utter excuses you cut them off, you meanie. And it's understandable that when filling out a survey form on you, they give you low ratings as a coach.

Fortunately the initial coaching of your new high performer *is easy* because they do most of the work, and the dice are loaded so that it's hard *not* to make this a very successful, energizing, fun session. The main reason this is such an easy and fun coaching session is that . . . *it's easy to coach high performers.* After the extensive hiring process, trust is high, you really *are* interested in them, you have already shown you listen well (in interviews), and because you are doing the coaching you obviously are interested in their development. Congratulations, Super Coach!

The main reason this is such an easy and fun coaching session is that . . . *it's easy to coach high performers.*

NEW HIRE COACHING GUIDELINES

1. **Don't delay.** You promised feedback and coaching, your new A Player will always want it, so do it. After a little rapport building, restate the purpose—that you'll discuss the Executive Summary as a

springboard to the new hire formulating an Individual Development Plan for smooth onboarding, high performance in the current job, and long-term development.

2. **The hiring manager is the coach.** However, some hiring managers want their tandem interviewer (who oftentimes is a Human Resources professional with a lot of interviewing and coaching experience) to participate. No problem.

3. **Open the coaching session with a statement of the three goals (onboarding, productivity, development).** Reiterate that you'll share your Executive Summary, but it's the new hire's responsibility to take that report and to compose the Individual Development Plan (IDP), taking your suggestions and making it his/her plan. Explain that the IDP should include the items in Appendix G, which provides clear examples of what every IDP should contain. For each developmental activity your new hire should state What is to be done, Why, When, and How Results will be Measured.

4. **Review your Executive Summary** with the candidate—every word, every strength, every weak point, and every developmental suggestion. Make it an ongoing dialog. Ordinarily there is minimal disagreement—newly hired high performers are generally self-aware, eager for feedback, and very willing to take your feedback and create that Individual Development Plan.

5. **Hand your new hire your Executive Summary plus Appendix G, the Sample Individual Development Plan.**

6. **Read and discuss the development activities included in your Executive Summary.**

7. **Ask your newly hired A Player to create an Individual Development Plan (What, Why, When, and How Measured). This should only take a week or so.**

8. **Be sure the IDP includes quarterly reviews.** These can be informal, even over lunch, but it's a very positive message when the new boss commits to meeting every three months to review progress on the IDP, get current feedback, and hopefully receive continued support. Newly hired with Topgrading methods, A Players feel great about the job, themselves, and about you, the hiring manager. They are eager to write and finalize (with you) their IDP and they want your approval and ongoing support. So it's best if *they* say what they want to do and you then mostly agree, tweak the plan, and *you* offer support.

Congratulations! When you follow the above 11 Topgrading Hiring Steps, your new A Player is not only hired but coached to soar to great heights. Remaining is one more step, tracking Topgrading success.

TOPGRADING HIRING STEP #12:
ANNUALLY MEASURE YOUR TOPGRADING SUCCESS

As CEO, I believe annual measurements of our success in hiring and promoting people is essential. Several years ago we had some hiccups in our hiring process in a couple plants; we had too many mis-hires. In our analysis, we learned that most of our mis-hires were caused by skipping steps in the Topgrading process. We learned some important lessons and since that time we require full Topgrading process adherence to avoid similar misses.

—Curtis Clawson, President, CEO, and Chairman,
Hayes Lemmerz (recently retired since
acquisition by Maxion in 2012)

In Step #12 we close the loop on Topgrading in one sense—because we're sort of doing what we did in Step #1—we're measuring hiring success and costs of mis-hires. In Step #1 we measured pre-Topgrading results, a baseline, and the poor results motivate managers to Topgrade. In Step #12 we measure success Topgrading, and we do it annually.

What is the problem that this step solves? You can probably guess—without annual measurements there can't be real accountability for quality of hires, and without accountability, even the best of best practices wither and die on the vine.

So Step #12 is systematically measuring percent high performers hired and costs of mis-hires (and mis-promotions), pre-Topgrading and since Topgrading. Companies use a lot of different measurements, and here are some examples:

A Player/A Potentials in Management
(example with fictitious numbers)

	Year 1	Year 2	Year 3	Year 4
Number (%) A and A Potentials in Senior Management (N=10)	5 (50%)	8 (80%)	10 (100%)	10 (100%)
Number (%) A and A Potentials in Middle Management (N=60)	15 (25%)	30 (50%)	40 (66%)	55 (92%)
Number (%) A and A Potentials in Lower Management (N=200)	50 (25%)	80 (40%)	120 (60%)	170 (85%)

Note: Topgrading is top-down, with senior management Topgraded before middle management, which is Topgraded before lower management, so it is common that lower levels temporarily show less success than upper levels.

Hiring Success When Topgrading Is Used, and Not Used
(example with fictitious numbers)

	Topgrading Used	Not Used
Number (%) A or A Potentials Hired	20 (91%)	2 (17%)
Less than A or A Potentials Hired	2 (9%)	9 (75%)
Total	22	12

Every manager uses the Topgrading Cost of Mis-Hires Form (Step #1) whenever there is a mis-hire, and these costs of mis-hires can be aggregated across the company, and disclosed to all managers annually.

Total Cost of Mis-Hires Example
Total Costs of Mis-Hires

	2011	2012	2013	2014
Costs	$5,400,000	$3,800,000	$2,100,000	$1,400,000

In real life the results are always the same: Topgraders increase their percent high performers hired and promoted, from 25% to 50%, 60%, and steadily toward 90%, and the high costs of mis-hires goes down, down, down year after year. Every manager sitting with HR to analyze the costs of every mis-hire, by reviewing the total hiring file on the mis-hire or mis-promotion, sees that cutting corners on Topgrading methods is foolish because it is so costly.

"Hey Jack, you're VP Sales and you have 70% mediocre sales reps, but you continue to cut corners on Topgrading. You sometimes don't have a tandem partner and you typically call two rather than six references. None of the rest of us on the team will get our bonus this year unless Sales does the job, and if you don't start using Topgrading methods rigorously, you'll fail and we'll all suffer."

One case study company saw hiring success plummet from over 90% to 60%, and the analyses showed corner cutting. In this case, plants were opened in new countries and translations of the Career History Form and Interview Guides were not done until after the plants were staffed. Because Step #12 was performed, the decline in hiring success and sky-high mis-hire costs resulted in Topgrading being reinforced and of course hiring success shot up and costly mis-hires plummeted.

Once per year use the Topgrading Talent Projection Calculator (page 67) and the Cost of Mis-Hires Calculator (page 72) and ask your subordinate managers to do it, too.

These will show you your hiring/promoting success rates, calculate how many people you will have to hire to achieve your Topgrading goal (presumably 90% As), and determine the total costs predicted from the inevitable mis-hires. Why do this? It will further motivate the organization to stick with Topgrading disciplines.

START STEP #12 A YEAR AFTER TOPGRADING IS LAUNCHED

Why? Because it usually takes a year to determine if a manager hired or promoted has turned out to be an A Player.

Topgrading companies "stole the show" at an American Productivity and Quality Center meeting in which they described how they determine the quality of hires. One year after a person is hired, the hiring manager, Human Resources, and two others who worked closely with the person meet for an hour. The new hire's Job Scorecard is reviewed and the four decide how the person performed in relation to the stated accountabilities. If any 360-degree surveys were done, the results are reviewed. A conclusion is reached and the new hire is told, "We consider you an A Player" . . . or not, and if it is "not," the person is put on a performance-improvement plan.

A summary chart of costs of mis-hires annually reminds managers of the high costs, but when the aggregated costs are steadily declining, it's also a strong message.

Although several examples of annual measurements are provided above, there are plenty of additional measurements that you'll think of making . . . eventually. For example, if only 5% of your hires come from referrals from your people, you probably will launch a program to increase the referrals. And of course, by tracking the measurements annually you and your team will know whether your referral program is working or not.

To summarize, the advantages in performing annual measurements of quality of talent are as follows:

- It's necessary for accountability: Topgraders shine and non-Topgraders don't. Topgrading is on every manager's Job Scorecard, including the CEO's.
- It provides an opportunity for the CEO (or top manager) to reinforce the commitment to Topgrading.
- It's valuable learning for managers: the value of the company is related to Topgrading.
- Showing reduced costs of mis-hires makes all managers want to be better Topgraders.

Does following 12 Topgrading Hiring Steps seem onerous? As mentioned earlier in this book, you can shorten Topgrading hiring to creating a Job Scorecard, using the Topgrading Career History Form and Topgrading Snapshot, conducting the Starter Topgrading Interview, and performing reference checks; do just these steps and you will hire better performers. But I hope you will return to this chapter periodically to be reminded of the value of all 12 steps, so that you can enjoy close to perfect hiring.

Chapter 4

ADVANCED INTERVIEWING TECHNIQUES

It is not the strongest of the species that survives, nor the most intelligent; it is the one that is most adaptable to change.

—Charles Darwin

Tips on how to interview are on every page of this book, but this chapter highlights some of the most powerful, advanced interviewing techniques, ones worth your time trying to master. Topgrading Hiring Step #8 is where Topgrading interviewers, immediately following the Topgrading Interview, pull out the Interviewer Feedback Form and give each other a few minutes of feedback and advice about how to improve on interviewing techniques. And in that section you learned many of the basic interviewing techniques. But this chapter elaborates on the more advanced techniques that build rapport and produce the most valuable candidate insights. And there is a section with tips on how to comply with the law; although Topgrading has been thoroughly vetted for legality (we have heard of zero discrimination lawsuits connected to Topgrading), to stay out of a minimum-security prison (just kidding) be sure to follow these tips. Finally there is a section on validity, showing research supporting Topgrading methods.

In our Topgrading Workshops we of course pass on the best interviewing advice we can, and all attendees receive feedback and coaching as they conduct the tandem Topgrading Interview. This chapter summarizes "Brad's Top 10 Tips," what we have found over the years to be the most important methods to improve managers' interviewing skills.

Tip #1: Repeatedly inform candidates of the purposes of the thorough Topgrading hiring approach, and of the TORC Technique.

Okay, this is actually pretty basic, and you've learned a lot about it, but there are some subtleties that make using TORC somewhat advanced. We've learned that many beginning Topgraders are squeamish about threatening candidates, again and again, with what they consider a heavy-handed threat: "You gotta be honest because we're gonna check up on you and, by the way, *you're* gonna have to arrange calls with bosses." But experienced interviewers don't flinch, don't hesitate, and they make the gentle reminder repeatedly because A Player candidates love to hear it. They want to arrange the calls. It's an opportunity for them, not a threat.

So, at the beginning of the Telephone Screening Interview, Competency Interviews, and Topgrading Interview, take a minute to remind the candidate why this process is different, more thorough, and better not just for the company but better for high performers who join the company. You've already read suggested scripts, and you should change the words a bit to be spontaneous. But here is one more script, and as you read it, please envision yourself being calm, pleasant, and not at all threatening as you convey this message at the beginning of various interviews:

> This interview will give us the best insights so if you join us, there is a terrific chance you'll be a happy A Player, and by getting to know you well we can assure a smooth onboarding process and you can be more productive on the job faster because of the onboarding. And we can start the developmental planning process within weeks of your joining us, so your long-term development will be turbo-boosted. You should also know that a final step in the hiring process is for candidates to arrange personal reference calls with former managers and maybe others. Is all of this okay with you?

Companies routinely inform candidates that they embrace Topgrading, and encourage candidates to browse www.Topgrading.com. Why? Because A Players quickly realize this is exactly the sort of approach that will enable them to shine, and C Players realize they don't have a chance of being hired and they drop out. Good!

Tip #2: "Connect" with the interviewee.

New Topgraders are frequently so conscientious about asking all the questions that many come across as a bit cold, at least initially. It's no problem after you've done a few interviews, but initially remind yourself to connect with the candidate by calling the person by name, being friendly and cordial, showing sincere enthusiasm when the person discusses a major accomplishment, showing your sense of humor, and offering to take breaks every hour or so. After using the interview guides just a few times, you will loosen up. Your confidence will blossom because you will anticipate the next question, which follows a logical order, and the real "you" will engage with your interviewee.

Tip #3: Maintain control of the interview.

Every book on how to get a job says that interviewers are so bad at interviewing (that's generally true) that to get a job offer, interviewees must take control of the interview and tell interviewers how good they are, using well-rehearsed, self-promoting sound bites. Those books advise that, just like a politician on TV, candidates should answer the questions *they* want asked, which will not be the ones interviewers ask.

Tip #1 (above) helps you maintain control, for candidates realize you have a thorough and very structured process, and when they hear they will have the opportunity to talk about every job, including every accomplishment, sharp candidates realize that grabbing control will cause them to *not* get an offer.

There are three key ways to take back control if the interviewee either tries to take over or just wanders off on topics not of interest to you.

The first time you need to regain control, be gentle, but interrupt and restate your question.

The next time interrupt and explain, "Pat, our Topgrading process involves asking a lot of questions about a lot of jobs, and I'd really appreciate it if you focus on the question asked." Or, "Your running marathons sounds fascinating, but I'm concerned we won't have time to complete this interview if we don't get back to discussing your career."

And the third time say something like, "Joe, I'm wondering if you've read some books that say you have to take control of the interview. Please don't because I'm thinking that if you come to work for me, I will have difficulty getting you to answer my questions."

The gentle approach is almost always sufficient to regain control. If you are the hiring manager, can you imagine what it would be like working with someone who would try to avoid your questions, obfuscate, or flat-out change your agenda in a conversation? The third rather blunt and harsh approach is taken when you are about to reject the candidate and call off the interview. It is very fair, however, because it gives the candidate one last chance to "pass" the interview. I do this in interviews, essentially speaking for my client: "Susan, we've been together a couple of hours and I've found that sometimes I have to ask a question twice or three times before I get an answer. I know you want to put your best foot forward, but I'm thinking that if Jan hires you, she would be frustrated because she really insists that people on her team listen carefully to her questions and answer them directly." If interviewees then listen better and answer my questions, fine, and I put that in my report. And if I continue having to re-ask questions I also put in my report how I tried to inspire directness but found the candidate frequently not answering my questions.

Tip #4: Probe, probe, probe to answer the big question: SO WHAT?

Perhaps the single most important technique in interviewing is getting underneath the words to understand the true meaning of what was said and what the significance is, so you can validly rate a person on one or more competencies. This is so important, I'll provide many examples.

Every time a candidate makes a statement, make it your business to figure out the SO WHAT? You ask a question in the Interview Guide, and if you are sure you fully understand and believe the response, take notes and go on to the next question. But particularly during the last hour of the Topgrading Interview, when you are discussing the most recent and relevant jobs, to "fully" understand the response will require more and more probes.

> **Question:** *Why did you get your CPA?*
>
> **Answer:** Because at the time it was a requirement in my company to move up in Finance.

That's such a common and understandable response to a question very early in the interview, you don't need to probe for SO WHAT? But particularly when you progress to jobs in the most recent decade, almost all the questions about successes and failures will require follow-up questions to really pin down what occurred.

The figure on page 183 explains what I mean. Suppose for a job the candidate had 10 years ago you ask the standard question, "And what would Pat Smith say were your weaker points in that job?"A Level 3 response, "I sometimes procrastinated," is an example of an unclear shortcoming or weaker point. Everyone "sometimes" procrastinates (except you and me). So you probe with, "Can you use an example to explain how you sometimes procrastinated?"

Level 2 is a bit more specific. "I missed three deadlines last year" is a precise response, but again incomplete. Probe deeper—"Three out of how many, and what were the consequences in terms of your overall performance?" It makes a difference if it's three out of three, or three out of thirty, and more importantly we still need to know SO WHAT?—is missing three deadlines a terrible failure or maybe even a success? As it turns out the boss might criticize her procrastinating, but she still got a promotion!

Interviewer Probes

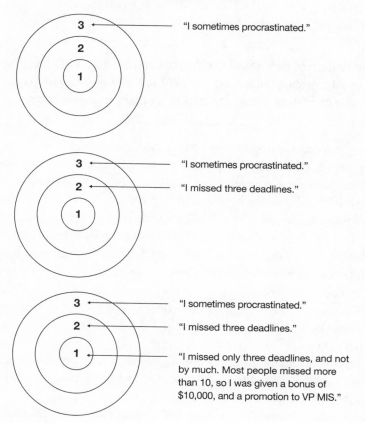

Level 2 and 3 responses are too vague to rate the person. Probes that produce the bull's-eye, the SO WHAT? answers, are Level 1 and what you need. The response in the diagram convinces you that procrastination is probably not a major shortcoming, but suppose she had said, "I missed all three out of three deadlines, and it was totally my fault; I got the reports in eight weeks late; consequently, we lost our best customer and I both lost my bonus and was fired." That answers SO WHAT?, a Level 1 response.

You get it—without probing and probing to answer the SO WHAT? you could easily arrive at terribly incorrect conclusions.

If you were discussing a job 10 years ago and the candidate has become well organized and has received top performance ratings, salary increases, and bonuses since then, great, it's no longer a shortcoming. But if a failure to get work done well or on time has occurred again and again, and very recently, would you hire the person?

The *pattern* of successes and failures revealed through a series of Level 1 probes answers SO WHAT? and will permit you to rate the candidate today, accurately, on many competencies.

The *pattern* of successes and failures revealed through a series of Level 1 probes answers SO WHAT? and will permit you to rate the candidate today, accurately, on many competencies.

Your probing for Level 1 "bull's-eyes" will also reveal *why* the person fails to meet deadlines. In this particular example, a very common reason (or excuse) given for not meeting deadlines is for people to fear saying no to bosses who load them up with projects: "If I tell my boss I can't handle additional projects, I'd probably be fired, but when I take on too much, both quality and on-time performance suffer." Most people have had an unreasonable boss, but if the candidate has missed deadlines in the past four jobs, and describes every boss as unreasonable in expectations, just maybe if you hire him you will be considered . . . you get it . . . "unreasonable." A Players develop confidence and figure out how to say, "Hey, boss, I'm working 70 hours per week and if I take on project X, I'll have to drop something else or I'll make mistakes and miss due dates."

It frankly takes a probing mind to dig out sufficient specifics to be able to arrive at valid conclusions. In Topgrading Workshops when we see interviewers getting a vague response and failing to probe, we suggest, "Whoa, let's stop—that response could mean 100 things, half good and half bad.

Interviewers, let's probe, probe, probe to be able to answer SO WHAT?" One of the main advantages of having a tandem interviewer is to have two brains working to realize when probes are needed and to think up the follow-up questions.

The sad fact is (at least in my opinion) that every business day thousands of hiring interviews take place and interviewers rarely get better than vague Level 3 responses, so when they sit down to rate the interviewee, all they have listed for possible weaker points is "sometimes procrastinates," "could communicate better," "need to study competition more," "impatient with himself," "probably works too hard" . . . and dozens of other responses that, if probed deeply, might have revealed that not one is in fact a weaker point.

Let's make this a game. You think up the probes.

Question: *How many did you produce that year?*

Answer: 75 widgets

Okay—so what are your probes?

Follow-up questions must nail down exactly what producing 75 widgets means, the SO WHAT?, so you can rate some competencies; thus, you should consider the following:

- (Job Scorecard and performance rating) *"How many widgets were you supposed to produce that year; what was the goal in your job description? What was your overall performance rating and what was the impact of producing 75 widgets on that rating?"*
- (Peers) *"How did your 75 stack up against your 20 peers in that job?"*
- (Industry standard) *"How did your 75 stack up against others in the industry?"*
- (Last year) *"How did 75 stack up against your previous year's performance?"*
- (Extraordinary circumstances) *"What were any factors we haven't discussed that might have made it easier or harder to produce 75— economic upturn or downturn, additional or fewer company resources to help you, better or worse competitive factors, or what?"*

Another example: Suppose the interviewee says, "My boss would say I should communicate better." Don't peek; let's make this another short game. What would *your* follow-up probes be to get Level 1 responses, the responses that answer SO WHAT?

Common follow-up questions are

- *What specifically would your boss want you to do to communicate better?* (And whatever you hear, you'll probably need to pin down: Oral communications? Written communications? Your communications in meetings? Public speaking? Keeping him better informed? Grammar? Inappropriate humor?)
- *So, what were the consequences for you and others?*
- *If we had video or audio tapes of your not satisfying your boss with communications, what would we see or hear?* (People are increasingly visual so I use this all the time—point to the wall and ask them to imagine a big flat screen, and what we would see, and they can relate to this and give revealing descriptions.)
- *What is your best guess as to how your boss will describe this in a call we will ask you to arrange if we move ahead?*

BRAD'S STRANGEST INTERVIEWS: PROBES DISCLOSE MAFIA CONNECTION

I was interviewing all the executives of a national company as part of a Topgrading Audit, and the vice president of Distribution had been struggling to get results because the union rates in warehouses were higher than what competitors paid. I was noting a weird pattern—he kept referring to the mob. This pattern became a red flag. I needed to—you guessed it—probe!

I didn't want to scare him away from mentioning the mob, so I let him bring it up and I didn't probe much during most of the interview. But at the end of the interview I figured out a gentle way to broach the subject. I was thinking, "Why the heck are you so preoccupied with the mob?" or "Are you in bed with mobsters?" so I asked, "Have you had any mob contact recently?" He said yes, two reputed hit men for the mob had been to the corporate offices and wanted to offer the CEO an "incentive"—make payments of $50,000 per month and the thugs promised that onerous union contracts would "go away." With the former head of the union in jail, I asked how the national union could enforce local contracts, and he made it clear that a local who refused to do what the jailbird "requested" would be killed. Got it—either the onerous parts of the contract would "go away" or the local union leader would, um, depart, and my Fortune 500 client would have indirectly hired the hit man.

I interrupted the interview and took the executive to visit the CEO, a charismatic man who wanted to turn the company around and then run for president of the United States. (No, not Donald Trump, Lee Iococca, or Ross Perot.) The CEO heard the story, declined to pay the bribe, and the onerous union contracts continued. The company continued to decline, and the board eventually replaced the CEO. If I had not discovered the VP's mafia contacts, one of the best-known companies in the U.S. might have become party to corruption and murder. And if that little tidbit became public during a presidential campaign, the CEO would have instantly disappeared from the political scene.

The lesson about probing is this: when an interviewee mentions something that shocks you, stay cool and ask, "Could you tell me more about that?" but don't frighten the person into holding back. Wait until later to aggressively probe. See if the strange topic comes up again, and maybe again. If it does, your pointing out the repeated reference will convince the interviewee you have discovered so much that the interviewee is likely to open up. And this is NOT Tip#5: Don't hire hit men (is that sexist?) to help you achieve your business goals.

Tip #5: Have at least 20% eye contact, but no more than 50%.

There is a common myth that interviewers should have constant eye contact with the interviewee but that's nonsense. When asked, interviewees like less than 50% eye contact, so that they can scratch an itch or just not feel stared at. Your mom taught you not to stare; she said it's impolite and she was right. With two interviewers taking a lot of notes and only having eye contact 40% with the interviewee, that's enough.

Tip #6: Constantly take notes, but be unobtrusive.

In workshops we see interviewers writing on their Topgrading Interview Guide with the Guide on the table, right in front of the interviewee. As soon as you are writing something negative, like a mistake or failure, the candidate will stare at your note taking, be concerned, and be less inclined to give you negatives.

In chapter 3 the use of a padfolio was recommended, but it's worth repeating: By propping up the padfolio at just enough of an angle that the interviewee cannot see what you are writing, you can write negatives such as failures or mistakes and it will not be obtrusive, interfere with rapport, or cause the interviewee to "clam up."

Top #7: Do a thorough summary at least every 10 minutes.

Summaries are super rapport builders and powerful clarifiers. When you summarize accomplishments, reasons for leaving, or whatever, it shows you're listening, and a summary will commonly trigger additional thoughts. "So, your reasons for leaving were more money, greater challenge, and to join more of a growth company" might trigger, "Yes, those are reasons, but I guess there was another one I don't like to talk about—I didn't get along with my boss."

Or you could summarize four accomplishments and the person could say, "Oh, I forgot the biggest one—they put me in charge of a product launch that saved the year for the division."

Tip #8: Use active listening at least every 15 minutes.

Active listening is incredibly powerful. Active listening is more than an echo, more than just playing back the facts stated. Active listening includes empathy, sensing what was not said but felt, and playing back to the person your understanding of the feelings.

For example, the candidate might say, "They changed bosses on me three times that year, and two of the three tried to use me politically in ways that were not good for me or the company." Wow, you really need to dig in and get specifics, and you could say, "Uh-huh," or "Tell me more." But those are rather cold probes. Active listening personalizes your interview and will provoke revealing disclosures. You could say, "Oh, Sarah, I once had a boss who sacrificed me politically anytime there was heat and my stomach was in knots all the time." If she felt stress, and she probably did, she'll appreciate your compassion and understanding, and she'll trust you a bit more.

More than 1,000 executives have participated in executive coaching with Smart & Associates, and if you were to read all of our recommendations for how they could improve as leaders, one would stand out as the most frequent recommendation—use active listening a *lot* more.

Tip #9: Know when and how to sell a candidate on taking the job.

Actually you "sell" every time the candidate sees you and your company, but most of the selling is indirect and subtle. High performers are attracted to jobs when the following factors are evident:

- Your company has a strong recruitment brand.
- Your Web site and Careers section are exciting.
- Your Telephone Screening Interview includes a credible "pitch."
- The competency interviews are well organized and the interviewers are impressive . . . and allow 15 minutes each for the candidate to ask questions.
- You promise to provide feedback and coaching in first couple of weeks, to help assure smooth onboarding, to be sure A Players are highly productive soon, and to begin a developmental process to help them grow (all key motivators for talented people).
- You and your tandem interviewer are positive and professional, and you allow some time at the end of the Topgrading Interview for the candidate to ask questions. And this is key: at the end of the Topgrading Interview, after you have learned about what the candidate has liked and disliked in every job, you know precisely what are the hot buttons to push to excite the candidate about the job. So, after the Topgrading Interview, perhaps during the days when reference-check calls are being made, it's time to tailor the offer to exactly what you now know the candidate wants.

As my son Geoff says in his best-selling book *Who*, high performers take the job when you satisfy them with respect to the 4 Fs—Family (spouse employment, kids, soccer teams, schools, etc.), Freedom (most A Players need to soar, to be empowered, to make things happen), Fortune (studies all show money is not the key factor in attracting high performers, but don't try to take advantage of people, because comp is a symbol of success and A Players value that symbol), and Fun (pay attention to creating an exciting, fun culture).

Many readers have also learned an important lesson: don't stop recruiting high performers until months after they have joined you. High performers have options and in many cases the companies they did not join are staying in touch so that if things don't go so well with you or your company, they might still hire the A Player.

Tip #10: Stay legal and valid by sticking with the Topgrading methods.

Let's address the legality of Topgrading first, and then validity. Before I pass the baton to top experts in employment law, it's disclaimer time. You don't want to violate the law, and because the law in the United States and everywhere else is constantly changing, please check with your attorney to be sure all your hiring practices are legal and defensible. We used the pros at Seyfarth Shaw LLP (www.seyfarth.com) to prepare this section of the book.

I know of no lawsuits dealing with any aspect of Topgrading. Not one. Years ago, a division of Royal Bank of Canada had an inquiry—someone had asked the Canadian equivalent of the EEOC if it's legal to request all dates of employment, because with that information it is possible to guess at someone's age. I explained that Topgrading is so thorough it looks at every success, failure, key relationship, and key decision for every full-time job, and without dates for a job, the interviewers wouldn't know if someone had accomplishments in three months or 10 years. They "got it," so the Federal Government of Canada hired me to train their top Human Resources professionals so that *they* could use Topgrading methods.

The simplest advice we give to clients is "stick with the Topgrading methods and Interview Guides." Later in this chapter Seyfarth Shaw elaborates on some particularly sensitive topics to avoid, and why. My "grocery list" advice is: When creating questions (follow-up probes, competency questions, etc.), **do not ask questions about any of the following:**

- Religion
- Race, Ethnicity
- Sexual Orientation
- Age
- Height/Weight
- Marital Status or Intentions
- Children or Intentions
- Arrests, Financial Problems
- Physical or Mental Problems/Disabilities
- Alcohol Consumption
- Certain Citizenship Questions
- Native Tongue
- Birthplace

Topgrading methods have been designed from their inception to be nondiscriminatory. EEOC strongly favors thorough job analyses resulting in what we call Job Scorecards. And EEOC favors structured interviews. The Telephone Screening Guide, templates for Competency Interviews, Topgrading Interview Guide, and Topgrading Reference Check Guide are the most comprehensive and structured guides of any hiring system we know of. The use of extensive note taking, tandem interviewers, and reports with ratings on competencies all help assure fairness.

Because we have not heard of a legal charge against any part of Topgrading, let alone a successful lawsuit, you might conclude you need not be cautious. But there are some legal banana peels, so now it's time for me to pass things to the professionals at Seyfarth Shaw. Please note that it is always prudent to consult with qualified legal counsel when making employment-related decisions.

Seyfarth Shaw Opinions and Advice

Topgrading methods are legal. We at Seyfarth Shaw have performed research and have found no Topgrading-related lawsuits in the United States.

Our bottom-line advice is to stick with Topgrading disciplines, Interview Guides, and advice. That advice works, not just to hire and promote top talent, but to do so in full accordance with the letter and spirit of the law.

Perform Thorough Job Analyses

To comply with the Americans with Disabilities Act (ADA) (and the more recent Americans with Disabilities Act Amendments Act), it is important to focus on the essential functions of each position and to document those essential functions as part of your ADA compliance. Always remember, the key to ADA compliance is not whether a disabled individual could perform the job, but whether that individual could perform the "essential functions" of the job when reasonably accommodated (for example, could a person who cannot walk do the job if walkways were modified to accommodate wheelchairs?).

Write Job Scorecards with Behavioral Competencies

Describe the job in terms of only the knowledge, skills, and abilities (KSAs) that are necessary for a trained or trainable person to perform the job. If the job analysis leads you to include peripheral activities that cannot be reengineered out, that's okay, but you need to consider that possibility. It is also critical for ADA-compliance purposes that the Job Scorecard states what you, the employer, consider to be the "essential functions" of the job.*

---

* Although the employer's view is not determinative as to what is considered an essential function of the job, the employer's view is taken into account under the EEOC Regulations.

When possible, Job Scorecards should include objective, measurable performance accountabilities. Specifying first-year bonus accountabilities, particularly for managers (production metrics, quality goals, productivity improvements, number of product launches, maintaining nonunion status, etc.), may offer some legal protection, by forcing a more detailed job analysis, a clearer Job Scorecard, and a focus on most essential competencies.

Most courts and the EEOC agree with the Fourth Circuit Court of Appeals* that competencies based on soft or subjective criteria such as quality of prior experience and personal, interpersonal, and motivational competencies may also be used where they are applied evenhandedly to all applicants for a position and when subjective competencies are job-related; that is, they meet the standard of business necessity.

Use Nondiscriminatory Language in All Hiring Forms and Guides

Application Forms: With the job analyzed and described with behavioral competencies and with various communications broadcasting your recruitment,† the next chronological step is scrutiny of completed application forms. The Topgrading Career History Form frequently becomes a company's application form, with the company logo and oftentimes some unique questions added; changes must be approved by Smart & Associates (to be sure Topgrading principles are not violated; clients take legal responsibility for the legal defensiveness of using any Topgrading forms or guides and for any changes made to them, approved by Smart & Associates or not). The Topgrading Career History Form and the Topgrading Snapshot produced from the Topgrading Career History Form are, in our opinion, legally defensible.

The new Topgrading Snapshot is a visual portrayal ("snapshot") of some of the most important Career History Form information, and at present it is not scorable. Companies wanting a scorable version, which will offer a prediction of likely success ("There is an 85% chance this candidate, if hired, would a year later be judged to be a high performer"), need to follow strict validation protocols; Smart & Associates provides this service.

The Topgrading Career History Form is not tailored for use in any par-

---

* Love v. Alamance County Board of Education, 757 F.2d 1504 (4th Cir. 1985).
† Keeping in mind that it is against the law for employers to limit advertising and recruitment in ways that would deprive applicants of opportunities for employment based on factors such as race, color, sex, or national origin.

ticular state or country, but Smart & Associates constantly makes changes requested by companies (so the Topgrading Career History Form appears to be a clone of the company application form, contains unique questions requested, is translated into any language, etc.). Smart & Associates must approve any changes for copyright protection, but the client company accepts full responsibility for the legality of the changes and the use of the form.

If you use the Topgrading Career History Form (tailored to your company or not) as your application form and if your state allows you to express that "employment at will" is your policy, then an acknowledgment provision conspicuously stating "I understand and agree that if hired my employment is of no definite period and may be terminated at any time with or without cause or prior notice" provides important additional protection in connection with "at will" employees. For additional protection, after the disclaimer we suggest you ask applicants to sign an acknowledgment that reads, "I read and fully understand the terms set out in this application for employment and I certify that all statements contained in this application are true and complete to the best of my knowledge." Since disclaimer laws vary from state to state, check with your legal counsel.

Interviews: With résumés and application (career history) forms screened, interviews come next. There is the Telephone Screening Interview (with a Guide), Competency (behavioral) Interviews (with Guides the company constructs from Smart & Associates templates), the Topgrading Interview (conducted with the Topgrading Interview Guide), and the Topgrading Reference Check Guide. All the Interview Guides are structured, require note taking, and focus on behaviors and results without asking legally risky questions. No Interview Guide assures that the interviewer won't deviate and ask a forbidden question or make an unacceptable comment, because interviews are conversations. The EEOC recommends the use of Interview Guides, so stick with them.

All questions and comments must meet one simple criterion: They must pertain to the essential functions of the job and qualifications that indicate a person's ability and willingness to perform those functions. Why would you want to know anything else?

If you wander from an Interview Guide, what exactly can you or shouldn't you ask?

Age: Avoid obvious age-related questions (that some people still ask), and beware of indirect questions that suggest age; for example, "Where were you when President Kennedy was killed?" Finally, watch out for "smoking gun" questions or comments such as, "We need young blood here." A statement of this kind can imply that you're looking for young people and that older people need not apply.

Is it permissible to identify information, such as age, that could be used for illegal discrimination? The answer is "probably." For example, the Topgrading Career History Form requests (but does not require) graduation date from college, in order for interviewers to know how long it took to complete college and to be sure all jobs are accounted for. Precise dates (month and year) for all jobs permit you to understand how rapidly and deeply competencies have been inculcated by knowing when each life segment occurred, minimizing gaps in chronology. If you do not account for all dates, you might (for example) hire a convicted thief (who hid prison time by not disclosing complete dates for jobs), who subsequently steals from one of your employees.

We suggest that you use the carefully prepared Topgrading Career History Form that does *not* request high school attendance dates or graduation dates. It does request but does *not* require post–high school attendance years or graduation dates. We encourage you to *ask* all education dates in interviews. In this manner, and with accompanying reference checks, you have been diligent in your efforts to cover gaps in the applicant's work records and education history while minimizing potential exposure to an age-discrimination claim that might result from using forms that might raise concerns to those who don't understand the appropriateness of having that information.

Arrest Records: Arrests without conviction can be irrelevant. Anyone under suspicion can be arrested for a crime he or she didn't commit. Even asking about arrests that did not result in conviction is illegal in some states. On the other hand, you do need to protect yourself if a person has been arrested and convicted of a crime that affects his or her ability to perform a specific job. If you are hiring a controller, you have the legal right *not* to hire a convicted embezzler.

In fact, if you don't pursue conviction records, hiring a convicted felon can leave you vulnerable to a repeat crime or can lead to lawsuits charging negligent hiring. However, be sure you have a good business reason for asking about convictions: "Have you ever been convicted of a crime related to this kind of work?" and "Have you ever been convicted of a violent crime?" are legitimate questions. That doesn't mean you should never hire an ex-convict, but if you do, it may be wise to assign that person to work that reduces the potential for the individual to repeat the offenses or injure other people.

Religious Affiliation or Group Membership: Only if religious affiliation is a Bona Fide Occupational Qualification (which is very rare) should you question a person's religious practices, and you should question a person's group membership only if such group membership is job-related and not connected to a protected classification.

Health or Disabilities: Under the ADA, during a screening interview or anytime before offering a person a job (for example, on the application for a job), it's illegal to ask for his or her

Medical history (family or individual),

Prescription drug use,

Prior workers' compensation or health insurance claims,

Work absenteeism due to illness, or

Past treatment for alcoholism, drug use, or mental illness.

You can ask whether the applicant is able to do the job, with or without reasonable accommodation, but nothing else about any disabilities or health conditions.

Questions About Drug Use: Except for positions that are safety-sensitive and governed by regulations from the Department of Transportation, Nuclear Regulatory Commission, or Department of Defense, drug testing is not mandatory. Likewise, it's best not to ask an applicant during a selection interview if he or she has ever experimented with or used any kinds of drugs (prescription or illegal). However, universal testing for illegal drugs for all new hires is acceptable as a condition of employment. Furthermore, it is permissible under the ADA to ask about an applicant's current illegal use of drugs.

Diversity: To achieve more diversity in management, for market or legal reasons, be sure you select from a diverse pool of candidates. As obvious as that may sound, too often diversity goals are not achieved because recruiters did not look in the right "pools."

Bottom line, the laws on discrimination are supportive of what Topgrading is all about—clear Job Scorecards with measurable accountabilities and competencies spelled out, structured interviews with Interview Guides, note taking . . . and generally being sure that every question and hiring or promoting action is job-related.

Topgrading Methods Are Valid

This section might be a bit arcane for you, if you are a "doer" without much patience with theory, but many large companies have Ph.D. Organizational Psychologists on staff and they have a legitimate interest in knowing what research has been done on whether the recommended methods are valid. We contend that Topgrading is *the* most valid hiring method, by far. If that's all you need to know, jump to the next chapter. But if you want a tour through the history of research related to Topgrading, read on!

When I completed my Ph.D. in 1970, I had read every study on interviewing validity, and the results were pathetic—interviews did not predict job success. In preparation for my 1983 book, research continued to show interviews to be invalid; they still did not predict job success. And yet, I was sure I had created a magic bullet.*

I was sure that the Topgrading Interview could achieve 90 to 95% good hires. Beginning around the early 1980s, research began confirming that interviews not only can be valid, but done properly can be the most valid predictor of job performance. Research, for example, showed job analysis is essential. During World War II, armies (literally) of psychologists took job analysis to stratospheric heights. At lower levels of organizations, job analysts, industrial engineers, and systems professionals joined with compensation specialists to promote efficiency and productivity.

Years later, job evaluation specialists such as Hay Associates, who became quite proficient at assigning pay points to job grades, found themselves competing with McKinsey MBAs looking to reengineer processes. But, somehow, job analysis rarely crept into the most senior management positions. It is still a casual undertaking in most companies. Nonetheless, all current research supports the importance of pinning down exactly what the job is (through job analysis).

"State of the art" today is commonly a process consisting of a job analysis, behaviorally anchored competencies, and then some sort of semi-

---

* One book on interviewing influenced me early on: *The Evaluation Interview,* 4th ed., by R. A. Fear and R. J. Chiron (New York: McGraw-Hill, 1990). It's still a classic, but seriously flawed. For example, whereas I might recommend a four-hour interview, Fear says one and a half hours is too long, producing "a lot of unnecessary and irrelevant information" (p. 71). Furthermore, by discouraging asking about performance appraisals for every job (p. 107), Fear misses the most powerful lever for understanding negative—the TORC Technique.

structured interview format, so that questions focus on what is important to do the job. Topgrading offers even better approaches, but in most companies, assessment continues to consist solely of invalid, unstructured interviews. Unstructured interviews include one or more of the following characteristics: lack of question format, short (less than an hour), casual questioning ("Tell me about yourself"), unplanned (no job analysis, no job description, no written competencies), and no systematic analysis of data (the hire/no hire conclusion is made in minutes). In 1988 Wiesner and Cronshaw* found structured interviews over three times more valid than unstructured, in a review of 150 studies. Structured interviews are most valid when interviewers are trained, according to Pulakos et al.† Psychological testing is less valid than structured interviews, according to Van Clieaf.‡

A study by McDaniel et al.§ analyzing 86,000 interviews by leading researchers in 1994 concluded, "Structured interviews were found to have higher interview validity than unstructured interviews." My graduate school colleague Frank Schmidt was an author of this study; he has done many meta-analytic studies of interviewing and tells me that the jury is definitely in: Interviews must be structured if they are to predict job performance. Perhaps you wing it in interviews because a tightly structured interview seems unbecoming, not as collegial as top-level interviews should be. Trouble is, the "wing it" interviews can't address all of the competencies, so 250 of such interviews might be necessary for valid conclusions about a single interviewee.

Let me cite two more studies. Pulakos and Schmitt⁵ found historical

---

* W. H. Wiesner and S. F. Cronshaw, "A Meta-Analytic Investigation of the Impact of Interview Format and Degree of Structure on the Validity of the Employment Interview," *Journal of Occupational Psychology* 61, no. 4 (1988): 270–90.

† E. D. Pulakos, N. Schmitt, D. Whitney, and M. Smith, "Individual Differences in Interviewer Ratings: The Impact of Standardization, Consensus Discussion, and Sampling Error on the Validity of a Structured Interview," *Personnel Psychology* 49, no. 1 (1996): 85–102.

‡ M. S. Van Clieaf, "In Search of Competence: Structured Behavior Interviews," *Business Horizons* 34, no. 2 (1991): 51–55.

§ M. A. McDaniel, D. L. Whetzel, F. L. Schmidt, and S. D. Maurer, "The Validity of Employment Interviews: A Comprehensive Review and Meta-analysis," *Journal of Applied Psychology* 79, no. 4 (1994): 599–616.

⁵ E. D. Pulakos, N. Schmitt, D. Whitney, and M. Smith, "Individual Differences in Interview Ratings: The Impact of Standardization, Consensus Discussion, and Sampling Error on the Validity of a Structured Interview," *Personnel Psychology* 49, no. 1 (1996): 85–102.

experience–based questions ("What were your accomplishments and failures in that job?") to be better predictors of job performance than hypothetical situational questions ("How would you restructure the finance department here?"). The Topgrading Interview approach does both, and why not? Campion, Campion, and Hudson* report a respectable validity coefficient (.50), with a 30-item interview, half-historical, half-future questions. An interview consisting of 30 questions could take half an hour. Add half an hour to sell the candidate, and the interview would take an hour, which is the length of time scheduled for 90% of all management interviews. The one-hour time frames exist because interviewers don't know how to interview and because lawyers have frightened managers into avoiding so many questions. The Topgrading Interview approach, originated over 30 years ago and described meticulously in the two earlier versions of this book, can easily ask 200 questions. In this book I argue that there are more than four dozen competencies necessary (not just desirable) in any management job, so asking a lot more than 30 questions is necessary.

The tandem interview has yet to be researched to any degree. Having discussed the tandem approach, my opinion is that a "solo" Topgrading interviewer who is very experienced is apt to be more valid than a tandem of moderately experienced interviewers. Pulakos et al. found multiple interviewers to reduce harmful effects of interviewer bias, but only if the interviewers did not share the same biases.

A huge frustration I've personally had is that the academic community has ignored Topgrading. I have talked with dozens of professors, offering to open doors to Topgrading companies so they can do master's and doctoral research, but so far I've had no takers. With over 40 case studies prepared for this book, a University of Illinois professor said he would be glad to unleash his doctoral students to vet the cases, but he quit and is not consulting. Topgrading is so popular that hundreds of master's and doctoral theses could produce practical insights, something horribly missing in the many industrial/organizational journals. I won't give up; as of this writing I have a scheduled call with another professor who has expressed interest.

---

* M. A. Campion, J. A. Campion, and J. P. Hudson, "Structured Interviewing: A Note on Incremental Validity and Alternative Question Types," *Journal of Applied Psychology* 79, no. 6 (1984): 998–1002.

Chapter 5

TOPGRADING INNOVATIONS: CASE STUDIES

Topgrading changed my business, and as a small business owner,
by extension, Topgrading also changed the quality of my life.
—Kenneth Munies, CEO, Education, Inc.

This chapter answers the question, "So what—what does Topgrading achieve?" There are dozens of case studies, with companies and top executives named and quoted, all providing examples of the book title: Topgrading is indeed a proven method to hire and promote people, and according to the CEOs, Topgrading indeed turbocharges their companies' success. But there's more . . .

Remember the ad line, "Everything goes better with Coke"? You don't? Maybe that was before your time. Oh, well. Anyway, the case studies in this chapter provide significant and positive proof that Topgrading will benefit you, no matter whether you have one subordinate or 100,000, no matter what country you are in, no matter whether you are a CEO or run a tiny department, no matter what type of organization you're in. Additionally, the case studies are proof positive that surrounding yourself with high performers will likely boost your career success.

As frosting on the cake, Topgrading will likely improve your quality of life. We Topgrading professionals hear it all the time—"Before I Topgraded, I worked 75 hours per week, mostly sweeping up after low performers; my marriage and relationships with my kids suffered and I never made the time to work out; but since Topgrading, I have mostly A Players I can delegate to, and feel less stress because they perform so well; I work fewer hours and get a lot more accomplished, and I have a lot more time to devote to my family and personal stuff."

Unlike the 2005 edition of *Topgrading* that mostly focused on mega companies such as General Electric, Honeywell, etc., this chapter features companies of all sizes, but mostly the small and medium-sized companies that create most jobs and which are at greater risk with just a few mis-hires. With 40 case studies, this could be a 200-page chapter. So we've tried to be a bit creative, offering you several different ways to read case studies:

A Master Chart of 40 mini case studies (pages 202–204), shows the broad range of companies and, in a nutshell, their Topgrading success. You might want to glance through this chart first.

Appendix F provides one-half-page versions of the case studies in the Master Chart. Each mini case study provides the name of the company, a quote (generally by the CEO) on how Topgrading improved company performance, how many employees are in the company, the industry they are in, and highlights of the case study including the improvement in hiring and/or promoting success with Topgrading. Also in "highlights" are creative Topgrading innovations. This will provide enough information for you to decide which of the long-version case studies you want to read.

www.TopgradingCaseStudies.com contains the latest, updated, far more complete case studies. These include advice and insights from executives, details of what they have done, and innovations you'll find intriguing. Bookmark it. If you are reading this 2012 edition in 2018, you can go there and read updated case studies. With your smart phone and a QR Code, you can go to this site directly by holding your phone up to:

We'll keep www.TopgradingCaseStudies.com well indexed, so you can easily locate the case studies of greatest interest. Many of the case studies provide you with Topgrading forms and guides tailored to unique requirements of companies and specific jobs (such as entry-level hiring). These long case studies all have the best insights and advice from their top executives. For case studies to be included in this Web site, Smart & Associates and a company officer must approve them in their entirety; otherwise the case study is removed. You will see many different styles of writing for the case studies, and here's why: Companies want to be case studies so that their recruitment brand will be fortified, and more A Players will want to work for them. Therefore I'm allowing them to be highly creative in composing their case study. All I want to be sure of is that the reported statistics on Topgrading success are "for real." And they are.

Eight of the full (www.TopgradingCaseStudies.com) case studies are also in this chapter, and show some of the most innovative approaches to Topgrading:

- Hiring entry-level employees and store managers (Roundy's, a regional grocery store chain)
- "Do it yourself" Topgrading that was so successful a high-tech entrepreneur made $170 million (Mint.com)
- Improving education by using Topgrading to hire A Player administrators and teachers (North American Nursing Education, a fictitious name because the company wishes to remain anonymous)
- Improving restaurant performance with all Topgrading methods, including the Topgrading Snapshot (K&N Management, owner and operator of restaurant chains)
- Rolling out Topgrading to help a global company come out of Chapter 11 and become one of the most respected automotive suppliers (Hayes Lemmerz, the world's largest wheel manufacturer)
- Attracting A Players with "best company" awards and internally certifying managers as Topgraders (Access Development, seller of discount programs)
- Dramatically improving entry-level hiring (Caregiver franchise for Home Instead, a rapidly growing assisted living alternative)
- A final story is not actually a case study, but a historical event in which an A Player launched a country (that's no typo).

How to roll out Topgrading is the final section in this chapter. Although the case studies show how companies did it, and with what talent and business results, this section distills their advice into practical steps.

CASE STUDY MASTER CHART

Let's begin by looking at the 40 case studies for this edition, including some revisited case studies from the 2005 edition.* For the 2005 case studies that have not been updated, the short case study in this book merely excerpts the 2005 case study with no changes. There are 40 companies, some with separate case studies within the company.

The average improvement hiring and/or promoting people using Topgrading methods is from 26% to 85%.†

Master Chart of Topgrading Case Studies

	Pre-Topgrading	With Topgrading
Access Development	33%	94% (total company)
American Heart Association (2005 case study)	25%	95% (upper management)
Argo	51%	96% (Assist. VP and above)
Azura	??%	75% (total company)
Batesville Casket	60%	80% (total company)
Benco Dental	27%	60% (management)
Carestream Health	Est. 30%	74% (total IT department)

(Continued)

---

* Some case studies from the 2005 edition of this book are General Electric (current statistics are estimated by recently retired head of HR, Bill Conaty); Hayes Lemmerz (update is current); Hillenbrand ('05 was total company case study; the company reorganized and Batesville is current case study); Virtual Technology (the company was acquired and the case study is not updated); American Heart Association (not updated); and EMC (Topgrader left so it is not updated).

† These statistics (26%, 85%) are averages of the Pre-Topgrading and With Topgrading columns and are not weighted by size of the organization Topgraded. When management could not calculate pre-Topgrading success, "??%" is inserted; when management made an educated guess the pre-Topgrading % might read "Est. 33%"—or whatever—and 33% is entered for the statistical calculation; for start-ups, "Start-up" is entered; for "confidential," no number is entered.

	Pre-Topgrading	With Topgrading
Columbus McKinnon	??%	85% (exempt jobs, globally)
Corwin	33%	92% (non-entry jobs)
DenTek	10% 0%	92% (staff) 100% (management)
DPT	17% 20%	75% (hired, total company) 80% (promoted, total company)
Education, Inc.	12% ??%	78% (teachers) 89% (corporate staff)
EMC (2005 case study)	27%	95% (sales reps)
General Electric	??%	More than 80% (high potential managers)
ghSMART	Start-up	100%
GSI	Est. 22%	90% (executives)
Hayes Lemmerz	??% ??%	85% (managers promoted, globally) 74% (managers hired, globally)
Hillenbrand (2005 case study)	Low	81% (management)
Home Instead (franchise)	25%	88% (caregivers)
JT Foxx Organization	2%	80% (total company)
K&N Management	21%	86% (total company)
Labsphere	30%	70% (total company)
Los Niños	50%	85% (total company)
MarineMax (total company)	25% 30%	95% (dealership general managers) 100% (region managers)
Mint.com	Start-up	90%
Netsurit	9%	75% (promotions, management)

(Continued)

	Pre-Topgrading	With Topgrading
North American Nursing Education (fictitious name)	19%	87% (school deans)
Nurse Next Door	??%	85% (corporate and caregiver)
OnyxMD	10%	90% (total company)
Anonymous pharmaceutical company	33%	75% (sales reps)
ProService Hawaii	45%	91% (total company)
Red Door Interactive (total)	20%	90% (total company)
Ron Santa Teresa	25%	74% (total company)
Roundy's	20% ??%	80% (store directors) 100% (senior management)
Sigma Marketing	45%	90% (total company)
Southern Tide	15%	67% (total company)
Synergia One	57%	83% (total company)
Tekmore (name changed; 2005 case study)	??%	95% (managers hired/ promoted)
Triton	2%	80% (total staff)
Virtual Technology (2005 case study)	??%	98% (total company)

EIGHT HIGHLY INNOVATIVE TOPGRADING CASE STUDIES

These are current case studies, as of the printing of this book. They can be revised and updated at any time for www.TopgradingCaseStudies.com.

1. ROUNDY'S: A GROCERY CHAIN ACHIEVES A TURNAROUND, TOPGRADING AT ALL LEVELS AND CREATING SUCCESSFUL INNOVATIONS IN STORE MANAGER AND ENTRY-LEVEL HIRING

There is no doubt about it—the company as a whole has performed better because of Topgrading. A Player executives do a better job of setting direction, four times as many A Player store directors of course get better results, and when we've Topgraded entry employees and the social media rave about how positive and energized the whole store is, record sales no longer surprise us!

—Bob Mariano, CEO

The Roundy's case study is the most detailed and extensive in this book. Reading it will help you understand what to do and how to do it for all levels of a company.

The Company: Roundy's is a privately held grocery chain of 160 stores, operating under five banners in Wisconsin, Illinois, and Minnesota. The newest banner is Mariano's Fresh Markets, which in the Chicago area has achieved unprecedented praise from the media (including social media) and has achieved unprecedented results, in part because of the Topgrading innovations.

A private equity company needed a new executive team to turn the company around and hired Bob Mariano, who was involved with Topgrading in the mid-1980s, when he was a SVP with Dominick's.

Topgrading Roundy's: Mariano Topgraded Roundy's, top to bottom. His first step was to Topgrade the executive ranks, and he recruited the right way—attracting A Players he had worked closely with in the past. It is to his credit that he has been so successful recruiting, for many new executives came to Roundy's because they had (and have) so much respect for Mariano.

Topgrading was implemented with two-day workshops for Store Directors and all managers through senior executive, plus shorter Topgrading workshops (with more pre-reading required) for managers within the stores. Roundy's has implemented all 12 Topgrading Steps, throughout the entire company, and at all levels.

This means that in the stores, for example, not just the Store Director but the entire team of managers is chosen with Topgrading methods, and beginning recently, all entry-level employees in the new Mariano's Fresh Markets are being hired with Topgrading. This is probably the first retail company to use Topgrading to hire and promote 100% of store employees.

For entry levels (cashier, stocker) there has been simplification of the Topgrading methods. And at senior levels Topgrading professionals help guide Topgrading implementation and occasionally assess and coach managers.

An internal executive (Carmel Pender) participated in the Smart & Associates Train-the-Trainer program. She conducts Topgrading workshops as new managers are hired and promoted.

> *Topgrading of all employees within a unit has created a culture of A Player employees with energy, enthusiasm, and passion for their work, our company, and our customers. Any business with quality products is brought to life by its employees—A Players excite customers with their infectious attitudes, customer engagement, and their desire to satisfy the customer's needs. A Players create a vibe within the workplace that is contagious . . . and our customers love it! Customer word-of-mouth builds a business—and our customers tell us daily how much they love our wonderful stores and our amazing employees that came to us through the Topgrading process.*

> —Carmel Pender, VP Service Operations

Topgrading Results:

- The executive team now has 100% A Players.
- Store Director hiring has improved from **26% to 90%** who turn out to be A Players when rated after one year. Store Director promoting has improved from **17% to 63%,** and combined hiring and promoting success for Store Directors has improved from **20% to 84%.**
- Entry hiring (stockers, cashiers, etc.) has improved dramatically, though no performance appraisals are done at that level. Customer survey results have improved from a company average of **83% to 95%.** Mystery Shopper (outside service of people pretending to be shoppers, hired to rate customer service) are the best the company has seen.

TOPGRADING INNOVATION: STORE MANAGER (CALLED STORE DIRECTOR) HIRING PROCESS

Topgrading has given us a preferred method of hiring individuals across all of our stores. We now have a consistent method and a process of how to conduct an interview. As an organization, we are making better hiring decisions as a result of using Topgrading.

—Don Rosanova, EVP Operations

In past decades Smart & Associates trained district managers of many retailers to use Topgrading methods to assess existing store managers and assess replacements, with improved results. But John Boyle, Roundy's Group Vice President Retail Operations, wanted to do better. He entered his position and found masses of statistics on store performance, but with massive holes so large he could not distinguish the As from the Cs. Working with Topgrading professional Chris Mursau, a very accurate, thorough, practical Store Director Job Scorecard was created. Said Boyle, *"I finally had valid measurements, so I could judge results."* He traveled to meet store directors, interviewed them, and used Topgrading professionals for a "second opinion" on some.

We have made a cultural shift across all of our more than 150 locations from merely filling positions to filling them with the best available candidate, and it is entirely because of Topgrading. While intellectually we knew the investment of additional time in the process on the front end to select the best candidate would have a tremendous ROI, we weren't certain those on the front line would buy in. Having utilized the process and seen the difference in the quality of people they now have on their teams, they are believers and wouldn't do it any other way. Topgrading has been the enabler to transform us into the "A" Player culture we so desired.

—John Boyle, Group VP, Retail Operations

The statistics cited above tell the story—combined hiring and promoting success for Store Director has improved from 20% to 84%.

Instead of a vague job description, Roundy's has a Store Director Job Scorecard that is used to measure performance quarterly, resulting in overall performance ratings of Outstanding, Excellent, Meets Performance Expectations, Below Performance Expectations, and Unsatisfactory. An A Player is someone rated Excellent or Outstanding.

Supplement to this case study: Please go to www.TopgradingCase Studies.com if you would like to see the complete Store Director Job Scorecard. Here is just a fraction of that Job Scorecard:

Job Scorecard for Store Director

Accountability	Metric	Standard	Points	Comments
Driving Financial Performance Running a profitable and operationally efficient business			25 Points	
	EBITDA	Equal to or greater than X% actual sales		
	Sales	Sales to budget		
	Controllable Shrink	Less than or equal to X% of actual sales		
	Labor Efficiency	Less than or equal to X% of actual sales		
	Supplies	Less than or equal to X% of actual sales		
Delivering the Customer Experience Creating a compelling and memorable experience			25 Points	
	Customer Interviews & Surveys	90 points or greater		
	Mystery Shops	90 points or greater		
	Merchandising			

(Continued)

Accountability	Metric	Standard	Points	Comments
Creating Great Teams Ensure the right people are in the right place at the right time to deliver business results. Creates an environment where employees feel as though they are respected, recognized, and empowered.			25 Points	
	Hiring Success Rate	At least 75% hiring success rate*		
	% A players	At least 80% A Players all roles*		
	Bench strength	A Player replacements for each manager position*		
	Employee engagement	Measured by annual survey		
Leading Driving financial performance, delivering the customer experience, and creating great teams in a positive way, inspiring followership and fostering a high-performance culture			25 Points	
	Leadership	Competencies rated by DAO		

* Measured by quarterly talent review with DAO

	Learning the Competency (5)	(3)	Highly Competent (1)
Connection and Coaching	• Doesn't take time to build connections with others • Style unsettles people; too direct, intense, impatient, or judgmental • Inconsistent in treatment and perceived fairness • Ineffective at dealing with conflict	• Connects well with most people • Generally good interpersonal style; approachable, genuine • Treats others fairly and consistently • Able to handle lower-level conflict or difficult situations	• Connects well with all types of people • Style puts people at ease; warm, friendly, inviting, genuine • Demonstrates high standards of personal integrity and fairness • Uses diplomacy and adept at addressing and resolving conflict

(Continued)

	Learning the Competency (5)	(3)	Highly Competent (1)
Personal Accountability and Ownership	• Inconsistent at holding people accountable for results • Blames others for failures or mistakes • Promotes dependence on boss for decisions • Manages strictly by rules and structure	• Usually holds people accountable for results • Accepts some responsibility for mistakes or missed results • Delegates low-level decisions or decisions related to routine/daily job duties • Allows people to try new ideas	• Consistently holds people accountable for results and presses for more • Accepts total responsibility for own actions • Delegates most decision making to store team and stresses ownership • Creates entrepreneurial culture; encourages experimenting with new ideas
Motivates and Inspires	• Rarely provides encouragement or positive feedback; critical and negative toward others, particularly in public • Discourages people from doing more • A micromanager; does not trust people and limits individual contributions • Expects people do enough to get by; expects all people to be self-motivated and do their job without having to provide them with recognition	• Generally provides positive feedback when deserved and tailors delivery appropriately • Encourages people to perform assignments and deliver results; removes obstacles • Trusts people to complete assignments; effectively oversees • Expects people to improve performance; applies routine approach with all people	• Appreciates and recognizes good performance; seeks opportunities to do so and tailors delivery to individual • Challenges and stretches people; encourages and enables people to do their best work • Does not undermine others; builds confidence through trust and transferring responsibility • Collaborates with individuals to understand motivators in order bring out their best

TOPGRADING INNOVATION: ENTRY-LEVEL HIRING

Topgrading has been the difference maker in the quality of peo-
ple that we hire for our stores. We have never received as many posi-

tive comments from our customers regarding the quality of our employees.

—Don Rosanova, EVP Operations

In the past year the executive team has launched an effort to Topgrade the entry levels. It's a "work in progress," with simplification of Topgrading methods and efforts to create a Job Scorecard. The Topgrading methods being used include the following:

- The Topgrading Career History Form, which only requests information on part-time jobs going back eight years (so completing the form is easier for someone with 20 part-time jobs dating back many years), though all the usual information on full-time jobs is requested.
- A Store Operations Manager (SOM) conducts the Topgrading Interview, and after being trained and conducting some tandems, the SOM is quite capable of conducting the interview "solo."
- The Topgrading Interview typically lasts an hour, but is complete; without management jobs, and with typically redundant entry jobs, a complete interview in one hour is enough.
- Only two reference calls are done, and they are typically with bosses within the past two years.

The press has been very complimentary, and social media have, too. Mariano's Fresh Markets has the most friendly, hardworking, customer service–oriented employees company management has ever seen, anywhere, in any chain. Instead of working in a grocery store as the job of last resort for not-so-cool kids, employees say working at Mariano's is cool. Typical comments from customer surveys include the following:

"Everyone was so friendly—the store was a treasure."

"Best of all was the stellar service . . ."

"Each employee I interacted with was friendly and enthusiastic."

"The staff was extremely friendly."

Business Results: The company is owned by private equity, and financials are confidential. However, from the Mariano quote at the beginning of this case study, you can get a sense that Topgrading is credited with contributing to the success of the company.

> *Topgrading provides a method to learn more about your candidates and to understand if they really fit your organization. The Topgrading interview allows you to dig deep into the person and really understand who they are. Topgrading separates the "A" players from the rest of the group.*

> —Don Rosanova, EVP Operations

Topgrading in the Future: The Roundy's management team never stops raising the bar. They are constantly tweaking and improving the talent systems, including hiring and promoting at all levels.

Best Insights and Advice from Executives to Would-Be Topgraders

1. Topgrading when implemented correctly produces A Player leaders.
2. Hiring only A Players provides a larger pool of promotable candidates with quality leadership skills.
3. Eliminating poor hiring choices eliminates expensive turnover and business costs.
4. Believe in and follow the Topgrading process! Hiring A Player leaders who attract A Player subordinates creates a culture of A talent employees with a desire to succeed and be successful.
5. Follow the Topgrading process and do not take shortcuts. Plan and prepare for proper execution of all interviews.
6. Ensure the Topgrading Interview is uninterrupted.
7. Ensure that candidate agrees to arrange for personal references with former supervisors.
8. Present yourself as an A Player to the candidate to be interviewed. Give your time and sincere attention to the candidate. At the conclusion of the interviews, will this A Player want to work for you and your company?
9. Don't underestimate the power of your enthusiasm and professionalism. The candidate is also interviewing you and your company.
10. Do not skip steps in the Topgrading process.
11. Do not settle. . . . Choose only A Player talent!

Supplement to this case study: Go to www.TopgradingCaseStudies. com to see the entry hiring system, and some of the Topgrading forms and guides modified for entry levels, and a lot more customer and employee comments.

2. MINT.COM: A DO-IT-YOURSELF TOPGRADER MAKES $170 MILLION!

This is a short case study without all the Topgrading details, but with an exciting message: some people indeed can do it themselves, without (gulp!) attending our Topgrading Workshops, hiring Smart & Associates for "second opinion" interviews of senior candidates, or buying our videos.

Meet Aaron Patzer, founder of Mint.com. He is still in his twenties and has sold his company to Intuit in 2010 for a cool $170 million. I read that he attributed some of his success to using Topgrading methods. So I called Aaron, and this is a brief version of his story.

Aaron grew up in Indiana, got into computers at age six, paid for school by designing Web sites starting at age 16, graduated from Duke University in computer science and electrical engineering, dropped out of a Ph.D. program at Princeton, and received an MSEE instead.

He joined IBM, got three patents on PlayStation, and quit because IBM seemed to promote people on the basis of seniority and Aaron guessed he would not have a fun job for more than a decade. He joined a start-up, writing code, and soon he was interviewing candidates on the phone.

With about a 600 IQ, Aaron wasn't satisfied with his interviewing skills, and he picked up the 2005 version of *Topgrading: How Companies Win by Hiring, Coaching, and Keeping the Best People.* I suspect he memorized the book, particularly the Topgrading Interview Guide. He asked the questions about education years and then investigated a person's career by asking about—for EVERY job—successes, failures, bosses ("I figured if a candidate's last three bosses were jerks, I'd rather not be the fourth"), boss appraisals, and reasons for leaving. Aaron "got it," the power of gleaning patterns and the importance of asking "why?" and "so what" 1,000 times. He used the TORC (Threat of Reference Check) Technique to encourage all candidates, even weak candidates, to be honest, and asked finalists to arrange reference calls with past bosses.

Aaron says Topgrading is "the best business book I've read," although he says the first part included too much name dropping of famous companies that Topgraded, and too much "selling" of Topgrading. (Aaron's viewpoint caused me to downplay Global 100 Topgraders in this book.) He instructed his managers to read the practical advice in the book.

The Company: Why did Aaron start Mint.com? At age 25, Aaron was working 75 hours per week and frustrated with the additional hours necessary to manage his personal finances using Money or Quicken. Then a bolt of lightning struck—he decided to create the best personal finance software. So he did it, he launched Mint.com, with occasional self-doubts. After all, he was attacking Microsoft and Intuit with no business experience, no leadership experience, no knowledge of Java Web services, and by the way—no money. Aah, but he already knew how to hire A Players. In particular he used the Topgrading Interview to not just hire great engineers, but ones that were outstanding in customer service. He wanted his A Players to literally sit with customers to be sure Mint.com was not just debugged, but fabulously user friendly. Thank you for the advice, Aaron, for Smart & Associates has used it to make the Topgrading Snapshot super user friendly. To see how user friendly Mint.com is, Google it. You'll see details of his business, videos of how someone can enter a few super secure credit card and bank accounts in six minutes and immediately begin saving money and time. And it's free.

So, at 26 years of age Aaron started hiring people for Mint.com and had 40 employees at the time he sold it to Intuit, where he now heads their personal finance division.

Topgrading Results: And what was his track record? Four mis-hires out of 40. Not bad! A couple of others quit for good reasons—involving family emergencies. It looks like a 90% success record, with successful hires not just "okay," but true high performers. As Aaron put it, "I don't think Mint.com would have succeeded without my Topgrading and having only a few mis-hires."

Aaron Patzer makes assembling a team of outstanding performers look easy. He just got the book and became a "do it yourself" Topgrader. He didn't happen to mention one small factor that actually does make Topgrading "easy"—he's clearly an A Player.

3. NORTH AMERICAN NURSING EDUCATION, INC. HELPS IMPROVE NURSING EDUCATION IN AMERICA

Note: This company chooses to remain anonymous, for several reasons, among them not wanting to inspire competitors to Topgrade. Therefore the industry and the names of the company and its company officers have been changed.

I believe that a focus on talent with Topgrading as a foundation has been foundational to our growth and success over the past seven years.

—Alice Johnson, Vice President, People Development

North American Nursing Education is a real case study, except that, as stated, we are using fictitious names (company name and names of officers quoted herein). This case study was written, revised, and at the last minute not approved for use with real names, so the words and all the numbers are correct and only the company, job title, and officer names have been changed.

This case study is presented because it is representative of a category of Topgrading case studies that is exciting: hiring better professionals including doctors, psychologists, teachers, lawyers, and consultants. It is too often assumed that because of shortages in a profession, it's almost impossible to select out the low performers. For example, looking at the mediocre performance of U.S. public schools, there is evidence that too many C Player teachers are hired and retained. Another case study is Education, Inc.—the company's real name. It is a private company that improved its success hiring A Player teachers from 12% to 78%. Despite seemingly insurmountable obstacles to hiring outstanding professionals, clients have figured out solutions.

Company: North American Nursing Education (NANE) has 4,500 employees and currently operates approximately 70 nursing schools in the United States and Canada. NANE recognized that as a people-intensive business, their success would rely, in large part, on the quality of the nursing instructors at each site. The selection of school deans was vital as they are responsible for building culture, managing people, leading instruction, and of course hiring the best teachers—all critical to the success of a school.

Topgrading History: As a rapidly growing organization, NANE's leadership team participated in a seminar for growth companies, where they first learned about Topgrading.

With instructor talent considered crucial for success, a more systematic and effective hiring process seemed to make sense, because in a talent review, less than 50% of the instructors and only 19% of the school deans hired had turned out to be A Players. The leadership team made talent a top priority and proved it by taking action.

The team, led by then COO John Smith (now President/CEO) and the new Vice President of People Development, Alice Johnson, was trained in a Smart & Associates Topgrading Workshop.

Topgrading Methods: Similar to the Roundy's case study (above), NANE embraces all 12 Topgrading Hiring Steps. However, unlike Roundy's, Smith already had an A team at Corporate (hiring mostly A Players he had worked with in the past) and initially focused on hiring A Player deans. Smith: "The senior team agreed that A Player deans would eagerly learn Topgrading and hire A Player nursing instructors, but only 19% of our deans were considered A Players." Smith and Johnson dedicated two half-days each week strictly to dean hiring and conducted tandem Topgrading Interviews and reference checks for all finalist candidates.

Topgrading Results: From 2006 to 2011 the percent A Player Deans improved from 19% to 87%. "Our hiring success rate has skyrocketed since we implemented Topgrading across the organization, but we are not satisfied with 87%," said Johnson.

	2009	2009%	2010	2010%	2011	2011%
A	9	56%	13	59%	13	87%
B	4	25%	7	32%	2	13%
C	3	19%	2*	9%		
	16		22		15	

* One of the 2 Cs was predicted by Topgrading but hired by the school.

Definitions:

The talent review process distinguishes between performance and potential. Individuals are rated on both scales.

PERFORMANCE

A = Top 10% for the job in the market
I would enthusiastically rehire this person.
I would work for this person.

B = 65th – 89th percentile for the job in the market
This person understands their job, but does not consistently meet / exceed expectations.

C = Below 65th percentile for the job in the market
I would not re-hire this person.
This was a hiring error.
This person is not in the right position to perform at an acceptable level.
This person is not on the right team to perform.

Note: Ratings based on manager perceptions

The chart doesn't convey the way NANE deals with chronic low performers: talent reviews. Johnson said, "At the beginning of 2011, we identified four C Player deans and have successfully managed them out of the organization. The talent review is used to track our hiring success, but also to call us to action with individuals who are underperforming expectations as well."

Johnson said, "Using the tandem Topgrading Interview approach has been hugely beneficial for us not only because it has allowed us to hire better, but because it allows us to go back when we make hiring mistakes to see what we missed and adjust our process to ensure that we do not make that mistake again. Going back after a hiring mistake has also helped us realize which characteristics are coachable and which are not."

Throughout the business world when there are mis-hires, there rarely is a systematic analysis of the mistake. Isn't this odd? If a new retail store concept, a high-tech product, or a pharmaceutical product fails, the analyses are very thorough. When someone fails, however, there are usually bad results that someone has to explain, and the hiring manager is asked, "Why did you hire that jerk?" The defensive manager blames Human Resources, and HR says, "We weren't given a high enough salary to offer." After a brief round of finger pointing, the focus is on putting out fires ("Someone had better get over to our best customer and patch things up!") and figuring out how to fill the open job as soon as possible. When Johnson and Smith analyze a mis-hired dean they review all the interview notes, from all the interviews from the phone screen to the reference-check calls, to see what they missed. NANE's experience proves that analyzing mis-hires creates insights that prevent some costly mis-hires.

Johnson's quote ("Going back after a hiring mistake has also helped us realize which characteristics are coachable and which are not") actually tells you what their mis-hire analyses reveal. Typically they recognized the person's shortcomings but overestimated the person's ability to overcome them. The point is, analyzing mis-hires makes them able to avoid future mis-hires by more realistically predicting the extent to which weaker points will be overcome.

NANE understands that successful deans genuinely care about the people they manage, have a strong achievement drive, and are resourceful; those qualities are not very coachable. Some failed deans seemed to be very people-oriented in interviews, but reference checks disclosed problems. Johnson: "People can fake warmth and caring in interviews, but if recent references only rate the person Good rather than Very Good or Excellent, we've found that Good is not Good enough. But if dean candidates exhibit those three qualities and have a willingness to learn, we can typically help them develop into a highly successful dean."

With Topgrading, the team of deans is maturing nicely, and naturally Topgrading methods are beginning to be used for Nursing Instructor hiring. "Our goal for both Dean and Nursing Instructor hiring is 90% A Players," commented Johnson.

Business Results

> *From a financial perspective, we are primarily a capacity utilization business; every seat we fill in a school generates revenue. From a quality perspective, we are focused on delivering outstanding student learning results across all our schools. Our capacity utilization has set records over the past three years while academic achievement metrics have increased steadily. As we have increased the percentage of A Players in our organization, employee satisfaction ratings have also consistently improved as we ensure we have more of the right leaders in place.*

> —Alice Johnson, Vice President, People Development

One way of getting a handle on business results is to measure the cost of mis-hiring a dean. NANE estimates the cost of a mis-hired dean to exceed $1 million. And they estimate that a mis-hired dean results in a 10% decline in enrollment in a school, and with the average school having 700+ students, the losses are potentially huge.

Topgrading Advice to Would-Be Topgraders from NANE Executives

1. Take a look at your historical hiring success—the case for Topgrading builds itself.
2. Commit to the process—just having a consistent process improves your likelihood of success.
3. Start by building Job Scorecards—you have to identify your target before you can assess candidates against it.
4. Jump in—don't wait to jump into the process. The sooner you start, the sooner you start making higher-quality hires.

5. Look for help—find a Topgrading professional or network with other Topgrading companies to learn from them.

6. Commit the time—we find most people don't think they have the time to commit to the full interview process, but apparently they'd rather spend 10 to 20 times that amount of time managing bad hires.

7. Follow through—the selection process isn't done when the interview ends. Follow through with the reference checks. We learn as much through this as we do through the interview.

8. No candidate is perfect—the amount of information you gather in a Topgrading Interview can be overwhelming. Because there is no perfect candidate you have to use the thorough Topgrading methods. When you're less thorough in your selection process, you are less discriminating about evaluating talent.

9. Identify the critical competencies—learn which competencies are deal breakers and which ones are star makers for your organization. Put them in the job scorecard.

10. Once you make the hire, start coaching—the goal of getting great talent is getting great performance. Topgrading gives you a great tool for learning about the talent you choose to bring into your organization. Once you select the talent, commit to helping them succeed by coaching them to greatness.

11. Analyze every mis-hire by reviewing all notes.

4. K&N: RESTAURANTS IMPROVE RESULTS TOPGRADING

Our Rudy's "Country Store" & Bar-B-Q restaurants increased average unit sales from just over $3 million in 2000 to $8 million in 2011 (for food sales only). From its inception in 2007 through 2011, Mighty Fine Burgers, Fries and Shakes increased annual unit sales from just over $2 million to more than $3.5 million in 2011, triple the unit sales of its best competitor. These results would not have been possible without Topgrading.

—Ken Schiller, President and Co-Owner

The K&N case study is one everyone can relate to. It's a small growth company, and it runs restaurants we all are familiar with. I've chosen K&N as one of the featured case studies because the business is understandable and the case study shows how "work in progress," doing the basic Topgrading steps first and gradually embracing the remaining steps, succeeds.

The Company: K&N Management is a retail food company with two brands—Rudy's "Country Store" & Bar-B-Q, and Mighty Fine Burgers, Fries and Shakes. There are 500+ employees in eight stores. The company was founded in 1994 by Ken Schiller and Brian Nolen.

Topgrading at K&N Management: In 2006 Schiller read a magazine article on Topgrading and, frustrated with hiring failures, he and Nolen launched Topgrading. The Topgrading Director, Danielle Robinson was hired. Smart & Associates conducted a workshop for senior managers, and store managers read *Topgrading* and met in order to plan how to implement Topgrading in the stores.

Using the Topgrading Cost of Mis-Hires Form, the average cost of mishiring an entry-level employee was estimated to be $28,000, and for a store manager, $320,000. K&N was one of the first companies to use the Topgrading Snapshot to prescreen candidates.

Topgrading Results: Hiring of entry-level A Players has improved from 21% to 86%, and for management, the improvement has been from 62% to 92%. Success promoting people has improved from 65% to 90%. The A/B/C Player determinations are derived from Job Scorecard ratings, part of the performance-management system.

Additional Business Results

K&N Management was a recipient of the 2010 Malcolm Baldrige National Quality Award. Like other case studies in this book, K&N sees the award as building its recruitment brand. It is sure to attract more A Players because intuitively people associate super quality with super people, so I encourage all companies, big and small, to go after "best company awards," although I have a caveat. I've seen some companies spend so much time and money getting such awards that actual business results were harmed.

As mentioned above, K&N Management operates two high-volume, fast-casual restaurant concepts with over 500 team members. The restaurant industry is well known for knee-jerk hiring practices that result in extremely high turnover. Every reader can relate to this fact—"Huh? A Players in fast-food restaurants?" Schiller points out that K&N stores are a notch up from fast-food outlets, but he believes that having A Players visible to the public in industries where C Players are the norm must be good for business. Schiller: "Topgrading is the turnkey hiring process that guarantees we are using the discipline required to select the right people that will follow our processes, embrace our culture, and delight our guests."

When was the last time you ate at a restaurant that obviously had a lot of employees who were trainees? Yesterday? Me, too. And we all probably have a favorite family restaurant—no, not a store that serves mostly families but one in which the family members are long-term, dedicated, service-minded A Players.

Danielle Robinson, with the interesting title of Topgrading Director, said,

> Since we started using Topgrading, we have decreased the number of involuntary terminations within our company from 37% in 2009 to 14% in 2010. We have been able to do this as a result of hiring A Player team members and implementing an effective coaching process. We have also increased our number of internal promotions; 63% of our General Managers were once hourly team members. Topgrading has allowed us to promote people already familiar with our culture and expectations, rather than always having to search outside the company for A Player managers.

PROGRESS ON THE 12 TOPGRADING HIRING STEPS

As stated, the company is a "work in progress," meaning that some of the Topgrading steps are done extremely conscientiously and some are just beginning to be implemented. Specifically:

Step #1 Measurement: Done—see above.

Step #2 Job Scorecards: Done.

Step #3 Hire from Network: About 40% of new hires in the stores come from referrals. Employees get "bounties" of $500 ($10 when a person starts the job, and the rest over a period of 1 year).

Step #4 Career History Form/Topgrading Snapshot: Used for management. *"I love the Topgrading Snapshot. It is such a time-saver! It takes seconds to see the most important information and reject weak candidates, rather than having to read the entire résumé."* (Danielle Robinson)

Step #5 Telephone screens: Not used, but will soon be tried.

Step #6 Competency Interviews: Competency questions are used in the Topgrading Interview for management applicants and entry positions.

Step #7 **Topgrading Interviews**: Used for management; Danielle and HR are the typical interviewers. A scaled-down version is used for entry positions.

Step #8 **Interviewer Feedback Form**: Not used, but not needed because the Topgrading interviewers are so experienced.

Step #9 **Executive Summary**: Not done, *"but we should."*

Step #10 **Candidate arranges reference calls**: Done.

Step #11 **Coaching** in first couple of weeks: Done at 90 days but will be tried earlier.

Step #12 **Annual Measurement:** Not done yet, but are considering doing annual talent reviews and getting stats on success hiring and estimated costs of mis-hires.

Best Insights and Advice from Executives to Would-Be Topgraders

1. It is immoral not to redeploy C Players.
2. A Players attract other A Players.
3. C Players will cause A Players to leave.
4. You raise starting pay when you are not satisfied with the top 10% willing to work for current pay being offered.
5. Do not hire a person that does not align with your culture.
6. Topgrading helps you learn how to break down and define life balance.
7. It was challenging, at first, to get buy-in from some of our managers, but as they saw the results, they realized the process worked very well.
8. Using the TORC process is a great way to keep candidates honest with what they are telling you.
9. The Topgrading process may take longer than you are used to, but stick with it, because it works.
10. The Topgrading Snapshot is an invaluable tool when it comes to reviewing candidates. It drastically cuts down on the amount of time spent on this task.

A "Chat with a Topgrader" Conference Call with Danielle Robinson, Topgrading Director

Every other month I interview a Topgrader (CEO or head of HR, typically), and the first 250 people to RSVP can attend, hear the Topgrader explain their experience, and then attendees can e-mail me questions I pass on to the Topgrader. To get invitations sign up for the e-book and Topgrading Tips on the home page of www.Topgrading.com. And to read the transcript of my free-flowing interview with Danielle, got to www.TopgradingCase Studies.com, where you'll see the case study you just read, but with the interview transcript at the end.

5. HAYES LEMMERZ: A GLOBAL INDUSTRY LEADER TOPGRADES ITSELF OUT OF CHAPTER 11

Note: In 2012, Hayes Lemmerz was acquired by a stratagic owner, Iochpe Group, parent of Maxion Wheels. Curt Clawson retired and long-term Hayes Lemmerz executive Fred Bentley became President and CEO, Maxion Wheels.

> *The company emerged from Chapter 11 one of the strongest automotive suppliers, and Topgrading contributed to that success. Hayes Lemmerz competes in one of the toughest markets in the world: the global automotive OEM supply industry. We slug it out all over the world in head-to-head competition against the Asians, Europeans, Indians, and Latin Americans. In this tough industry with demanding customers, powerful suppliers, and relentless competition from low-cost countries, we have to have the best people to be successful. Therefore, Topgrading is a central part of our culture and the most important of our core competencies. We can't win if we miss on people.*

> —Curtis Clawson, President, CEO, and Chairman, Hayes Lemmerz (recently retired since acquisition by Maxion in 2012)

This case study almost makes it seem that Topgrading can save any company from bankruptcy. I've known the Chairman and CEO Curt Clawson for more than a couple decades, watching him successfully lead divisions of Allied Signal, then turn American Can Company around, before joining Hayes Lemmerz in 2001, Topgrading and applying lean manufacturing principles to vault the company out of Chapter 11 bankruptcy protection to one of the most successful and praised (by the auto companies). While Curt says his Topgrading the company was essential in its success, I'd add that A Player Curt Clawson was essential too. For what it's worth, I doubt that anything less than a strong A Player could have pulled it off.

On a personal note, Curt has several times said, "Smart, I wouldn't approve this case study, but I'm letting you use it because you're a friend." Curt is a little embarrassed that he didn't exceed the 90% A Player standard, that he let Topgrading slip a bit. But he should give himself a break—the automotive world was collapsing and the crises Hayes and other automotive suppliers were facing were hair-raising and constant for several years! Curt always puts the points on the scoreboard in business, a pattern that started when he was a basketball player on a Purdue Big Ten Championship team. Several years ago he beat Michael Jordan in a contest to see who could make the most 30-foot shots. Some might have bet on Jordan winning against an . . . um . . . aging, has-been jock. Anyway, thanks for permitting me to include this case study, Curt, which has great advice for all Topgraders!

Note that Curt is listed as "recently retired," as a merger took place with Maxion Wheels. Fred Bentley is the new CEO of Hayes Lemmerz division of Maxion. I've coached Fred for years and have watched him grow into a fine A Player successor to Curt.

The Company: Hayes Lemmerz International, Inc. today is a premier automotive supplier, with #1 market share worldwide in wheels. The Company has operations in the U.S., Germany, Italy, Spain, Turkey, India, Thailand, Czech Republic, South Africa, Japan, Mexico, and Brazil. The company was a case study in the 2005 edition, and the short version was that even in a troubled industry and a troubled company, in a troubled city (Detroit), Topgrading can enable a company to survive and even flourish. But then the Big Recession hit, and as everyone knows, the automotive industry was smashed, with bailouts provided to help save some companies. Hayes Lemmerz, like all the other suppliers, didn't receive government bailouts, and as demand for vehicles plummeted, many suppliers went out of business.

Hayes Lemmerz entered Chapter 11, but has emerged, is once again a premier supplier, and in fact has record EBITDA. Having recently talked with board members, Joint Venture Partners, and three levels of management, I cannot think of a more talented total group, with such a high level of mutual respect. And why not? In the most dire of circumstances, they figured out how to do more than just survive. That's worth repeating: Curt and his team turned around a company with four strikes against it— location, industry, Chapter 11, and recession.

Operations around the globe have succeeded, new products have been successful, and Best Supplier Awards testify to the company serving its customers.

Topgrading Methods: If there were a Black Belt in Topgrading, Curt Clawson would have it, and he has needed it, because most of the previous executive team had to be replaced. Upon joining Hayes late in 2001 he tapped his personal Network, attracting A Players to key Business Unit president and corporate positions, hardly using search firms. Despite restructuring the company, Clawson has retained most of his A Players. It is frankly one of the most impressive Topgrading cases ever. The top team is superb, with COO and President of Global Wheel Group Fred Bentley (now President and CEO of Maxion Wheels) playing a major role in driving operations and implementing Topgrading.

Initially Topgrading professionals (I and some on my Team) assessed and coached internal managers and candidates for hire or promotion. Topgrading Workshops were held, and over time and with support from my company, Smart and Associates, the top three levels of management in the U.S. proved they could Topgrade with only occasional use of Topgrading professionals.

Tim Welcer, Vice President Human Resources, participated in the Smart & Associates Train-the-Trainer program and initially, with the support of Chris Mursau (Smart & Associates), conducted a number of Topgrading Workshops. Welcer went on to conduct well-received Topgrading Workshops all over the world, training down to the level of managers reporting to plant managers. Welcer and his team have conducted Topgrading Workshops as well as refresher training in virtually every country where Hayes has offices in order to drive the Topgrading methodology throughout the organization.

Hayes locations in many countries have taken the primary materials and translated them into local language formats. Welcer and/or members of his HR team review Topgrading summaries and coach local managers toward continuous improvement in embracing the concepts. Managers are aware that the CEO, president/COO, and/or Business Unit executives will request to review the Topgrading reports during visits to audit the process as well as use the reports to learn about the new hires before meeting them.

Welcer and others often participate in local-country interviews as they travel and time permits as an observer to calibrate the effectiveness of those team members actually conducting the tandem Topgrading Interview.

How A/B/C Player Ratings Are Made: Hayes Lemmerz senior management team conducts an annual two-day Management Resource Review (MRR). Participation consists of the CEO, COO/president, the senior leadership team, Business Unit executives, and top Human Resources staff. The group reviews every functional area, taking time to discuss each person to review (reviews are conducted on each executive, functional leaders, their direct reports, and plant managers on a global basis). The discussions are very energized and open among the entire team. This is a separate process (also known as succession planning) from the performance-management process. Information from that process is used to roll up into the MRR.

Prior to this top-level MRR meeting each Business Unit conducts a similar process with all functional areas and plant locations for all white-collar staff. Results from these lower-level reviews are used to identify talent and high-potential employees in the upper-level talent review meetings for succession planning purposes.

Topgrading Results: Talent meetings have documented a major improvement in talent (see Figure 5.1). Nine out of the top ten executives are new, and it's an A team: 100% A Players. Among the top 77 managers, from plant manager to CEO, the percentage of A Players has skyrocketed from 38% to 89% . . . and is continuing to improve.

In 2003 talent reviews placed only 38% of managers in the A or A Potential groups. Within a year, after launching Topgrading, the executive team had 100% A Players, and the top 77 jobs in the company improved to over 80% A Players.

Annual talent reviews have shown the following results: In a 2011 talent review, hiring and promoting success was systematically measured. Because it's appropriate for a manager to be on board for at least one year in order to categorize the person A/A Potential or Non-A, statistics were computed for 2008 and 2009 hires and promotions.

The current results: Of the 137 managers hired globally, 74% have turned out to be A/A Potentials, and of the 96 managers promoted, 85% have turned out to be A/A Potentials. Combined, managerial hiring and promoting success in recent years has been 79%.

Figure 5.1
Topgrading Hiring and Promoting Results

	Pre-Topgrading (2001)	2003	2011
A/A Potential Hired	35%	94%	74% (N=137)
A/A Potential Promoted	N/A	N/A	85% (N=96)

Note: The table above states 2011 in the right column; however, those results are from 2008–2009.

Business Results: Losses of $211 million in 2001 were replaced by break-even (2002) and earnings from operations of $62 million (2003). Adjusted EBITDA has shown the same trend. In recent years EBITDA has been:

2008 $157.2M

2009 $ 54.5M

2010 $154.9M

2011 $193.3M

Best Advice and Insights from Executives to Would-Be Topgraders

1. I initially Topgraded the U.S., which was struggling, and left other parts of the world alone, because they were quite successful. In retrospect I should have Topgraded them sooner, since those A Players could have been even more successful. (Clawson)

2. Tell people the truth. With a Topgraded company we were faced with plant closings, and by telling people the truth it showed the respect they deserved, and people performed extremely well, even when plants were to be closed. (Clawson)

3. It may seem contradictory, but Topgrading empowers As to make decisions, and I travel constantly to drive the A Player standard. Fred, Tim, and I all travel and reinforce Topgrading while meeting employees, coaching and reviewing management, and meeting customers. (Clawson)

4. Expect to be tested every day, from every corner of the earth. There are always credible reasons to let a chronic low performer have third and fourth chances, but any company, even a global one, will quickly understand if B performance is suddenly okay. (Bentley)

5. Don't cut corners. There have been times, and even I've been guilty, that a supposedly well-known person has been given a promotion, only to fail. Do the tandem Topgrading Interviews and oral 360 interviews with co-workers and you'll avoid costly mistakes. (Bentley)

6. If you're in HR, insist on being involved in the tandem Topgrading Interview for key hires. You can become more experienced than all other leaders in the company. Don't shirk this responsibility and you can make a big contribution to success of the company. Also, be there to coach your managers during their initial tandem Topgrading Interviews to make certain they utilize the skills and training and are calibrated to the process! (Welcer)

7. Push back on your bosses if you see them making a talent mistake. HR generally has the reputation for going along with whatever the

C-suite executives want, and not fighting for what you professionally know is right. (Welcer)

A "Chat with a Topgrader" conference call with Curt Clawson can be read at www.TopgradingCaseStudies.com. As you read in the K&N Management case study, every other month I interview a Topgrader (CEO or head of HR, typically), and the first 250 people to RSVP can attend, hear the Topgrader explain their experience, and then attendees can e-mail me questions I pass on to the Topgrader. To get invitations sign up for the e-book and Topgrading Tips on the home page of www.Topgrading.com. To read the transcript of my interview with Curt Clawson, go to www.TopgradingCaseStudies.com and at the end of the case study you just read is that transcript.

6. ACCESS DEVELOPMENT: "BEST COMPANY" AWARDS AND CERTIFYING TOPGRADERS INTERNALLY BOOST COMPANY PERFORMANCE

During the last three years of the Big Recession we have continued to grow revenue, we've been one of Utah's fastest-growing companies, and we've won multiple awards as a "best place to work." Having 94%+ "A players" at Access is one of the key reasons for this success. Topgrading has been the foundation to help us attract, hire, and retain these "A players."

—Larry Maxfield, CEO

This small company is a case study because of their superior Topgrading results, their excellence in using "best company" awards to attract A Players, and their creative use of internal certification of managers to motivate them to learn and successfully apply Topgrading methods.

The Company: Founded in 1984 and based in Salt Lake City, Utah, the Access mission has been to inspire consumer loyalty through the world's best affinity marketing programs. The company has 165 employees.

Topgrading Methods: Fortunately for readers, Access management is willing to share not only their good results and advice, but candid recognition of ways they could Topgrade even better. You've learned the 12 Topgrading Hiring Steps and following is Access's status on the 12 Steps. Reading what they share will give you insight into what steps tend to be taken early on.

Step #1 Measurement: The pre-Topgrading estimate was 55% high performers hired, but since Topgrading Access, standards have become both clearer and higher. So senior management went back to review talent and decided the pre-Topgrading hiring success rate was only 33% across the company. In ratings, all employees are deemed to be A Player, A Potential, or Non-A.

Every quarter, every manager sends Travis Isaacson, Director of Talent Development, a Talent Review Form with all of their people rated and ranked. The ratings (A, A Potential, Non-A) come from a quarterly Scorecard Review with each employee. Travis compiles all the data from everyone and provides an Executive Summary that goes to the CEO, COO, and president.

Step #2 Job Scorecards: Done well.

Step #3 Recruiting from Networks: 89% of hires in the past year came from Networks. Every employee's Job Scorecard contains a requirement to have at least 10 people in their Networks. LinkedIn is encouraged. "Bounties," payments for referring someone who is hired, are $100 to $500, but not for managers.

Step #4 Career History Form: The Topgrading Career History Form is the company's application form.

Step #5 Telephone Screen: Done.

Step #6 Competency Interviews: "It's our weakest part." Done occasionally, and only after the tandem Topgrading Interview.

Step #7 Tandem Topgrading Interview: This is required. Normally the tandem interviewers are the hiring manager and another manager that will interact with the new hire (the hiring manager's supervisor, a manager in a related department, etc.). The Interview Guides and any additional notes are retained for two reasons. One, to help the hiring manager, who periodically reviews the notes to best understand and manage the new hire. Two, to analyze how a (rare) mishire might take place.

Step #8 Interviewer Feedback Form: Generally both tandems use it to give each other feedback for five minutes following every interview. Some feedback is received, however, through the Bronze, Silver, Gold certification process.

Step #9 Executive Summary Report: "We could do this better." Candidates are scored on the Job Scorecard and there usually are some notes on why the candidate was or was not hired.

Step #10 Reference checks with bosses, arranged by the candidate:
Done, and calls are made by the hiring manager, not HR.

Step #11 Coaching and IDP: As indicated in the certification process,
new hires receive feedback and coaching, and create their IDP, within
45 days of when they were hired.

Step #12 Annual Measurement: Once per quarter Travis Isaacson meets
with all (30) managers to do talent reviews, with all their people designated A, A Potential, or Non-A. Once per year another overall talent review is done.

Topgrading Results: From 33% to 94% A Players hired and promoted,
company-wide.

TOPGRADING INNOVATION:
CERTIFYING MANAGERS AS INTERNAL TOPGRADERS

The senior team looked for ways to help integrate Topgrading into the Access culture. Without something that accomplished this, a fear was that
Topgrading would be reduced to a "program-of-the-month" and would be
adopted by only a few managers and never fully adopted by everyone. Giving someone an official-looking certification seemed like a good incentive
and a way to track who has adopted it and how much.

So, the senior team reviewed the Topgrading steps, practices, and
expected outcomes and divided them into three categories (beginning
certification/Bronze, intermediate/Silver, advanced/Gold). To show every
manager the importance of Topgrading, certification achievement is part
of every manager's Job Scorecard.

An example, the Gold Level of certification requirements, is shown
below; Silver and Bronze certification requirements can be seen in their
entirety at www.TopgradingCaseStudies.com.

Topgrading
Gold Level Certification

Topgrader Information

Name: Title: Completion Date:

Signatures: Manager   HR   Organizational Development

PREPARATION

❏ Complete Silver Level requirements

❏ Reread the Work History script and questions page in the Topgrading Interview Guide) within 24 hours of conducting an interview for at least one interview

❏ Review Job Scorecards for direct reports and make changes/updates as needed

❏ Demonstrate ways your Scorecards have been calibrated with the local economy and job market

❏ Identify at least 25 people on your virtual bench

❏ Source your virtual bench for candidates

❏ Suggest new recruitment and job posting sources to HR

❏ Hold a review session with the HR Manager

❏ Hold a review session with the Sr. Director of Organizational Development

INTERVIEWING

❏ Demonstrate a consistent track record doing the following:

❏ Screens candidates by matching résumés up against the Scorecard

❏ Receives completed Career History Form from candidates

❏ Conducts screening interviews using the official screening interview form (or qualified replacement)

❏ Acts as a tandem Topgrading Interviewer

❏ Reviews candidate's résumé and Career History Form before the interview

❏ Uses the Topgrading Interview Guide questions

❏ Scores candidate against the Scorecard: overall rating, recommendation, accountabilities, and competencies

❏ Personally conducts reference checks

❏ Uses the Reference Check Guide questions and form

❏ Acts as a tandem Topgrading Interviewer on at least 5 additional interviews

❏ Receives interviewing feedback, from a Gold Certified Topgrader, on at least one more interview, using the Interviewer Feedback Form

MENTORING

❏ Provide interviewing feedback on at least two interviews using the Interviewer Feedback Form. Topgraders: _____ and _____

❏ Share your hiring best practices with at least one other hiring manager. Topgrader: _____ Best practice: _____

❏ Encourage those on your team to use their virtual benches

(Continued)

RESULTS

❏ Achieve at least 90% success in hiring/recommending A Players for at least 3 hires

❏ Details: at least 90% of at least 3 candidates you hired or recommended for hire that were actually hired are still A Players after 6 months of employment.

Access Development is one of several Topgrading companies with Topgrading certification. Some companies reinforce Topgrading methods and the A Player standard in their culture by having ongoing Topgrading training (through the online version of the Topgrading Toolkit with seven hours of DVDs). Many companies use annual talent reviews in which the CEO personally requires that A Player standard and reminds managers that they must use Topgrading methods. Bill Conaty's book *Talent Masters* shows how some of the best companies in the world at talent management drive high performance standards and grow A Players.

A "Chat with a Topgrader" conference call with Travis Isaacson can be read at www.TopgradingCaseStudies.com, at the end of the case study.

7. A HOME INSTEAD FRANCHISEE BLOWS AWAY THE INDUSTRY WITH ENTRY HIRING EXCELLENCE

Topgrading has allowed us to triple the projected sales for the office. A Player caregivers impress clients, who refer us, and A Players refer other A Players for us to hire.

—Michael Steinberg, Franchise Owner

With most of my career devoted to picking and coaching senior executives and only in the past decade cascading down to even entry-levels, people sometimes ask, "Does it make sense to Topgrade part-time employees?" Well, I'd bet my mother's life on it, or at least her quality of life.

In November of 2011 my 94-year-old mother passed away, and Home Instead Caregiver Lynn Geiger made the last year of Mom's life much fuller and richer. In a note to the franchise owner (not this case study franchise) I said Lynn had become like a super caring daughter, and in her eulogy Lynn said Mom had become her second Mom. How's that for "personal customer service"?

But that's not why this case study is included. The Roundy's case study showed you modifications of Topgrading for hiring cashiers and stockers, and theirs was a large-company process. This case study presents hiring methods for a small franchise of a large company. If your company hires entry-level employees, studying both case studies, including the forms and guides they use, might help you improve hiring. At the end of this case study you'll see the Caregiver Job Scorecard and portions of the modified Topgrading Career History Form and Topgrading Interview Guide.

The Company: Home Instead Senior Care provides caregivers through 900 franchises worldwide. The Wichita franchise, this case study, was launched in 2011 by Michael Steinberg and his wife, Ewelina.

Topgrading History: After corporate executives attended a Topgrading Workshop, I volunteered the services of Smart & Associates to help a couple of franchises simplify and abbreviate Topgrading methods for hiring caregivers. My interest obviously stemmed from my mother's needs. Michael Steinberg attended a Topgrading Workshop in 2010 and worked with Smart & Associates to tailor Topgrading hiring to the Caregiver role.

Topgrading Results: A Player hiring of caregivers has improved from an estimated 25% to 88%, since 44 out of 50 caregivers hired with Topgrading have turned out to be A Players.

A caregiver must remain with the company at least 90 days to be considered an A Player. Turnover is 100% in the industry, yet the Wichita office has experienced only 40% turnover so far.

Modifications of the 12 Topgrading Hiring Methods for Hiring Caregivers:

THE 12 TOPGRADING HIRING STEPS

Step #1 Measurement: Done.

Step #2 Job Scorecard: An excellent Job Scorecard (below) was created to reflect accountabilities not just for an "adequate" Caregiver, but a true A Player Caregiver. The Job Scorecard becomes the basis for annual performance appraisals.

Step #3 Recruiting through Networks: Even without an economic incentive, Home Instead caregivers are so proud of the company that they have referred 25% of our new hires.

Step #4 Topgrading Career History Form: The Topgrading Career History Form (below) was modified to emphasize education less and add questions specific to caregiving.

Step #5 Telephone Screening Interview: Not done, for a good reason. Caregiver candidates are willing to visit the office and it is most efficient to screen candidates in person.

Step #6 Competency Interviews: Competency questions are included in the Topgrading Interview.

Step #7 Topgrading Interview: The Topgrading Interview lasts 1½ hours and is conducted solo by Ewelina Steinberg. Part of the modified Topgrading Interview Guide is shown below.

Step #8 Interviewer Feedback: This is not done, because there is a full-time interviewer who has mastered the techniques.

Step #9 Executive Summary: Notes are taken but no formal report is written, and so far, has not been needed.

Step #10 Reference Checks: Finalists arrange for six professional references, including three bosses.

Step #11 Coaching New Hire: New hires are coached to be the best caregivers they can possibly be. A 4-hour orientation program also certifies candidates and is for caregivers hired "provisionally," and it is typical for 40% of new hires to wash out in this step. With candidates hired using Topgrading methods, the office experiences almost no failures at this step.

Step #12 Annual Measurement: Will be done.

TOPGRADING INNOVATION: ENTRY-LEVEL JOB SCORECARD

Caregiver Job Scorecard

Accountability	Metric	Standard	Rating (A, B, C)	Comments
Administrative/Reliability/Punctuality				
	Starts shift +/- 8 min. from schedule	100%		
	Uses call-in time clock	100%		
	Follows handbook policies	100%		
Communication				
	Communicates any emergency or changes in client immediately	100%		

Accountability	Metric	Standard	Rating (A, B, C)	Comments
	Returns messages within 60 min.	100%		
	Min. 4 hours' notice for call-offs	100%		
	Communicates schedule changes in advance	100%		
Customer Service				
	Service continuation	Cancellation of service other than for death, relocation, health change, financial, or end of assignment		
	Customer complaints	Receives no customer complaints		
Upholds Home Instead/North Shore Senior Care's values				
	Competency ratings	Average rating of 4, with no competencies rated "1"		
Availability				
	Able to work, sometimes on short notice	75% "yes" when request was during stated availability		
Training				
	Training completed on time	Initial training within 90 days. Ongoing training within 1 month.		

Competencies

Rating Scale: 5-Excellent; 4-Very Good; 3-Good; 2-Only Fair; 1-Poor

Medium: Easy to Improve; Dark: Very Difficult to Improve; Light: In-Between

	Definition	Rating	Comments
Compassion	Sympathetic to client needs Focuses on the client Truly cares about the client		

	Definition	Rating	Comments
Rapport and Relationship Building	Sets the client at ease Engages the client in conversation Acts like a guest in the client's home Can "win clients over"		
Likability	Warm and friendly Able to relate to their clients Makes the client feel as though the client is in change		
Professionalism	Physically presentable Does not involve client in personal affairs or get involved in the client's personal affairs Does not share personal information with the client that may burden or stress the client Does not share personal contact information with the client and does not have contact with the client outside work hours		
Adaptability/ Flexibility	Adjusts behavior to client behavior and mood Able to change shifts at last minute Allows client to live life the way the client wants to Responds quickly and effectively to emergency situations		
Communication	Proactive communicator Able to understand clients Consistent message to client, office, and family Asks questions when they don't understand or are unsure of a communication Consistent communication with the office		
Integrity	Trustworthy Refuses inappropriate gifts Does not try to "get away" with things Keeps promises to office personnel and clients		
Initiative	Performs necessary tasks without needing to be asked Finds things to do that helps the client Recognizes that they need to "earn their keep" Actively does things that help the client's situation		
Patience/Stress Management	Interacts positively with co-workers (in the office) Calm under pressure; does not show a temper with the client Able to separate work and personal life Asks for help when necessary in stressful situations		
Track Record (hiring)	Evidence that they can stay with a client No significant career gaps Good references/relationships with previous supervisors Minimal call-offs		

TOPGRADING INNOVATION: MODIFIED CAREGIVER TOPGRADING CAREER HISTORY FORM

The standard Topgrading Career History Form is used, but the following modifications show less emphasis on education (few caregivers have college education) and more questions about caregiver experience and work availability.

III. EDUCATION: (Please circle the highest grade completed)

Grade School: 6 7 8

High School: 9 10 11 12

College: 13 14 15 16 16+

Certifications or Accreditations _____

IV. CAREGIVING EXPERIENCE: (Write the number of years of experience you possess for each task or condition listed below)

_____ Personal Care Assistance (Male)

_____ Transferring Assistance

_____ Visual Impairment

_____ Personal Care Assistance (Female)

_____ Ambulation Assistance

_____ Hearing Impairment

_____ Incontinence

_____ Meal Preparation (light snacks)

_____ Diabetes

_____ Bathing Assistance

_____ Meal Preparation (full meals)

_____ Alzheimer's

_____ Dressing Assistance

_____ Dementia Parkinson's

_____ Showering Assistance

_____ Stroke

_____ Short-Term Memory Loss

_____ Medication Reminders

_____ Congestive Heart Failure

_____ Pulmonary (lung) Disease

V. AVAILABILITY: (Please indicate the *earliest* and *latest* times
that you are available to work)

Hours Available	Sunday	Monday	Tuesday	Wednesday	Thursday	Friday	Saturday
From:							
To:							

How many hours per week do you wish to work? _____

When are you available to begin work? _____

Please indicate the type(s) of work that you would be willing to work:

❏ Days   ❏ Evenings   ❏ Overnights   ❏ Live-In

Please indicate the areas in which you are able to work:

❏ North Wichita   ❏ South Wichita   ❏ East Wichita   ❏ West Wichita

❏ Valley Center   ❏ Bel Aire   ❏ Derby

❏ Haysville   ❏ Mulvane   ❏ Goddard

❏ Cheney   ❏ Mount Hope   ❏ Bentley

Please indicate the caregiver duties you are willing and able to perform:

❏ Companionship   ❏ Meal Preparation   ❏ Walking/Standing   ❏ Dressing
                                                Assistance   Assistance

❏ Bathing Assistance ❏ Laundry   ❏ Transportation   ❏ Errands

❏ Light Housekeeping ❏ Toileting/   ❏ Personal Care
                        Incontinence Care

Do you have any reservations about providing service to a client with pets?

❏ No   ❏ Yes   ❏ Cats   ❏ Dogs

Do you have any reservations about providing service to a client who smokes?

❏ No   ❏ Yes

VI. OTHER:

❏ No   ❏ Yes   Do you have the legal right to work for any employer in the United States?

❏ No   ❏ Yes   Would you be willing to arrange reference calls with supervisors you've had in the past decade, as a last step before a job offer?

❏ No   ❏ Yes   Have you had any moving traffic violations? If yes, please describe:

❏ No   ❏ Yes   Have you used any names or Social Security numbers other than those on this application?

❏ No   ❏ Yes   Have you ever been convicted of a felony and/or misdemeanor? If so, please describe below.

Incident

City/State

Charge

TOPGRADING INNOVATION: CAREGIVER TOPGRADING INTERVIEW GUIDE (PART OF IT IS SHOWN)

Applicant Name

Date

Interviewer

PART 1: JOB REQUIREMENTS AND INTEREST

How did you hear about us?

Why are you interested in HISC?

What type of hours/shifts are you looking for?

# Hours	Days	Evenings
Overnights	Live-In	Weekends

What parts of the job are you comfortable doing?

❑ Companionship	❑ Meal Preparation	❑ Laundry/Housekeeping
❑ Bathing Assistance	❑ Meal Prep	❑ Toileting/Incontinence Care
❑ Driving	❑ DL/Car	❑ DL/No Car
❑ Male	❑ Female	

❑ No	❑ Yes	Would you be able to pass a criminal background check?
❑ No	❑ Yes	Would you be able to pass a DMV (if applicable)?

(Part II is an abbreviated look at education.)
Part III is Work History:

> Spend no more than 15 minutes talking about the candidate's work history prior to the most recent 3 jobs, asking about:
> • Accomplishments
> • Mistakes
> • Boss's opinion of Strengths, Weaknesses, and Overall Performance

Work History Job # 1　　　　　　　　　　　　　　**Notes**

Start here with the third most recent job and come forward to the candidate's present job.

Record from Application/Career History Form: Company name, job title, and beginning and final levels of pay

1. Why did you take the job?

2. What did you do well there? What are you proud of?

3. What mistakes did you make, or, looking back, what would you do differently?

4. What's your best guess as to what this boss would say were your *Strengths? Weaker points? Overall performance rating?*

5. Why did you leave the job?

(Part IV is Plans and Goals for the Future.)

8. AN A PLAYER LAUNCHES A NEW NATION . . . AMERICA!

Thus, out of small beginnings greater things have been produced by His hand and as one small candle may light a thousand, so the light here kindled has shone to many, in some sort to our whole nation.

—William Bradford, 31 times elected Governor, Plymouth Colony

The final story is not really a case study but rather a historical event Americans (particularly) might appreciate; it's one of those "interesting Topgrading stories" to help readers avoid brain cramps. This account brings home, literally "home," as in our country, the importance of talent. Without some extraordinary A Players led by a governor who Topgraded in his own way, we probably would not be an English-speaking nation. (For many international Topgraders, please forgive this patriotic diversion!)

The story is almost 400 years old. America's first great leader, William Bradford, was, in his own way, a Topgrader.* Before telling his Topgrading story, let me intrigue you with a brief assessment of this man that you might not have heard of. William Bradford is one of a handful of leaders in history who was both pure of heart and very successful at changing the world. Gandhi and Lincoln were two others. It is an exclusive club. My interest in William Bradford stems from the fact that I'm named after my grandfather, 11 generations removed.

Here's his background: Within a year after the *Mayflower* landed at Cape Cod in 1620, William Bradford was elected governor of Plymouth Colony, the first leader elected on American soil, and he was reelected 30 more times. Under his leadership America was truly founded 150 years before the Revolutionary War. Bradford led his team of A Players (Winslow, Brewster, Standish, and others) as he

- **established what John Quincy Adams called the world's first true democracy.** The Greeks had slaves. Puritans flooded the New World after the Pilgrims showed families could survive, but the Puritans had a the-

---

* Bradford D. Smart, "America's First Great Leader: William Bradford, Governor of Plymouth Colony," *Mayflower Quarterly* 62, no. 1 (1996): 6–19.

ocracy. Bradford's creation of democracy led the way to our Revolution and the spread of democracy throughout the world. Bradford's annual "town meetings" are still held throughout New England and other parts of the United States. In those town meetings it was decided to approve property rights for women (so if their husbands died, they, and not their husbands' male relatives, got the property), and the Pilgrims used trial by jury.

- **abandoned socialism for free enterprise.** In 1621 the Pilgrims were near starvation. Their contract with European venture capitalists required a form of socialism in which all Pilgrims would send back almost all the money to Europe to pay off the debt. People weren't motivated. Bradford, in America's first privatization, let each family sell a portion of its goods on the open market after contributing their share to the common store. The GNP of Plymouth shot up, the Pilgrims stayed, and their prosperity attracted a flood of Brits to join the party, assuring an English-speaking New World.

- **began the first family Thanksgiving.** Bradford's free-enterprise effort was so successful, our holiday of Thanksgiving began in 1621. Because the natives had been good friends to the Pilgrims, Governor Bradford invited Chief Massasoit to enjoy the harvest celebration. The chief showed up with more than three dozen tribesmen, and they hung out, played games, and ate for three days.

- **assured separation of church and state.** Devout but no religious fanatic, Bradford insisted that rule by law, civil law, be separate from religious edict. So marriages in Plymouth were civil, not religious, services. Bradford advised the community in America's first town meetings not to elect religious leaders to political office, opining that religious leaders had enough power and adding political clout would make them too powerful.

One leader, William Bradford, led the Pilgrims to these foundations of our society 150 years before the signing of the Declaration of Independence. For fun, let's see how Bradford's Topgrading met some common Topgrading challenges:

- **Recruitment was difficult, because the job was "impossible."** Only 100 Pilgrims and hired hands volunteered and boarded the *Mayflower*. Quality, not quantity, permitted our nation to be founded. How's this for a selection test: risk your life fleeing a monarchy, face a horrible

Atlantic crossing and bitter winter, survive disease that will wipe out 50% of your team in the first year, face a mutiny by some hired hands, risk war with the natives . . . and in your spare time build a town, a government, an entire society. Any takers? Not many volunteered, but you can believe that those who stepped forward were strong in the essential competencies of Resourcefulness, Passion, Team Player, and many other A Player competencies. Bradford was the best and brightest—the A Player most respected to lead this miracle.

- **The Pilgrim team developed some C Players into A Players.** To have enough people to launch a colony, the Pilgrims recruited "hired hands," but the King only permitted the hired hands to be societal rejects, mostly criminals. On board the *Mayflower,* and upon arriving in the New World, the hired hands threatened mutiny. They were a mixed lot, including some A Players, but mostly B/C Players. The A Player Pilgrims were such a strong and capable team that they were sure their reason and pureness of spirit would win over the hired hands. They embraced the "strangers," as they called them, and coached them to join the team. Almost all accepted democracy in which they were made full voting citizens. Many apparent C Players grew into A Players and helped Plymouth become the first successful family colony in the New World.

- **Firing chronic C Players became necessary.** Some of the former lawbreakers were not coachable. Bradford was magistrate, and he banned repeated lawbreakers. Even this generous Christian removed C Players who threatened the viability of Plymouth Colony.

- **A change of organizational strategy required new talents.** Even as the Pilgrims attempted to sail to the New World, one final test separated the super resourceful from the merely resourceful. Here's what happened: There were plenty of reasons to abandon the voyage to the New World— lousy weather, merchant backers changing the terms and making the economic burden horrendous, a King trying to round up and jail a Pilgrim leader, and even after embarking, one of the two ships, the *Speedwell,* kept leaking. The *Speedwell* could not be fixed, and because the economic model the Pilgrims followed required trade, and the *Speedwell* was to be the only trading vessel (the *Mayflower* was just rented for the journey), a quick decision had to be made: Sail with only one of the two ships, abandoning the intended means of making a living (trade), or cancel the journey altogether. The less resourceful, the "loyal C Players," were nudged out. Every Wednesday before Thanksgiving since 1962 the *Wall Street Journal* reproduces William Bradford's account of what it was like to depart, with families weeping and expressing their love, knowing realistically that this journey into unknown lands, with stories of wild beasts and vicious natives, would mean many would not survive.

Bradford and other doers who chose to make the journey were betting they would be so resourceful they would figure out another means of making a living. Bradford and his team altered strategy, emphasizing farming and trapping. Changes in strategy work best with teams of A Players. Jim Collins, known for advocating "get the right people on the bus and then figure out strategy," might appreciate the Plymouth Colony version of his metaphor.

The Pilgims landed in the New World far north of their intended destination, and with snow on the ground, planting crops hardly looked like a viable foundation for an emerging economy. The fact that the Pilgrims were short on agricultural expertise was just another challenge. After natives ("Indians") had attacked them, the solution might surprise you: the Pilgrims made friends with the natives, who taught them how to grow corn, and were fast friends as long as Bradford and King Massasoit were leaders.

Okay, launching a new society is not exactly like running a business, but the principles are applicable. It is amazing that the Pilgrims succeeded as the first family colony in the New World for the A Players had to create a government (democracy), change the economic model (socialism to free enterprise; trade to agriculture), and survive a catastrophe (50% first year mortality).

SUCCESSFUL TOPGRADING ROLLOUT GUIDELINES

In the opening pages of this book you read Topgrading Lite, the steps to take to start Topgrading immediately. And a bit later I explained that the Topgrading Snapshot is enabling Human Resources or just about any manager to launch some powerful but basic Topgrading methods. As case studies of such approaches become documented, I'll insert them in www.TopgradingCaseStudies.com.

But in most of the case studies in this book you read how CEOs took the lead to Topgrade from the top down, and Topgrade the entire company. Successful Topgraders tend to do the same things, with variations. Distilling the Topgrading History and Best Advice messages within the case studies, the following steps are most common, and show a clear pattern:

1. Two senior managers, typically the CEO and head of Human Resources, attend a **Smart & Associates Topgrading Workshop.**

2. All senior managers **read** *Topgrading* (this new edition is recommended!) and/or *Topgrading 101* (the free e-book at www.Topgrading .com).

3. The top person driving Topgrading (usually the CEO) enlists the **support of senior A Players.** This "critical mass" of talent supporting Topgrading quells the inevitable resistance of C Players.

4. The **Topgrading Snapshot** is used immediately, even before an official rollout of Topgrading is announced. It is easy for everyone to understand and instantly saves time screening candidates while producing better candidates for interviews.

5. A **communications plan** for a Topgrading rollout is established, emphasizing the positive aspects of Topgrading—better hiring and promoting, and coaching, *not* firing underperformers.

6. **Senior managers participate in a two-day Topgrading Workshop,** which explains the Topgrading vision and rollout plans, and trains managers in how to conduct tandem Topgrading Interviews and other Topgrading methods. It includes a full day of coached practice, so that every manager leaves with a high degree of confidence: "I can improve my team with Topgrading."

7. **All remaining managers, and Human Resources professionals, participate in two-day Topgrading Workshops.** Companies with 500+ employees sometimes learn to conduct internal Topgrading Workshops, with the Train-the-Trainer program, using the Topgrading Toolkit with seven hours of DVDs which explain and demonstrate all 12 Topgrading Hiring Steps.

8. As soon as managers complete the Topgrading Workshop they are required to **use Topgrading methods to hire and promote people.**

9. **Topgrading cascades down,** throughout the organization, with the above steps repeated sequentially, until Topgrading is used for hiring at all, even entry, levels.

10. Topgrading methods are used before **every major promotion.**

11. All **12 of the Topgrading Hiring Steps are embraced,** driven by the CEO and Human Resources. Topgrading cannot be a "flavor of the month" program, but a profound cultural change that is tested daily and must be reinforced daily by top executives.

When to Use Topgrading Professionals

In almost all of the case studies, Topgrading professionals were used to conduct Topgrading Workshops (public workshops initially, and later internal workshops). Along with conduct of internal Topgrading Workshops is consultation with the CEO and HR regarding rollout implementation. Topgrading Professionals:

- help top management understand who are the As, A Potentials, and Non-As,
- help A Players remain A Players,
- help Bs and even Cs with A Potentials eventually qualify as A Players, and
- help B and C Players who will *not* become A Players realize the futility of their developmental efforts so that they either find a job internally where they qualify as an A Player, or leave.

In about one-third of the case studies Topgrading professionals are used to assess external replacement candidates for executive positions, to provide that "second opinion" when the stakes are so high, when mis-hires are extremely costly.

Chapter 6

THE ART OF TOPGRADING

*It is a paradoxical but profoundly true and important principle of
life that the most likely way to reach a goal is to be aiming not at
that goal itself but at some more ambitious goal beyond it.*

—Arnold Toynbee

What is your Topgrading goal—50% high performers on your team? Seventy-five percent? Or something like the 90% achieved by some Topgraders? Is Topgrading a key to achieving your bigger goal, a world-class organization?

For decades we have been innovating and fine-tuning Topgrading methods, and at a glance managers sometimes think that Topgrading is almost mechanical: follow the 12 Topgrading Hiring Steps and you'll get almost all high performers in the organization. However, after reading the case studies in chapter 5, and the advanced interviewing techniques in chapter 4, you know there is an art to Topgrading. So this chapter adds insights and advice, offering some additional Topgrading approaches and perspectives that might inspire you to set your Topgrading sights very high.

And because reading experts say busy A Players skim, skim, skim reading material, this chapter also serves as a summary of key Topgrading principles and methods already covered in this edition . . . and hopefully enables you to achieve your goals by not overlooking some of those key principles!

THE BEST WAY TO AUDIT CURRENT TALENT AND TO PROMOTE PEOPLE WHO SUCCEED IS . . . TOPGRADING!

In previous editions of this book, I said succinctly that to figure out what talent you have in the organization, use Topgrading methods, with the only difference being that there is no Job Scorecard (because you just want a broad view of the person's passions and talents), and the reference checks are not external but internal, with bosses/peers/subordinates. And I said that to improve success promoting people, use the Topgrading methods with a Job Scorecard for the promotion job, and with internal reference checks. I cryptically explained, "Hey, when you've learned Topgrading hiring methods, just use these minor tweaks and you'll both figure out what talent you have and your success promoting people will shoot up." And not many people paid attention. Of all the case studies, perhaps half the companies use Topgrading methods for promoting people, and very few use Topgrading Auditing methods to get a better understanding of who are the A/B/C Players now. Shame on me for writing the first two editions of this book without elaborating enough on the huge benefits of these methods!

So in this section, I fully explain these methods and why they are so important to use. At the risk of oversimplification: if you don't use Topgrading Promotion methods, most of the people you promote will disappoint you. And if you don't use Topgrading Auditing methods, chances are you will underutilize people, many of whom are square pegs in round holes.

To keep your interest and hopefully spark your commitment to using these methods, I tell a story of how these methods were perfected at General Electric and other companies. Note to small company managers: although I give the GE history, I promise I'll provide suggestions for how you can adapt the methods for your organization.

Almost all companies large and small are even more casual and superficial in their approaches to both auditing and promoting people than hiring people. Most companies figure out what people resources they have by relying mostly on the annual performance appraisal in which a busy boss checks a box indicating the performance rating and listing a few strengths and areas for improvement. And most companies decide whom to promote by looking at the same performance appraisals, specifically what box a boss checked indicating someone's promotability to . . . well, no job in particular. That's why the #1 Human Resources executives in Global 100 companies admit that 75% of the people they promote turn out to be disappointments, failures.

Topgrading Auditing provides outstanding insights into the strengths, weaker points, and potentials of internal people. What is the problem this solves? As companies look at their business strategy, naturally they must be sure they have the talent to achieve it, and sifting through performance appraisals provides shallow conclusions. For example, the Big Recession caused many companies to change strategy in the face of likely declining revenues. Strategic goals and ways to achieve them with fewer people resulted in many companies using talent audits to figure out if the same people who were A Players in growth markets are apt to be A Players when belt tightening is necessary. Put crudely, they didn't want to rely on superficial performance appraisals to figure out whom to keep . . . and not keep. Some Topgraders used the Topgrading Audit to get deep and accurate insights, making the keep/not keep decisions the right ones.

In the Topgrading Audit, there is no Job Scorecard, but an expansive look at what people's passions and capabilities are, and in relation to a lot of possible jobs in the company, where is there both a need and a good match—job(s) where they can function as an A Player. After the Topgrading Audit a couple of jobs (not necessarily promotions) look like a good fit, and the Topgrading interviewers study the Job Scorecards and see if they need to ask additional questions of the interviewee, or to ask additional questions of those who were internal references, to make a decision. Companies using Topgrading Auditing find that *most* of the people who go through the process (Topgrading Interview, co-worker interviews, e-mail 360 survey, coaching) show they have talents and interests that are a total surprise, and a good surprise, because it becomes clear in what jobs they'd be an A Player.

Topgrading Promoting methods are designed to solve the problem of high failure rates for those promoted. The processes are the same as with Topgrading Auditing, but from the start there is a Job Scorecard for the position to which someone might be promoted.

Are you getting lost in the "except for one thing" differences? Maybe this chart will help:

	Topgrading Method		
	Hiring	Promoting	Auditing
Job Scorecard	Yes	Yes	Initially no, maybe later
Tandem Topgrading Interview	Yes	Yes	Yes
Reference Checks	External	Internal	Internal
Coaching	Yes, new hire	Yes, whether promoted or not	Yes

History of Topgrading Promoting and Auditing

General Electric provided me the best and most visible opportunity to develop highly successful methods of promoting and auditing people. You've already read the results of the Topgrading Promoting methods—case study after case study in which success promoting people doubled, tripled, and even achieved 90%+ success. My work with GE began with improving methods to audit talent—to supplement boss ratings with a process that more accurately determined managers' present abilities and potentials. Next we used basically the same process to assess candidates for promotion to a specific job. And eventually Jack Welch decided to supplement promote-from-within with 25% of managerial jobs coming from outside hires—to "enrich the mix" of talent, to "bring in some new ideas." And that's when basically the same Topgrading methods used to audit and promote people were tweaked to hire people. Those hiring "tweaks" were not small. They included introducing the TORC Technique (obviously not needed when internal candidates know the interviewers will be talking with boss/peers/subordinates) and methods for external reference checking.

In short, General Electric was the testing ground for years that resulted in the Topgrading hiring methods you've studied but for the first few years all the focus was on assessing internal talent and doing a better job of promoting people.

CEOs of small companies, beware! Initially you know everyone pretty well, but by the time you have 20 employees I'll guarantee you, you do *not* know your people nearly as well as you should in order to put people in jobs where they can be A Players. I know this because after Topgrading Audits, CEOs marvel at how they did not know of some wonderful skills and passions some people have . . . how burned out some people are . . . how many "square pegs" there are in "round holes" . . . what significant developmental needs high-potential people have . . . and what huge talent deficits exist, given the CEO's ambitions. In small companies, there is rarely a good performance-management system, let alone a culture of coaching and developing people. Topgrading Audits, modified for the size of company, provide the full talent portrait of the company CEOs need to Topgrade effectively, to have the right organization, with the right Job Scorecards, to hire and promote the right people into those jobs.

Returning to the GE story . . . a Human Resources leader, Don Lester, showed up at one of my workshops and seemed to love the concepts, so when I asked him what was up, he said, "Jack Welch asked me to find the best assessment and coaching method in the world. I scoured the world and found nothing good enough for Jack, until I saw your book (1983 publication, out of print) in London, and I knew you had what Jack wanted. Would you like to meet him?" Hmm, let me think about that . . . hmmm, would I like to meet the most respected CEO on the planet? I guess so.

Jack Welch was the perfect client—I could disagree and he'd listen, and we almost always ended up agreeing. We never had a contract—I just sent invoices and he paid them. But the day I met Jack he was visibly ticked off. Or maybe he wasn't ticked off, just impatient and frustrated. "Too few of the people we promote turn out to be A Players," he lamented, "and we have the best people management and development programs in the world." Jack knew that GE wasn't unique; no company had seemed to crack the code on how to pick A Players.

GE was hardly alone, as indicated in the 75% failure rate in promotions top HR executives admit. Why does it happen? I've already mentioned overreliance on one boss's annual ratings. But it is also true that people get promoted to their level of incompetence. People who do a super job are given promotions because they "deserve the chance," and rarely are they assessed thoroughly for the higher-level job. Years ago a book called *The Peter Principle* documented how companies do this—promote people until they are incompetent in a job and then leave them in that job. We all know of a top sales rep who was promoted to sales manager and was a horrible manager.

Jack's solution initially was to have Human Resources professionals individually go to a different part of the company (where they would be independent of politics), conduct a competency interview with a manager, and then submit a report to the company (HR and Jack) and to the individual interviewed.

HR hated it! GE executives were not and are not exactly shy, so they argued and negotiated with the HR person who assessed them, naturally trying to have the report portray their abilities and potentials more favorably. And Jack hated it, because the competency-interview-based assessments were shallow and didn't predict well who would succeed or fail.

GE Audit/Promotion Innovation #1:
Replace Competency Interviews with the Topgrading Interview

So, the first thing I did was scrap the superficial competency interviews HR was doing—the ones that led to the assessment reports that the interviewed executives argued over, the ones that had no validity. The Topgrading

Interview was much more thorough and credible to the assessed executives, and having covered every success, failure, decision, and relationship in the executive's career, the reports were more accurate. And developmental suggestions were taken more seriously.

However, the managers still argued and fought with the HR manager over content. "How the heck can you tell me I confuse my team with changes in direction, when you haven't even talked with them?" But at GE there was no accepted method of finding out from subordinates what the boss was like; there were no surveys and no interviews with subordinates. I changed that.

GE Audit/Promotion Innovation #2:
Conduct Interviews with Boss(es), Peers, and Subordinates

For years as a Topgrading professional, when I was asked to assess candidates for promotion or do an audit to find out what a manager was best suited for, I'd follow the Topgrading Interview with interviews with bosses, subordinates, and peers. But everyone at GE said, "Forget it, Brad, it's counterculture at GE to ask anyone to rat on their boss, and Jack and Larry (Bossidy, Vice Chairman and future CEO of Honeywell) would never agree." Being somewhat naive I said, "I've been using co-worker interviews for years, and that process improves accuracy, validity, and credibility with the manager assessed; this process will improve GE's promotion success, and because the shareholders will benefit, I'm sure Jack and Larry will approve."

So I changed the program—without asking Jack or Larry. I started by personally doing an audit on one of GE's most prominent executives; we'll call him Pete. Pete balked when I asked him to arrange my interviews with his current and former bosses, peers, and all of his direct reports, but I said this: "Pete, I've interviewed thousands of executives, and I am certain you have some areas for improvement that you don't recognize. For example, I'm sure you confuse the hell out of your team when you change direction without communicating nearly enough with them, but here's the problem: you think I'm full of crap (I used to talk that way), so you won't change, your performance will suffer, and GE's stock price will be a bit lower than it could be. But let me talk to your team and, maintaining confidentiality, we'll find out the truth. And let's just do it without getting Corporate approval—I promise you that you will be more successful if we do this because you'll find out the truth and I'm sure you'll work to improve."

So we did it; it worked. Twelve of 15 direct reports said Pete confused them with his sudden changes and incomplete communications, so he immediately made changes in his communications. His team became more productive.

Jack and Larry were amazed because I hadn't requested permission, and more importantly, my report was a lot more accurate and useful than the reports they had seen, the ones based on (shallow, superficial) competency interviews. The report was more useful to Jack and Larry, because they could make better decisions regarding how best to use Pete in the future, and the report was far more useful to Pete because all of his areas for improvement were credible to him because instead of just Brad or just his boss suggesting he improve something, 20 people he worked with closely weighed in.

So GE's culture was instantly changed—I did get permission to change the program for HR people to assess candidates for both audit (no specific job in consideration) and promotion (to a specific job). GE went on to institute annual e-mail 360 surveys in which every manager would get feedback on dozens of competencies, with confidential ratings and comments by subordinates, peers, and bosses. And Jack instituted "skip level meetings," in which executives would go to a location and have frank and open meetings in which subordinates of a manager would talk about that manager, who wasn't in the meeting.

I encourage every leader to use e-mail 360 surveys and/or skip level meetings to gain insight into every manager's strengths and weaker points as perceived by three groups: their subordinates, their peers, and higher-level people. Later in this chapter I'll offer some guidelines.

The HR professionals were thrilled. Instead of a war with the executive they assessed, HR was viewed as a partner. Instead of HR saying, "You confuse people," and the executive saying, "Bull—you don't know that," the executives they assessed were convinced that the weaker point was for real, and they were appreciative of learning how to improve their effectiveness.

Jack decided to use the HR professionals, not just to audit managerial talent, but to offer their opinions on whether a manager should be promoted to a specific job. Their results were good, but (this sounds awful) not as good as mine. Jack was visibly frustrated . . . again. "We don't have enough Brad Smarts around here, so how can our HR managers do better?"

GE Audit/Promoting Innovation #3: Use a Tandem Partner in the Topgrading Interview, Including a Trained A Player Manager Plus HR

You've already read this part of the history. I said, "Jack, we use two interviewers in the Topgrading Workshops, and they do a lot better than one interviewer—shall we try it?" Jack said yes instantly, and after several years of fine-tuning the Topgrading Promoting processes at GE, the company improved dramatically.

And GE HR professionals were thrilled:

- Their success predicting who would be an A Player if promoted shot up.
- The tandem approach was much easier than a solo interview (probing tough GE executives is easier two-on-one).
- The operating executive who was the tandem partner with HR offered insights the HR person couldn't.
- With two people writing the report, the reports were better than solo reports.
- When sitting down with the manager for feedback and coaching, the tandem pair was more credible and influential than either could have been individually.

Frankly, in recent years not much has changed in our recommended methods to audit talent and assess candidates for promotion. The only tweaks we've learned are how entrepreneurs and managers in small business can do it and how the processes can be made simpler for even the lowest levels in an organization. The case studies explain those innovations.

SUMMARY OF TOPGRADING METHODS TO AUDIT AND PROMOTE PEOPLE

1. **Train operating managers and HR managers in the tandem Topgrading hiring methods.** (Small company CEO—get training through a workshop, the Topgrading Toolkit, or if nothing else, mastering this book.) External hiring methods and internal audit and promotion methods are almost identical. The main difference is that external reference calls are made for hiring, and internal confidential interviews with boss/peers/subordinates are used for audit/pro-motion.
2. **Choose the tandem Topgrading interviewers** from different parts of the company (so they are not politically involved). (Small company CEO—pick an A Player who will read this book and study the Topgrading Interview Guide.) For most companies a tandem pair of operating manager and HR manager is used, and after a couple of years the HR managers become so experienced and good at the Topgrading Interview that they "carry" the less experienced operating managers as interviewers.

3. **Ask the interviewee to complete the Topgrading Career History Form**, which produces the Topgrading Snapshot, and use the Topgrading Interview Guide with all the Career History Form information inserted. (Small company CEO—do the same.) The "picture" of the person's career, and the Interview Guide with all the information about the career inserted right along with the questions to be asked, makes interviewing relatively easy.

4. **After the tandem Topgrading Interview, tandem interviewers talk for an hour each with boss(es), peers, and direct reports of the person.** (Small company CEO—do the same.) The format is simple. Say your comments are anonymous and confidential and basically there are three questions:

   What are (manager's) strengths?

   What are (manager's) weaker points?

   What is your best developmental advice for (manager) in terms of things to do more of, less of, or learn?

   Just take notes, follow up with questions, and use all of those advanced interviewing techniques learned in chapter 4.

5. **Supplement #3 with an e-mail 360-degree survey.** (Small company CEO—do the same.) The co-worker interviews are good for generating spontaneous insights, opinions, and advice, but if you ask for ratings on competencies those interviews will become sluggish. So use any of the online surveys (Google "online employee survey tools") and e-mail the survey to two groups: direct reports and "other."

   The initial average ratings will serve as baselines, so that when you provide feedback and coaching, specific numeric targets are set. And follow up e-mail surveys will document progress. For example, if the manager gets a low initial average rating of only 4 (Only Fair) in Listening, the manager should set a minimum goal of 7 and the Individual Development Plan should include ways to improve.

6. **Write an Executive Summary**, and the same report goes to Human Resources, the company, and the manager. (Small company CEO—do a brief version, which you'll discuss with the person.) It should include a summary of the person's background, potentials, strengths, weaker points, and developmental recommendations. (See Appendix G, page 323, for a sample.)

7. **Coach the manager.** (Small company CEO—you can do this!) Both tandem interviewers meet with the manager and share all the information you have, including the e-mail survey results, (confidential)

opinions of co-workers interviewed, and of course the opinions of the interviewers. Give the sample Individual Development Plan (IDP, Appendix G, page 323) to the manager, ask the manager to write one, approve it, and at a minimum one of the two interviewers meet quarterly with the manager to track progress and tweak the IDP.

That's it! Two sharp managers trained in Topgrading methods can do a terrific job auditing internal talent, assessing candidates for promotion, and then coaching managers.

Whenever You Enter a New Job, Use the Topgrading Audit Approach. (Small company CEO—do this if you become CEO of another company and require your managers to do it soon after they move into a different job.) Why wait to "learn from experience" who are your As, Bs, and Cs? Find out in the first month who are the As you can embrace and keep, and find out who are the chronic underperformers you'll probably replace.

Whenever you have a new job, conduct Topgrading Audits in order to figure out your talent challenges in the first few months.

All managers: At a minimum, do a solo Topgrading Interview without the e-mail survey or co-worker interviews. This "lite" version is better— much better—than slowly working with people and taking a year to find out who are your As, Bs, and Cs. Just announce: "In order to get to know you, I'd like to sit down with each of you in the next few weeks and take you through a chronological interview covering your education years and all your jobs—what you did, how you did, how you like the job, what your bosses thought of you, and why you left. And I want to know your career goals and what advice you have for me for how I can best lead the team." A Players will love having their "audience with the Pope."

OBSTACLES TO TOPGRADING AND HOW TOPGRADERS OVERCOME THEM

Many managers are committed to the idea of employing only highly talented people, but find Topgrading challenging. In preparing case studies for this book, and frankly in daily communications with Topgraders for decades, I have asked thousands of senior managers to describe the challenges they faced and their best advice for how to meet them. At www.TopgradingCaseStudies.com every case study ends with "best advice" to would-be Topgraders from the top executives.

Every other month we conduct a Chat with a Topgrader (CEO or head of HR) conference call for those who subscribe to Topgrading Tips newsletter. People e-mail their questions to me, mostly about how to overcome obstacles to Topgrading but also what lessons they've learned. And during the Chat with a Topgrader call, while the CEO or head of HR is telling the story, people e-mail questions, which I ask the Topgrader.

Following are what we've learned to be the major obstacles to Topgrading, along with solutions. I think you'll find this a useful summary of main principles of Topgrading.

1. **"My B/C Players aren't as good as my A Players at hiring A Players."**

   Solution: Implement Topgrading, but don't let the B/C Players make hiring or promoting decisions without your approval.

   Let B and C Players know that they have to become A Players to independently Topgrade. Weaker managers can hire some As, but rarely all As, because A Players don't want to report to a low performer who will stifle their ideas and take credit for their accomplishments. However, with direction from above, B/C Players *will* use Topgrading methods diligently, because they realize that Topgrading is one of the few actions they can take to eventually qualify as an A Player . . . and keep their job.

2. **"We think we're hiring high performers, but most turn out to be mis-hires."**

   Solution: Use Topgrading methods.

   When managers e-mail me such statements, I know they have not used Topgrading methods. As mentioned in this book, it's smart for those with a 25% success rate replacing low performers to . . . "live with" B Players. It isn't worth the costs and hassles to remove a B Player with only a 25% chance the replacement will be an A, and the average cost of a mis-hire is six times base salary. At that rate, the typical hiring manager of $100,000 managers would mis-hire three people, and waste $1.8 million, to hire one A Player. With 90% As hired using tandem Topgrading Interviews, however, A Player managers are smart to replace Cs and Bs, smoothly and quickly building a team of all As.

3. **"Our Human Resources people are understaffed, so they just don't get enough candidates for us to hire only high performers."**

    Solution: Recruit your own A Players from your Networks.

    Don't blame HR if you can't find talent. I've interviewed hundreds of managers who were fired for failing to achieve their numbers, when their excuse was, "I wanted to Topgrade, but HR didn't find me A Player candidates." Curt Clawson could not have pulled Hayes Lemmerz out of Chapter 11 if he hadn't filled most of the top jobs with A Players recruited from his Networks. Jason Chandler, Regional Director at UBS, turboboosted his career by personally recruiting top financial planners on a daily, that's right, *daily*, basis.

4. **"Search firms just don't produce enough high-performer candidates."**

    Solution: Require search firms to use Topgrading methods and never accept a report that fails to state, for every job, mistakes, failures, and candidate guesses as to how bosses would appraise their strengths, weaker points, and overall performance. And even though search executives will do reference checks with former bosses if you require them to, you should perform tandem Topgrading Interviews and personally conduct duplicate reference checks yourself.

    Does this sound like overkill? Get this: Topgrading professionals frequently conduct the third—yes, third!—Topgrading Interview. The search firm does the first (solo), the executive team does the second, and because the costs of a mis-hire are so high, they ask the Topgrading professional for a third Topgrading Interview. And after we submit our report, if the client wants to move ahead, they conduct reference calls with former bosses that the search executive has already talked with. THAT is how you avoid multi-million-dollar hiring mistakes! Do A Player candidates consider three Topgrading Interviews excessive? No, they love the "walk down memory lane," reflecting on how successful they've been.

5. **"I want to raise the talent bar, but the A Players I recruit are undermined by people in the company."**

    Solution: Provide new A Players with air cover, protection from undermining by existing personnel.

    This is a common problem. A talent-oriented manager realizes her company, unit, or department is far from world class and rolls out Topgrading. The low-performance culture is often characterized by lack of accountability, fear of change, minimal innovation, and lots of excuse making. It reinforces itself with an incestuous promote-from-within policy. B/C Players chew up and spit out A Players, who say, "Gee, too bad, just didn't fit in here."

It is critical to seek out and employ A Players who will help drive the culture-change process with finesse, not a sledgehammer. Those A Players must have the competencies, skills, and attitudes to simultaneously earn the respect of the present culture while creating the new, *desired* culture. That's a tall order; A Players can be rejected by the old culture unless you provide them protection. Make it clear to the others that these new hires have your full support, monitor that support, reward active supporters, and quickly correct those who plant land mines to destroy the "outsiders."

6. **"We can't afford to hire A Players."**

Solution: Yes you can—you already pay for *all* A Players.

This was a trick question; did you get the correct answer? If not, please reread chapter 1. A Players are available at *all* compensation levels: They are people above the 90th percentile of overall talent of all potential candidates at every compensation level. You already are paying for A Players, whether or not you get them. That means that a company that is paying its C Player marketing director a $90,000 base salary could hire an A Player for the same salary. The definition of A Player is closed, airtight; you cannot *not* pay for an A Player. Is this a semantic game? No!

Perhaps you mean you can't afford to hire an A Player *at a higher salary level*. Aha! That's different. You need a higher-talent A Player at $150K to beat the competition, and A Players at $90K probably won't cut it. In other words, you think you can afford to hire only a B Player for an A league, but realize that you need an A Player to compete in an A league. Figure out a way to afford it, or expect to suffer— 100-hour workweeks yourself, burnout in the person you under-hire, or failure by the person you hire. At best you'll hire a B with A potentials, perhaps someone short on experience but highly resourceful and on a rapid learning path . . . and your long hours carrying and developing that manager will eventually pay off.

Given our definition of A Player, can you afford to not hire A Players? Perhaps, if your competition will guarantee they will *not* Topgrade. Don't count on that.

If you still think it might be too costly to Topgrade, please use the Topgrading Talent Projection Calculator (page 67). Compare the costs of retaining underperformers vs. Topgrading. A Players all conclude, "We can't afford *not* to Topgrade."

7. **"I don't want to fire loyal Cs and Bs."**

Solution: Redeploy chronic B/C Players. Do a Topgrading Audit and hopefully identify a job they want where they can be an A player. If, however, they underperform in any job and coaching and training don't help, and they know they can't remain a chronic underperformer but don't quit—in such a rare instance, fire them.

Painful as it is to fire someone, failing to do so is almost always more painful—to the company, your career, and the underperformer. In every economic downturn thousands of companies go out of business faster because executives don't want to remove the low performers. In a real sense, then, if you don't fire C Players, they end up firing everyone, including you.

It is immoral *not* to remove B/C Players and imperil the jobs of everyone else.

Theoretically, everyone can be an A Player. The best organizations ask the question, "In what sort of role (and for what level of pay) can this person be an A Player?" Such organizations creatively align individuals' responsibilities to be consistent with their strengths, weaknesses, and interests.

Companies go out of business for many reasons, but deficient talent is almost always a key factor. CEOs tell me all the time that their biggest failure is not moving fast enough to remove long-term underperforming managers. Just as A Players provide an uplifting force to an organization, B/C Players can sink the ship. The best way to avoid firing loyal, beloved B/C Players is to not hire or promote them over their head.

I know a man who owns his company, and his kids (grown, with their own kids) actually run it and want to Topgrade because some C Players are in key jobs and stifle company growth; those C Players burden the few A Players, who instead of maximizing their strengths, spend a lot of time preventing the Cs from causing problems and sweeping up after them when they do cause problems. The man says he can't fire the long-term loyal employees, and of course I say that's okay *if* you move them aside with a nice title but narrowed responsibilities so that they no longer hurt the company.

Move loyal, long-term, underperforming employees aside with narrowed responsibilities.

---

8. "We have big problems but have engaged a major strategy company, so we hope their solutions will make it less necessary to Topgrade."

Solution: Topgrade first.

In *Good to Great*, author Jim Collins noted that all 14 newly appointed CEOs of companies they took from good to great *first* assembled their A teams, *then* launched new strategic initiatives. Great management initiatives combined with a cast of A Players can reasonably be expected to increase a company's performance. However, expensive consulting engagements typically fall flat when the company managers lack the talent to drive successful implementation. In chess, great strategy will not prevail if one player has all pawns while the opponent enjoys a board full of royalty. Talent is a necessary ingredient to making management initiatives convert to shareholder value. Indeed, talent is the grand enabler of all management initiatives. I cringe every time I hear about an undertalented company trying to implement Six Sigma or some other initiative and push decision-making responsibility down in the organization to 75% low performers. Underskilled or undertalented employees are given decision-making authority and end up making bad decisions. Performance inevitably suffers.

In contrast, organizations that Topgrade are able to drive improvements in strategy, productivity, innovation, quality, customer service, and speed to market. They experience greater success in these areas because they have the most competent employees on whom to rely. Having consistently strong operational performance can be a powerful force in building shareholder value. Of course, other factors such as macroeconomic trends, currency fluctuations, industry changes, and customer preferences can all affect share-holder value as well.

At the end of the day, you bet on people, not on strategies.

—Larry Bossidy

I am not saying talent is the only driver of shareholder value, but that it is a key one—and one of the few that managers can directly control. Ratcheting up the talent level of a company is a lot easier than trying to affect the strength of the U.S. dollar.

The idea behind Topgrading is so simple, I am continually shocked that so few companies do it. Far too often, managers at all levels make the costly mistake of trying to "manage their way" to excellence with underperformers on their team. That is truly a losing strategy.

9. **"My subordinates vote thumbs down when I try to hire an A Player."**

   Solution: Don't let them vote. Make the hiring decision yourself.

   Having your subordinates interview a prospective peer of theirs is desirable, almost necessary. A Player candidates might insist on it. But don't forget obstacle #1 ("I can't get my B/C Players to hire A Players"), because a corollary is "A Player peers might not want the competition of other A Players." So, get the peers' opinions, but don't give them a vote.

   Your job is not to preserve the status quo. Get the A Players in, help Bs to rise to the occasion, and remove the untrainable B/C Players who drain the energy from your group. If your A Players don't want competition, that's too bad, but you are paid to make the tough calls. Maybe if you changed the compensation system so all are paid bonuses on team performance, A Player peers will be more welcome. Always make it clear that hiring A Players for your team is not a de-mocracy—it's your responsibility and you will meet it.

10. **"We are downsizing and my job is on the line, so I don't have time to Topgrade."**

    Solution: Improve short-term results *by* Topgrading.

    For years I have noticed a dangerous "death spiral" that can occur when organizations become leaner. Survivors of massive downsiz-ings have more work to do; stress levels increase; the more marketable people, the A Players, quit. Managers may not feel that there is time to find A Players. A futile mistake is to try to squeeze A Player results out of the remaining B and C Players. Stress increases even more and drives the best of the remaining talent to quit, causing the "death spiral" to continue. "Death spiral" may be more than a metaphor; more people seem to have heart attacks and strokes in high-pressure companies, and I wonder if Topgrading might have alleviated some pressure and health problems.

11. **"I know I should redeploy a B/C Player, and I have confidence that by using tandem Topgrading Interviews an A Player will be a replacement, but I just can't pull the trigger."**

    Solution: Recruit the A Player replacement *now* and *then* you'll find it a lot easier to remove the B/C.

    It's amazing how easy it becomes to make a change when an eager, sharp A Player is ready and willing to take the job. It's "the devil I know is better than the devil I don't know" syndrome that causes managers to limp along with marginal talent. So . . . get to know an A Player replacement and you'll no longer tolerate the B/C devil.

    If you have As in your Networks, it's easy to talk informally, then talk some more, eventually do a tandem Topgrading Interview, and *know* the replacement will be much better in the job. If the alternative is to sign a contract for a search fee, it's understandable that you might want to give the B/C "six months more" to move into the A category. It's understandable, but usually regrettable, to delay the inevitable.

12. **"Even my A Players aren't calibrated; they don't accurately judge who are the As, Bs, and Cs."**

    Solution: Get them calibrated by conducting talent reviews once or twice per year and have them read this book.

    Inbred organizations or those in remote locations can have A Players who are simply out of touch with the talent marketplace. They don't know how much talent might be available, for how much money, because they haven't experienced much turnover and when they do, they recruit within the community, or stay narrowly within their industry.

    In some companies with multiple locations the CEO and corporate HR people travel to conduct talent meetings. They become calibrated, and help those in the field become calibrated.

13. "The board of directors is more inquisitive about talent, following scandals in recent years, and I fear they will restrict my Topgrading efforts."

Solution: CEO, Topgrade and keep the board fully apprised.

Boards of directors increasingly *require* Topgrading. Directors are increasingly held accountable for misdeeds of CEOs, CFOs, and other executives, as they should be. The CEO should welcome board pressure to Topgrade, do it, and communicate both processes and conclusions. When boards understand the thoroughness of Topgrading processes and the accuracy of assessments, they have more, not less, confidence in the CEO and his team.

14. "I understand that Topgrading can improve talent, and I know I have some B and C Players, but for all that work, I don't think Topgrading would really make a difference in my career."

Solution: Think again.

There is no clearer truth to a Topgrading professional than this:

The single most powerful lever for career success in management is Topgrading.

. . . and its corollary:

There is no more certain career impediment in management than failing to Topgrade.

Successful careers all have a common pattern: creating more talented teams accounts for better results, earning managers more promotions. Thousands of Topgraders know this to be true: the single most important management skill is not coaching, building teams, getting organized, or leading change; it's Topgrading, because with a team of A Players, all managerial best practices are more successful. This is a corollary of, "Everything goes better with Coke." Sometimes the managers I spoke to admitted they were lucky—they inherited an A team because a boss assigned them the "best and brightest," or they went to work for a Topgrading company that taught them how to do it. Most were motivated and resourceful, figuring out how to develop or replace Non-As.

The vast majority of managers I have interviewed experienced stutter steps in their career, failures to Topgrade and resulting failures to perform that led to career stagnation for a while or, in some cases, getting fired. Ralph's (not his real name) story is typical. As Vice President of Sales and Marketing, he inherited a mix of two A/A Potentials, four Bs, and two Cs, as well as stretch goals for the year. The company had trained all managers in Topgrading. The president of the company and I implored Ralph to Topgrade, but all he did that year was develop one C into, maybe, a B-minus. A couple of underperformers convinced him they had "irreplaceable" relationships with customers. Ralph complained that Human Resources wasn't recruiting A Player replacements. This happened to be true, but he should have done his own recruitment. His feedback to his team was soft and ineffectual. When he failed to generate the sales results he committed to, he was fired.

**Never blame HR for not recruiting A Players for you.
Be your own recruiter by using your Networks.**

I talked to Ralph after he was fired, and he was mad—at himself. "I was a C Player because I didn't Topgrade," he admitted. Ralph got a VP Sales and Marketing job at another company, Topgraded at warp speed, and was promoted to President. He blossomed from a non-Topgrading C Player into a Topgrading A Player, and his career became much more successful. Instead of blaming HR for not recruiting A Player candidates, Ralph and his team all took the stance that all managers are their own recruiters, and have to develop their Networks to be sure they have a "bench" when they need replacements.

HOW C PLAYERS FIRE THEMSELVES

Puleeeze, do not think of Topgrading as something you "do" to C Players; do not think of Topgrading as a method of firing people. Think of Topgrading as methods to hire, promote, audit, and coach people, and if you have chronic underperformers, it's up to you to create a performance-management system that deals with them. If you want to keep underperformers and roll out Topgrading just to improve hiring and promoting, your company will certainly improve and you don't risk scaring people who otherwise will think of Topgrading as firing Cs.

However, if Topgrading means packing teams, even the entire company, with A Players, then it usually involves the departure of chronic C and B Players. In Topgrading companies, only rarely are people fired because so many people hired and promoted turn out to be A Players. That said, initially most Topgrading managers help underperformers fire themselves by doing the following:

- Having a Job Scorecard so that the C Player knows selling 75 widgets (or whatever) is a condition of employment.
- Having regular coaching and performance review sessions, to reinforce the necessity of selling 75 widgets and provide the training and other resources so that the C Player believes the manager is very fair.
- Nudging the C Player who is not improving to take time off to explore other job opportunities (including within the company). Any C Player knows it's a lot easier to get a job when they have a job.
- Having a nice going-away lunch when C departs.

Is it being nice to people to tolerate their underperformance? As Debra Dunn, former Vice President of Strategy and Corporate Operations at Hewlett-Packard, said: "I feel there is no greater disrespect you can do to a person than to let them hang out in a job where they are not respected by their peers, not viewed as successful, and probably losing their self-esteem. To do that under the guise of respect for people is, to me, ridiculous." Or, to give people higher performance ratings than they deserve and *not* give them honest feedback about their weaker points can leave them in the dark. That dishonesty can continue for years, particularly if a company is doing well. Then a company falters, the performance-management system is tightened to weed out C Players, and fired people are understandably indignant: "Why didn't you level with me 10 years ago? I could have been working to overcome the shortcomings you now say are so serious you're firing me. Thanks a lot!"

It is immoral treatment of B/C Players to leave them in the dark regarding their weaknesses and leave them in the job in which they fail.

The War for Talent (Harvard Business School Press) provides some shocking statistics:

- Only 19% of managers surveyed believe their company removes low performers quickly and effectively.
- Only 16% say their company knows who the high and low performers are in the senior ranks.

Hanging on to chronic underperformers hurts the company, division, managers of the B/C, and the B/C Players themselves. And surely a nation of Topgraded companies is apt to be more productive than a nation of companies with 75% Non-As.

BRAD'S STRANGE INTERVIEWS: ATTEMPTED MURDER, OF SWEET LITTLE OL' BRAD?

Speaking of firing people, my last strange interview story is about when a chap threatened to fire me . . . fire real bullets at me!

I was using the chairman's (Joe's) office, interviewing a candidate for an executive position. Halfway into the Topgrading Interview my interviewee admitted that he had "disagreements" with Las Vegas mobsters, and he was looking for another job to "disappear." I wondered if my Topgrading Interview might be interrupted by mobsters who might have a beef with this guy. Let's call him Mr. Run from the Mob.

Just as Mr. Run from the Mob admitted the Mob was after him, I heard screams from the outer office; the door banged open, and there stood a Clint Eastwood look-alike with not one but two pearl-handled .357 Magnums. Let's call him Mr. Twin Guns. "Good grief," I thought. "Tony Soprano is here to take this guy out, and as a witness, maybe I'll be shot too!" I know—it doesn't make sense. At least in the movies the mobsters don't burst into offices with dozens of witnesses.

Mr. Twin Guns glowered at me and barked, "Are you Joe? I'm gonna kill ya!" Both of his hands clutched the guns that were fortunately still holstered. "No," I burbled. "Joe's out of town!" Then he barked, "Are you sure you're not Joe?" As scared as I was, I almost laughed at his stupidity, which would have proven I was even more stupid. Then, like a flash, Mr. Run from the Mob jumped up, pulled some karate moves, and my would-be assailant was on the floor. *Phew!*

Mr. Twin Guns was arrested, of course, but the company did not press charges, fearing that Mr. Twin Guns would then be certain he was the victim and maybe come after the chairman again. Mr. Twin Guns had just been fired for repeatedly getting into fights in the warehouse. Chairman Joe had never met the guy and wouldn't have recognized him, but Mr. Twin Guns was somehow convinced that Joe was out to get him. Why press charges and prove Joe *was* out to get him? He was fired, and the company decided to leave it at that.

Mr. Run from the Mob was my hero for the day, but he was not offered a job. His Mob connections were very suspect, and the last thing the company needed was for a fired hothead paranoid worker to seek revenge and get into another fight with Mr. Run from the Mob.

Joe sold his company a few years later. Last I heard, Mr. Twin Guns still lives in the same town and he's still a hothead, constantly getting into fights. I have no idea what has happened with Mr. Run from the Mob.

Is there a Topgrading lesson in this? Actually, yes. The company had strict rules against fighting and Mr. Twin Guns got into fights monthly with no consequences. Although underperformers fire themselves for failing to meet accountability, strict firing rules (for fighting, unethical behavior, etc.) have to be followed rigorously.

The Magic Potion That Makes Coaching "Work" Is a Simple, Inexpensive E-mail 360-Degree Survey

Throughout this book I've said how valuable and inexpensive e-mail 360 surveys can be. Many companies administer them annually to see how managers are viewed by others (subordinates, peers, and others), and to help coach people to improve. The surveys are part of Topgrading Auditing and Topgrading Promoting, to supplement oral interviews with a few bosses/peers/subordinates; it's an inexpensive way to get useful insights from dozens of people and help reveal who are the As, A Potentials, and Non-As. And the surveys provide ratings that serve as baselines when improvement is called for. But how, exactly, do surveys function as a "magic potion" to motivate change?

In several client companies managers are expected to achieve a minimum 7 rating on a 10-point scale on the interpersonal aspects of leadership, or they could lose their job. That might seem harsh, but a company's organizational culture is clearly shown in the aggregate ratings on the surveys. CEOs naturally want their organizational culture to attract and hold A Players, and to stimulate maximum performance. A positive, exciting organizational culture is impossible if a lot of managers are given low ratings in how they treat people, coach, communicate, keep confidences, listen, work with others, show passion, etc.

Suppose the survey shows that Pat, your subordinate, publicly berates her people, and that lack of respect is causing A Players to quit. You can coach her to improve, and use the e-mail 360 survey of her people as the scorecard. In your coaching session say, "Pat, I won't recommend you for promotion until you earn ratings of at least a 7 on a 10-point scale on Listening, Team Player, and Treats People with Respect," and Pat will likely improve, if she is A Potential.

The survey, which can be repeated again and again inexpensively (Google "buy e-mail survey") is a "magic potion" because Pat will think of the survey as a camera that videotapes her every action all day, every day on the job. She knows that if after six months the "tape" shows her cutting off people and berating them publicly—just once or twice—people will talk about it and her ratings will fall short of a 7 rating, so she will not get a promotion.

Indeed, when we coach people who must improve in order to be successful, we elaborate on the camera scenario: "Pat, every day think that a camera is on you—look up in the corner of the room and imagine it's taping you now and every second you're on the job. Do you have that image? Okay, now let's take your weaker points—sarcastically putting someone down, interrupting them, and cutting them off so they can rarely make their point. Let's call all of these one thing—blasting people. It scares the hell out of your people, and as you now know from reading the Written Comments in the survey, your people retreat to their office, lick their wounds, and are much less productive for days and days. And when you interrupt and show sarcasm, they are more inclined to blame others, which hurts teamwork. In your IDP you have agreed that you will achieve an 8+ on Treating People with Respect, and here's how to motivate yourself to stay on your good behavior: Think that the camera is on you, Pat, every moment of every day. Blast someone publicly or maybe even privately, and do so with sarcasm, and everyone in the department will hear about it, and in the very next e-mail 360-degree survey you'll be rated low in Treating People with Respect. You can be on your best behavior 99% of the time and one dramatic episode will be talked about and remembered and your survey results will suffer. By the way, not only will your Treating People with Respect be rated low, but you can bet that just because of one time you ripped someone's head off verbally, many other survey items such as Team Player, Inspiring Followership, Fair Minded, A Good Coach, A Good Listener, and Clear in Direction will be rated lower."

Be careful, because e-mail 360 surveys can be abused. If, for example, Pat inherited a team of C Players, she might get low ratings when doing what she has to do—hold them accountable for performance. Perhaps her average rating on Treating People with Respect is only a 5. But her C Players consider her realistic expectations to be unrealistic, and when she confronts their nonperformance they'd like her to be more warm and fuzzy. Maybe she should be, but we at Smart & Associates have seen thousands of surveys of very popular C Players; they receive high ratings in leadership because they are warm and fuzzy but don't hold their team accountable. So, the tweak to the minimum 7 rating standard is "Managers must achieve that level (higher for integrity and Topgrading) *when rated by A Players.*"

So, the tweak to the minimum 7 rating standard is "Managers must achieve that level (higher for integrity and Topgrading) when rated by A Players."

Another common problem with the surveys is they are too darned long. What would you do if you were required to fill out 15 surveys, each 100 items long? Yeah, me too—I'd do them Saturday morning (before the kids are up), zooming through them at warp speed, hardly reading the items and not writing any comments.

At Smart & Associates, we favor 20-item surveys, with requests for explanations after every item. And we use software that produces the full ratings distribution, so that you can see how many rated the person 1, 2, 3, etc. Many surveys provide just the means for items. But if Pat has worked to improve her leadership style and a couple of years later her Topgraded team of As give her a rating of 7, what does that mean? With the full distribution of ratings displayed, plus many comments reproduced for each item, Pat might learn that most of her team gives her 8+ ratings but there are three who give her very low ratings. Their comments might express that she is two months late conducting performance appraisals, or she promised coaching but hasn't done it, or she forgot to inform her team of some change others were told about, or whatever. The point is, the full ratings distribution and comments provide the specific feedback to Pat so she can improve.

The point is, the full ratings distribution and comments provide the specific feedback to Pat so she can improve.

"CHEETAHS" OUTPERFORM "LAMBS"

Various scenarios in this chapter suggest a value system—don't be an autocratic SOB, and don't be Mr. Nice Guy, who fails to hold people accountable. The art of Topgrading has a lot to do with your leadership value system, so perhaps this section will put the issue in perspective.

There seems to be a common myth that top executives, including CEOs, need more Emotional Intelligence than results-orientation. ghSMART was studied by the University of Chicago researchers (Steven Kaplan, Mark Klebanov, and Morten Sorenson). They found that CEOs who were extremely results-oriented (and "good" in Emotional Intelligence) delivered much better financial results than CEOs extremely high in Emotional Intelligence (but only "good" in results-orientation).

CEOs who were extremely results-oriented (and "good" in Emotional Intelligence) delivered much better financial results than CEOs extremely high in Emotional Intelligence (but only "good" in results-orientation).

Are you surprised at this politically incorrect result? I'm not. The press seems enthralled with Emotional Intelligence, as though it were the most important competency. But two-thirds of CEOs fail to meet the objectives they were hired to achieve, and the average tenure for a CEO these days is only 18 months. I think the two lines of research are related—that high-level managers are hired with too much weight placed on Emotional Intelligence and not enough importance put on getting results.

Here are some research details: In the September 15, 2008, issue of the *Wall Street Journal* (WSJ) there was an article that reported findings in which three University of Chicago professors (Kaplan et al.) studied the ghSMART Inc. assessments of 225 CEOs hired by private equity firms. The question was—what are the strengths of CEOs who made more . . . or less . . . money for the shareholders. WSJ: "The findings are sure to intensify debate about how much toughness is appropriate in a CEO." With tough CEOs at General Electric, IBM, and Hewlett-Packard replaced by CEOs high in Emotional Intelligence, and with hundreds of studies of EI in the psychological archives—almost all seeming to sing praises for EI—the results indeed break with conventional wisdom.

As you might expect, the private equity firms researched, including

Blackstone and Bain Capital, are not shy about measuring the financial performance of CEOs they hire.

The results, among the high-scoring traits of CEOs delivering superior financial results, were following through on commitments, hiring A Players, setting high standards, holding people accountable, and analytical skills. Correlating less with financial performance were treating people with respect, listening skills, persuasion, creativity, and enthusiasm.

These results coincide with my experience—high-performing leaders are not necessarily super salespeople, but as Jim Collins points out in *Good to Great*, underneath the surface they are intensely motivated. And results-oriented "doers" are not necessarily *very* warm and empathetic, but people respect and follow them as leaders.

Mark Gallogly, a co-founder of Centerbridge Partners, suggests that CEOs of public companies need more soft skills to manage relations with the public, shareholder groups, analysts, governmental entities, and so forth. The ideal, of course, is to have both intense drive to produce results *and* warmth, understanding, and empathy. However, for any upper-management job, if there are two finalists, one who drives hard to get superior financial results and is "okay" on Emotional Intelligence, and the other who exhibits superior EI and is "okay" at driving for results, which would you hire? Me too.

The ideal, of course, is to have both intense drive to produce results *and* warmth, understanding, and empathy.

Geoff Smart's consultants performed all the in-depth assessments of the 225 CEOs, and he and I have discussed the results. In personal communications Geoff said that soft skills are important; however, the existence of the hard skills is what differentiated CEO performance.

In his book *Who*, Geoff refers to "cheetah" CEOs, who scored highest on being fast, aggressive, persistent, proactive, strong in work ethic, and holding people to high standards. And there are the "lamb" CEOs, who scored highest on showing others respect, listening, and openness to criticism. The "cheetah" CEOs met or exceeded their financial targets twice as often as the "lamb" CEOs.

The "cheetah" CEOs met or exceeded their financial targets twice as often as the "lamb" CEOs.

It may be that the tough skills are absolutely necessary to get results, and the soft skills are important to have at least in moderation, but not necessarily to an extreme degree. I personally cringe when boards value the soft skills over the proven ability to get results. But it's equally risky to hire the Type A, hard-driving SOB manager who is clearly deficient in Emotional Intelligence.

My hunch is that managerial hiring in recent years has been an extremely costly failure in part because of disproportionate emphasis on Emotional Intelligence and insufficient emphasis on getting results, and that the standard for hiring senior managers should be that they are good in Emotional Intelligence and great at getting results.

WHAT IS THE ROI OF TOPGRADING?

This is a self-serving section of the book, but people frankly ask us this question all the time. The short answer is this: since one managerial mis-hire is typically estimated to be $250,000 or more, avoiding just one mis-hire will assure a sky-high ROI if a company has sent a few people to a Topgrading Workshop, conducted internal workshop(s), bought some books or the Topgrading Toolkit, or rolled out the Topgrading Snapshot. The bigger costs are when Topgrading professionals are used to provide the "second opinion" on internal executives or candidates for C-suite positions. Frankly, reference checking us is the best way to estimate ROI; let other CEOs or heads of HR say if costly mis-hires have been avoided and whether the second opinions helped avoid them.

CONCLUSION

Thank you for taking this Topgrading journey with me! I hope this is just the beginning, and that you will consider this book a manual to be visited from time to time as you learn and apply Topgrading principles and methods. Sign up at www.Topgrading.com and you will be invited to Chat with a Topgrader calls, where we might talk and you can share your thoughts, successes, insights, and questions with me and others.

EPILOGUE

The 2005 version of this book proposed eight areas where Topgrading could make a contribution to the world. Actually, there has been progress . . . and there will be many more successful applications of Topgrading as the tipping point is reached:

1. COMMUNITY SERVICE

Zillionaires like Buffett and Gates have suggested that it's harder to get results from activities in foundations than in business. A major reason, I suspect, is that too many not-for-profits hire C Players, cheap.

Good news: Cass Wheeler, former CEO of the American Heart Association, wrote *You've Gotta Have Heart: Achieving Purpose Beyond Profit in the Social Sector,* a plea for not-for-profits to use business best practices. He suggests that not-for-profits can pay salaries similar to those in private industry if they have fewer employees but almost all A Players.

More good news: With a vision of Topgrade the World, Smart & Associates is giving not-for-profits Topgrading forms, guides, videos, and services (such as workshop attendance) at cost. Organizations such as World Vision, Feed the Children, American Heart Association, and Arthritis Foundation are taking advantage of this offer. Our LinkedIn Topgrading groups for CEOs/Presidents and heads of Human Resources will help not-for-profits Topgrade.

2. GOVERNMENT

Decades ago I picked managers for Mayor Daley—the dad. And from time to time a state would ask me to interview candidates for a job (head of Education Department, or whatever).

Bad news: My son Geoff and I each offered President Obama $500,000 in free assessments of candidates for key jobs, but he declined.

Good news: My son Geoff is doing pro bono work for the governor of Colorado, John Hickenlooper. He has asked Geoff to assess candidates for top spots and has said party affiliation is inconsequential—he just wants A Players.

3. CORPORATE GOVERNANCE

Bad news: Most boards of most companies do a terrible job of assuring that the top team consists of high performers. CEOs recruit buddies to sit on boards that control the Compensation Committee, which in turn "takes care of" the CEO. It's incestuous, unethical, and should be illegal; but remember, those same CEOs have lobbyists who . . . you get the picture.

Good news: Most of the private equity world is different in good ways. Combined, Smart & Associates and ghSMART have dozens of private equity clients, and they want one thing: for their acquisitions to be hugely successful. So they hire Topgrading professionals and consultants to assess teams of companies they are considering buying, and they get the "second opinion" assessments of candidates for replacing senior managers.

4. EDUCATION

Bad news: Secondary education in the United States is very weak, in part because schools don't attract and hold nearly enough A Player teachers, and teachers unions protect C Player teachers.

Good news: The North American Nursing Education (fictional name) case study (pages 214–219) shows nice progress here. So does Education, Inc., another case study (page 303).

5. TOPGRADING SUPPLY CHAINS

Bad news: The author of this book has been remiss in not doing more to encourage companies to Topgrade their supply chains. In a previous edition of this book the epilogue suggested Topgrading your nannies, cleaning ladies, and landscape people, with a brief nod to the supply chain.

Good news: The same clients to whom this book is dedicated have done it again, showing me an obvious innovation, and that, of course, is to Topgrade their vendors. It's almost as though a Topgrading bolt of lightning struck the world, because I've heard more and more companies say they are "getting serious" when insisting that companies serve them with . . . A Players. Topgraders can be like reformed smokers when someone lights up in their presence (a rarity except in a few countries). When an obvious C

Player messes things up and their supplier says, "Oh, well, just a mis-hire and everyone has mis-hires," the Topgrader pounces with questions about hiring methods. It was predictable—just as companies adopted Lean or Six Sigma and then required their vendors to do the same, of course they would do so with Topgrading. In the next year or so, supply chain Topgrading will be inserted in case studies at www.TopgradingCaseStudies.com.

Do you have any ideas for how Topgrading could be beneficial? Please share them with me!

Thank you!

SAMPLE JOB SCORECARD

Company: Cyber Learning International
Position: Chief Talent Officer
Location: New York, NY
Compensation: $175,000

Company Description

Cyber Learning International (CLI) is a growing, privately held $250 million company that sells a broad range of online educational programs to businesses, government, and nonprofits such as educational institutions. Based in New York City, CLI has sales offices in Atlanta, Chicago, Dallas, and Los Angeles. There are 350 employees, including creative content specialists, marketing professionals, technology specialists, project managers, sales representatives, and staff support. CLI's organizational culture is considered key to its success and can be characterized as open, entrepreneurial, nonpolitical, fun (wins are celebrated), and accountable (performance is measured; chronic nonperformers are redeployed). Employees are referred to as team members, and although individuality is highly valued, the vast majority of team members are enthusiastic, positive, highly resourceful, good team Players, and "winners"—successful in what they do.

Mission

The CTO reports to the president. The mission of the chief talent officer (CTO) is to pack the organization with superior talent at every salary level. The main challenge is growth, recognizing that companies outgrow their talent. The overall standard is to have 80% high performers (A Players) in all jobs. The CTO will have responsibility for creating and (with internal managers) implementing Topgrading best practices in hiring (recruitment, selection, recruitment "brand" for CLI), developing talent, succession planning, and retaining high performers. The CTO will also have responsibility for creating and implementing a highly effective talent management process that holds all personnel accountable for achieving measurable accountabilities. Consistent with CLI's organizational culture, the CTO will attract and hold talent with key competencies listed below.

Accountabilities

	Metric	Rating	Comments
		5 = Excellent 4 = Very Good 3 = Good 2 = Only Fair 1 = Poor, N/A	
Measure CLI hiring success pre-Topgrading	Senior team completes analysis by June 30: % A/A Potentials hired and promoted in past 5 years and cost of mis-hire forms completed on same group		
Quality of external hires	At least 80% A Players hired, determined by hiring manager, his/her supervisor, and chief talent officer 6 months after person is hired		
Quality of promotions	At least 80% A Players promoted measured by Annual Talent Review		
Increase the percentage of managers who are promoted within the organization	At least 75% of management placements in 2009 from within the organization.		
Implement and monitor comprehensive employee referral program to increase percent of new hires resulting from employee referrals	40% of external hires in 2009 come from employee referrals. All managers submit Network lists of 20 As, 15 Connectors		
Reduce recruiting expenses	Reduce external recruiter expense by 30% in 2009		
Succession planning	Assess and identify high-potential employees in top three levels of organization by end of fiscal year and have an IDP for each of them		

Internal credibility	CTO gets 7+ ratings (10-point scale) on survey of peers in all key competencies
Create a high-performing Talent Management Team	90% of team are A Players or have A Potential in the near future (2011 goal)

Key Competencies**

- Judgment/Decision Making
- Strategic Skills
- Leading Edge
- Track Record

- Integrity
- Resourcefulness/Initiative
- Selecting A Players
- Redeploying B/C Players

- Training/Development/Coaching
- Team Player
- Enthusiasm/Passion
- Change Leadership

The recent incumbent was excessively tolerant of mediocre performance both in the talent organization and management at Acme. At the same time the individual was autocratic with peers and condescending with his team. The new CTO must be able to drive change with best practices, improve talent, and be a positive, respected leader.

Competencies

Competencies	Definition	Minimum Acceptable Rating	Tandem Interviewers' Rating
Green = Relatively easy to change		5 = Excellent	
Yellow = Hard to change but doable		4 = Very Good 3 = Good	
Red = Very difficult to change		2 = Only Fair 1 = Poor, N/A	

Intellectual

1.	Intelligence	Ability to acquire understanding and absorb information rapidly. A quick study.	4	
2.	Analysis Skills	Indentifies significant problems and opportunities. Analyzes problems and people in depth. Sorts the wheat from the chaff, determining root causes.	4	

Competencies

Competencies		Definition	Minimum Acceptable Rating 5 = Excellent 4 = Very Good 3 = Good 2 = Only Fair 1 = Poor, N/A	Tandem Interviewers' Rating
Green =	Relatively easy to change			
Yellow =	Hard to change but doable			
Red =	Very difficult to change			
3.	Judgment/ Decision Making**	Consistent logic, rationality and objectivity in decision making. Neither indecisive nor hip-shooter.	4	
4.	Conceptual Ability	Deals effectively with not just concrete, tangible issues but with abstract, conceptual matters.	4	
5.	Creativity	Generates new approaches to problems or innovations to established best practices. Shows imagination.	3	
6.	Strategic Skills**	Determines opportunities and threats through comprehensive analysis of current and future trends. Comprehends the big picture.	4	
7.	Pragmatism	Generates sensible, realistic, practical solutions to problems.	4	
8.	Risk Taking	Takes calculated risks, with generally favorable outcomes. Does not "bet the farm."	3	
9.	Leading Edge**	Constantly benchmarks best practices and expects others to do same.	4	
10.	Education	Meets formal and informal educational requirements. Exhibits continuous learning.	4	
11.	Experience	Job specific	3	
12.	Track Record**	Successful career history. Generally earns performance ratings of "Excellent."	4	

Competencies

Competencies	Definition	Minimum Acceptable Rating	Tandem Interviewers' Rating
Green = Relatively easy to change Yellow = Hard to change but doable Red = Very difficult to change		5 = Excellent 4 = Very Good 3 = Good 2 = Only Fair 1 = Poor, N/A	

Personal

13.	Integrity**	Ironclad. Does not ethically cut corners. Earns trust of co-workers. Puts organization above self-interest.	5	
14.	Resourcefulness/ Initiative**	Passionately finds ways over, around, or through barriers to success. Achieves results despite lack of resources. Goes beyond the call of duty. Shows bias for action. A results-oriented "doer."	4	
15.	Organization/ Planning	Plans, organizes, schedules and budgets in efficient, organized manner. Focuses on key priorities.	5	
16.	Excellence	Sets high stretch standards of performance for self and others. Low tolerance for mediocrity. High sense of responsibility.	5	
17.	Independence	Willingness to take independent stand. Not swayed by last person talked with.	3	
18.	Stress Management	Stable and poised under pressure.	3	
19.	Self-Awareness/ Feedback	Recognizes own strengths and weaknesses. Not defensive. Does not rationalize mistakes or blame others. Uses feedback mechanisms.	3	
20.	Adaptability	Not rigid. Copes effectively with complexity and change.	4	

Competencies

Competencies	Definition	Minimum Acceptable Rating	Tandem Interviewers' Rating
Green = Relatively easy to change Yellow = Hard to change but doable Red = Very difficult to change		5 = Excellent 4 = Very Good 3 = Good 2 = Only Fair 1 = Poor, N/A	

Interpersonal

21.	First Impression	Professional in demeanor. Creates favorable first impression—body, language, eye contact, posture, etc.	3	
22.	Likability	Puts people at ease. Shows Emotional Intelligence. Warm, sensitive, compassionate. Not arrogant. Friendly, sense of humor, genuine.	4	
23.	Listening	Tunes in accurately to opinions, feelings, and needs of people. Empathetic. Patient. Lets others speak. Listens actively.	5	
24.	Customer Focus	Monitors client satisfaction (internal or external). Establishes partner relationship with clients. Visible and accessible to clients.	4	
25.	Team Player**	Reaches out to peers. Overcomes we-they. Approachable. Leads peers to do what is best for company.	4	
26.	Assertiveness	Takes forceful stand on issues without being excessively abrasive.	3	
27.	Communications— Oral	Communicates well one-on-one, in small groups and public speaking. Fluent, quick on feet, command of language. Keeps people informed.	4	
28.	Communications— Written	Writes clear, precise, well-organized documents using appropriate vocabulary, grammar, and word usage.	4	

Competencies

Competencies	Definition	Minimum Acceptable Rating	Tandem Interviewers' Rating
Green = Relatively easy to change Yellow = Hard to change but doable Red = Very difficult to change		5 = Excellent 4 = Very Good 3 = Good 2 = Only Fair 1 = Poor, N/A	
29. Political Savvy	Aware of political factors and hidden agendas, and acts effectively with that awareness.	4	
30. Negotiation Skills	Achieves favorable outcomes in win/win negotiations.	4	
31. Persuasion	Persuasive in change efforts, selling a vision. Convincing.	4	

Management

32. Selecting A Players**	Topgrades through effective recruiting and selecting at least 90% A Players.	5	
33. Training/ Development/ Coaching**	Actively and successfully trains people. Coaches and develops for promotion into positions where they succeed. People builder.	5	
34. Goal Setting	Sets fair stretch goals for self and others. Encourages individual initiative.	4	
35. Empowerment	Pushes decision making down to lowest level. Provides authority and resources to subordinates.	4	
36. Performance Management	Fosters high level of accountability through fair, hard hitting performance management system. Free with deserved praise and recognition. Constructive in criticism. Provides frequent feedback.	4	
37. Redeploying B/C Players**	Redeploys chronic B/Cs.	5	

Competencies

Competencies	Definition	Minimum Acceptable Rating	Tandem Interviewers' Rating
Green = Relatively easy to change Yellow = Hard to change but doable Red = Very difficult to change		5 = Excellent 4 = Very Good 3 = Good 2 = Only Fair 1 = Poor, N/A	
38. Team Builder	Achieves cohesive, effective team spirit with staff. Treats staff fairly. Shares credit.	4	
39. Diversity	Topgrades with diversity.	4	
40. Running Meetings	Demonstrates ability to organize and run effective meetings.	4	

Leadership

Competencies	Definition	Minimum Acceptable Rating	Tandem Interviewers' Rating
41. Vision	Provides clear, credible vision and strategy.	4	
42. Change Leadership**	Actively intervenes to create and energize positive change. Leads by example.	4	
43. Inspiring Followership	Inspires people to follow lead. Minimizes intimidation. Takes charge. Motivates by pushing appropriate hot buttons of individuals.	4	
44. Conflict Management	Understands natural forces of conflict and acts to prevent or soften them. Effectively works through conflicts to optimize outcome. Does not suppress, ignore, or deny conflicts.	4	

Motivational

Competencies	Definition	Minimum Acceptable Rating	Tandem Interviewers' Rating
45. Energy/Drive	Exhibits energy, strong desire to achieve, high dedication level. 60 hours or more per week probably necessary for results expected.	4	
46. Enthusiasm/ Passion**	Exhibits dynamism, excitement, and a positive can-do attitude.	4	

Competencies

Competencies	Definition	Minimum Acceptable Rating	Tandem Interviewers' Rating
Green = Relatively easy to change Yellow = Hard to change but doable Red = Very difficult to change		5 = Excellent 4 = Very Good 3 = Good 2 = Only Fair 1 = Poor, N/A	
47. Ambition	Desires to grow in responsibility and authority.	3	
48. Compatibility of Needs	Needs that are consistent with opportunities in foreseeable future.	4	
49. Balance in Life	Achieves sufficient balance among work, wellness, relationships, community involvement, professional associations, friendships, hobbies, and interests.	3	
50. Tenacity	Consistent reward of passionately striving to achieve results. Conveys strong need to win. Reputation for not giving up.	4	

Appendix B

TOPGRADING SNAPSHOTS

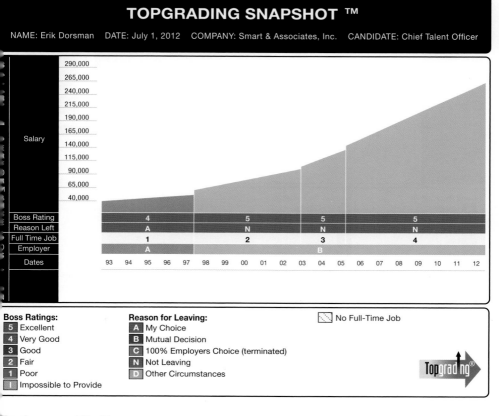

TOPGRADING SNAPSHOT ™

NAME: Erik Dorsman   DATE: July 1, 2012   COMPANY: Smart & Associates, Inc.   CANDIDATE: Chief Talent Officer

Salary	290,000			
	265,000			
	240,000			
	215,000			
	190,000			
	165,000			
	140,000			
	115,000			
	90,000			
	65,000			
	40,000			

Boss Rating	4	5	5	5
Reason Left	A	N	N	N
Full Time Job	1	2	3	4
Employer	A	B		
Dates	93 94 95 96 97	98 99 00 01 02 03	04 05 06	07 08 09 10 11 12

Boss Ratings:
- 5 Excellent
- 4 Very Good
- 3 Good
- 2 Fair
- 1 Poor
- I Impossible to Provide

Reason for Leaving:
- A My Choice
- B Mutual Decision
- C 100% Employers Choice (terminated)
- N Not Leaving
- D Other Circumstances

No Full-Time Job

Topgrading®

Employers and Positions:

A South Bend Community School
  1 Teacher, 8/1/1992 - 6/1/1997

B Educational Management Int'l
  2 Director Information Technology, 6/1/1997 - 12/1/2002
  3 VP Information Technology, 12/1/2002 - 4/1/2005
  4 VP People Development, 5/1/2005 - 7/1/2012

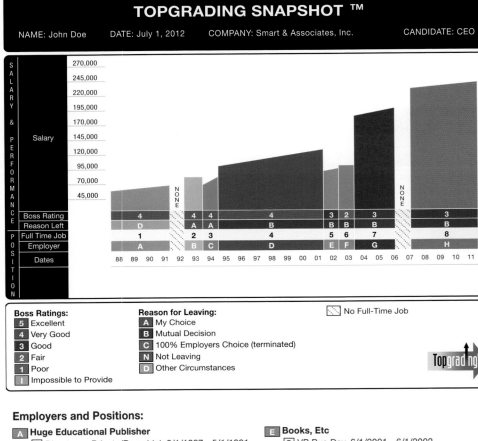

TOPGRADING SNAPSHOT ™

NAME: John Doe   DATE: July 1, 2012   COMPANY: Smart & Associates, Inc.   CANDIDATE: CEO

Boss Ratings:
- 5 Excellent
- 4 Very Good
- 3 Good
- 2 Fair
- 1 Poor
- I Impossible to Provide

Reason for Leaving:
- A My Choice
- B Mutual Decision
- C 100% Employers Choice (terminated)
- N Not Leaving
- D Other Circumstances

No Full-Time Job

Topgrading®

Employers and Positions:

A Huge Educational Publisher
1 Director or Private/Parochial, 6/1/1987 - 5/1/1991

B AAA Publishing
2 VP Marketing, 5/1/1992 - 7/1/1993

C Publisher
3 Director of Marketing, 8/1/1993 - 7/1/1994

D Religious Publishing USA
4 President, 7/1/1994 - 6/1/2001

E Books, Etc
5 VP Bus Dev, 6/1/2001 - 6/1/2002

F Major Books
6 SVP Marketing, 6/1/2002 - 6/1/2003

G Religious Health Assoc.
7 SVP, 6/1/2003 - 2/1/2006

H Ryan Publishing
8 President & CEO, 3/1/2007 - 7/1/2011

Topgrading Hiring Vision
12 Steps to 90% Hiring Success

Topgrading Best Practices in Hiring Sequence	Topgrading Skill	Result
1. Measure Company's Hiring Success (pre-Topgrading)	Calculate Percent A Players; Calculate Costs of Mis-Hires	Awareness of need to Topgrade
2. Create Job Scorecard	"Nail down" A Player performance accountabilities	Candidate and company are clear about job expectations
3. Recruit from Network	Build and maintain list of 20 As, 15 "connectors"	Quicker, better, cheaper than recruiters/ads
4. Use Topgrading Career History Form to Discover *truth* about Candidates	Analyze "Truth" document (Topgrading Career History Form)	Easy to sort C/Bs from As
5. Conduct Telephone Screening Interviews	Use Topgrading Career History Form/résumé to qualify candidates in 45-minute phone interview	Only invite in best candidates for face-to-face interviews
6. Conduct Four 1-Hour Competency Interviews	Learn a bit more about candidate; allow them to ask questions about the organization	Candidates "sold" more on the job
7. Use Topgrading Interview Guide to Conduct Tandem Topgrading Interview	Attain correct insights into (50) competencies	Learn most about candidates
8. Use Interviewer Feedback Form	Understand how to improve interviewing technique	Smoother, more professional interviews
9. Write Draft of Executive Summary	Analyze all data and arrive at valid conclusion to hire or not hire	Accurate, complete Executive Summary; right hiring decision
10. Candidate Arranges Reference Calls with Bosses; Finalize Executive Summary	Get former bosses to tell you the truth	Deeper insights and confirmation of conclusions

A PLAYER HIRED!

11. Coach Your New Hire	Convert thorough insight into practical developmental plan	Highly motivated new hire, with Individual Development Plan
12. Measure Company's Hiring Success (pre-Topgrading vs. post-Topgrading)	Calculate pre-Topgrading and post-Topgrading Hiring Success	Connect Topgrading success with company success, to ingrain Topgrading in company's DNA

 # Cost of Mis-Hires Form ©

Job title of person mis-hired or mis-promoted: _____

Dates person was in position: from_____ to _____

Reason for leaving:
Quit ___, Fired (or forced to resign) ___, Transferred ___, Demoted ___, Retired ___, Died ___, Other ___.

1. **Total costs in hiring the person:** $_____
   - Recruitment/search fees (any guarantee? if so, was money recovered?)
   - Outside testing, interviewing, record checking, physical exam
   - HR department time and administrative costs (for all candidates)
   - Travel costs (for all candidates, spouses, other executives traveling to meet candidate)
   - Time/expenses of non HR people (all candidates)
   - Relocation (moving household goods, purchasing house for candidate)

2. **Compensation:** (sum for all years person was in job) $_____
   - Base ($_____ x number of years)
   - Bonuses ("signing," performance, etc.) for all years
   - Stock options (realized for all years), benefits (insurance, 401k, etc.), car, clubs

3. **Maintaining person in job:** (sum for all years person was in job) $_____
   - Administrative assistant for all years
   - Office "rental" (incl. electricity, etc.) for all years
   - Furniture, computer, equipment, travel for all years
   - Training
   - Other "maintaining" costs

4. **Total severance:** $_____
   - Severance fee (salary, benefits, use of office), lawyer fees
   - Outplacement counseling fee
   - Costs in lawsuits caused by the person (EEOC, harassment, EPA, OSHA, etc.)
   - Administrative costs in separation, wasted time of people in separation

5. **Mistakes/Failures, missed and wasted business opportunities:** $_____
   (For example... drove a key customer away, impaired customer loyalty, launched three "dog" products)

6. **Disruption:** $_____
   (Costs of inefficiency in the organization, lower morale, lower productivity, impaired teamwork)

7. **Other:** $_____

8. **SUM OF ALL COSTS** (#1 through #7): $_____

9. **Estimated Value of Contributions** of the mis-hire: $_____
   (Even if a $50,000 per year store manager drove away customers and stole $1M, perhaps he contributed something — hired five excellent employees, came up with a merchandising idea worth $500K per year to the bottom line.)

10. **NET COST OF MIS-HIRE** (#8 – #9): $_____

"WASTED" Hours:
Number of additional hours you and others spent dealing with mis-hire's weak points — patching things up with customers, etc.

_____

Appendix E

STARTER TOPGRADING INTERVIEW GUIDE

This is by far the most important selection tool. This Guide is for beginning Topgrading interviewers.

Please take copious notes on a tablet, refer frequently to the candidate's Topgrading Career History Form, and have a partner, a tandem interviewer (two interviewers).

EDUCATION YEARS

Although we will spend most time on your career, and specifically your most recent jobs, this is a chronological interview, starting with your education years and coming forward to the present.

Please describe

- the schools attended (and dates), starting with your first school;
- grades;
- degrees awarded;
- high and low points;
- people who influenced you—your career interests, personality, and values; and
- meaningful work experience during school years.

Note: For those with college experience, start with college. For those without college experience, start with high school.

WORK HISTORY

Start with your first full-time job and come forward to your present job. For each job, please tell us

1. why you took the job;
2. about your successes and accomplishments (and how you achieved them);
3. about your mistakes and failures;
4. what you liked most and least about the job;
5. (for management job) how many A, B, and C Player direct reports you had when you entered the job and at its end; and what happened to change the talent mix—hiring, firing, coaching, etc.;
6. the name of your supervisor, and that supervisor's strengths and weaker points;
7. whether you agree to arrange reference calls for us. Please note that in order to receive a job offer, we may ask you to arrange reference calls with supervisors you've had in the past 10 years. Give us your best guess as to what that supervisor would say were your
   strengths,
   weaker points, and
   overall performance
8. the reason(s) you left that job.

SELF-APPRAISAL

Please list your strengths and weaker points, in detail.

FUTURE

What are your goals for your next job? What are your long-term career plans and goals?

Appendix F

SHORT CASE STUDIES

1. ACCESS DEVELOPMENT (165 EMPLOYEES)

During the last three years of the recession (2009–2012) we have continued to grow revenue, we've been one of Utah's fastest-growing companies and we've won multiple awards as a "best place to work." Having 94%+ "A Players" at Access is one of the key reasons for this success. Topgrading has been the foundation to help us attract, hire, and retain these "A Players."

—Larry Maxfield, CEO

Industry: Discount Programs
Highlights:

- Improved from 33% to 94% A Players hired and promoted throughout the company.

- Three levels of internal certification of Topgraders (for all managers; see complete certification criteria at www.TopgradingCaseStudies.com).

- "Best company" awards attract A Players.

2. AMERICAN HEART ASSOCIATION
(450 EMPLOYEES, 2005 CASE STUDY)

Topgrading helped us to raise $50 million more . . . Topgrading saves lives . . . we've improved from 20% A Players to 60%, and we're just getting started.

—Cass Wheeler, CEO (retired)

Industry: Not-for-Profit Association
Highlights:

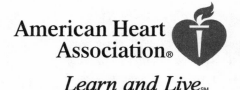

- Improved from 25% to 95% A Players hired and promoted to upper management positions.

- Topgrading 100% applicable to not-for-profits; don't lower the bar—pay comparably to for-profits and require A Players to be hired.

3. ARGO GROUP INTERNATIONAL HOLDINGS, LTD.
(1,300 EMPLOYEES, GLOBALLY)

Argo is more successful as a company because Topgrading has resulted in a higher percentage of A Players. For example, one business that we Topgraded is performing better because we didn't need as many people. So now we're remapping some of the workflows across the entire company because we're finding that we can be substantially more efficient and get just as much work done with, say, 20% less people, if they are A Players. And that's a material change that will make not just one division, but all of Argo Group more successful.

—Mark Watson, CEO

Industry: Global Insurance
Highlights:

- Improved from 51% to 96% A Players hired/promoted in management (AVP and above).

- Fewer people, but almost all As, is most successful.

- Train-the-Trainer for Topgrading Workshops.

- Topgrading helps B/Cs transfer to jobs and become As.

- Topgrading coaching helps some B/Cs become As in present job.

4. AZURA (220 EMPLOYEES)

Topgrading has definitely made the company more successful. We started the company with Topgrading and got great results hiring and in the business. We let Topgrading slip, we saw the business hurt, and so we've relaunched Topgrading, with great success.

—Tim Heronimus, Principal

Industry: Rehabilitation and Assisted Living Centers
Highlights:

- Pre-Topgrading hiring success unknown, but with Topgrading, 75% of all employees hired throughout the company have turned out to be A Players.

- Topgrading slipped, and hiring success declined to 40%, but because of the negative impact on the business, Topgrading has been reinstated.

5. BATESVILLE CASKET COMPANY (3,200 EMPLOYEES)

In the 42 months since becoming independent, Hillenbrand Industries, the parent company of Batesville Casket Company, has grown by nearly 50%—all during a very challenging world economy. We now teach the Topgrading methods in the companies we acquire. Stated simply, the best talent wins and Topgrading helps identify and hire the best talent. This is true for internal promotions and external hires.

—Ken Camp, CEO, Hillenbrand
(parent of Batesville Casket Company)

As a company that prides itself on having a strong culture of execution and delivering bottom-line results, we depend on Topgrading to ensure we have the talent necessary to win; the results speak for themselves.

—Philip Waddell, Vice President,
Human Resources, Batesville Casket Company

Industry: Burial Options
Highlights:

- Improved from 60% to 80% As hired/promoted in management.

- Improved A Player hiring effectiveness, throughout the company, from 60% to 80% in 2011.

- How to flourish in a declining market.

- How to measure quality of hire.

- Topgrading all levels in the company.

- Importance of CEO buy-in.

6. BENCO DENTAL (1,300 EMPLOYEES, GLOBALLY)

Implementing Topgrading throughout our organization has been integral to Benco Dental's growth and success. In the five years since we started our Topgrading journey (and it really is a journey), we've grown revenues by more than 30% while doubling operating income.

More important, Topgrading has helped us extend our continuous improvement culture to the way we select and develop people. It's given us a replicable process that our Human Resources team has implemented in every corner of our company, across the country and at all levels.

As leaders, we often say that people are our most important asset. Topgrading provides an invaluable template for managing that asset.

—Charles Cohen, Managing Director

Industry: Dental Supply
Highlights:

- Improvement from 27% to 60% A Player managers hired in recent years.

- With Topgrading, turnover in the company has dropped significantly.

7. CARESTREAM HEALTH IT DEPARTMENT (300 EMPLOYEES, GLOBALLY)

With a 4-year goal of 1.5% sales, our team has almost achieved it (1.57%) in only 3 years. Furthermore, efficiency has increased 10-fold and productivity is much improved. The only way we could have achieved those results is with Topgrading.

—Bruce Leidal, CIO

Industry: Health-Care Digital Solutions
Highlights:

Carestream

- Improvement from an estimated 30% to 74% As hired throughout the IT department.

- 100% of those hired for the leadership team have turned out to be A Players.

- How to Topgrade a department of a large company not using Topgrading (short answer—don't ask, just do it, and send corporate HR to a Topgrading Workshop and they become supportive).

- How to achieve cost reductions and improve service.

8. COLUMBUS MCKINNON (2,500 EMPLOYEES, GLOBALLY)

Topgrading has been essential in our international growth. Without Topgrading our growth and market share would not have been nearly as impressive. We've always had strong market share in the U.S., but our double-digit international growth in recent years would not have been possible without Topgrading. Topgrading first helped us pick A Player leaders for China and other locations, and Topgrading has helped us pick A Players for all the exempt jobs as well throughout the company.

—Tim Tevens, CEO

Industry: Manufacturer of Hoists and Cranes
Highlights:

- Pre-Topgrading stats unknown, but with Topgrading, 85% of all salaried employees—managers and nonmanagers—hired and promoted have turned out to be A Players.

- Excellent advice for Topgrading internationally.

- Excellent reminder to not cut corners (or there will be more mis-hires, costly mis-hires).

9. CORWIN BEVERAGES (100 EMPLOYEES)

Topgrading has provided a process and discipline that results in hiring quality employees who provide an immediate impact. These new team members have generated increased revenue and profits for Corwin when the economy was dictating otherwise.

—Vic Oenning, Senior Vice President, Sales and Operations

Industry: Beverage Delivery Industry
Highlights:

- Improvement from 33% to 92% A Players hired in nonentry jobs, using Topgrading.

- Value of persistence.

- Importance of CEO support.

- Topgrading in a down economy.

- Value of calculating costs of mis-hires.

- Value of Topgrading entry jobs (truck loader).

10. DENTEK (75 EMPLOYEES, GLOBALLY)

Topgrading has been an invaluable tool for DenTek in recruiting and retaining high-level performers. Over the past 6 years we have blossomed into a world-class Consumer Goods company with explosive growth and great opportunities, due largely to the hard work of "A" Players recruited through the Topgrading process.

—David Fox, President

Industry: Dental Equipment
Highlights:

- Improvement from 0% to 100% hired turned out to be A Players in management.

- 10% to 92% hired turned out to be A Players in staff jobs.

- Small company Topgrades globally.

- Topgrade at the top of the company first.

11. DPT LABORATORIES (1,000 EMPLOYEES)

Topgrading is the stealth bomber of the business world. It gives us a talent advantage which we believe is far superior to our competitors, and enables DPT Laboratories to provide a level of quality and service that is unparalleled in pharmaceutical contract development and manufacturing. Since we adopted Topgrading at DPT, we have developed and successfully implemented a strategic approach to the DPT business that includes a "people strategy" of hiring, developing, and retaining top talent. Over the past eight years we have averaged double-digit growth year over year. It's clear to me that we couldn't possibly have accomplished so much in such a short period of time without continuously Topgrading our talent.

—Paul Johnson, President and Chief Operating Officer

Industry: Pharmaceutical Contract Development and Manufacturing Organization (in semisolid, liquid, and sterile dosage forms)
Highlights:

- Improvement from 17% to 75% A Players hired, total company, with Topgrading.

- Improvement from 20% to 80% A Players promoted with Topgrading.

- Internal certification of hiring managers to use Topgrading methods.

12. EDUCATION, INC. (113 EMPLOYEES)

Since 2008, through Topgrading, our A Players have increased Education, Inc.'s shareholder wealth significantly and made us competitive on a national stage. We now operate with fewer, better people who have changed the game in EI's favor. Topgrading changed my business, and as a small business owner, by extension, Topgrading also changed the quality of my life.

—Kenneth Munies, CEO

Industry: For-Profit Special Education
Highlights:

- Using Topgrading, improvement from 12% to 78% A Player teachers hired.

- Using Topgrading, 89% of corporate staff hired turned out to be A Players.

- Using Topgrading, 76% of those promoted to corporate staff turned out to be A Players.

EDUCATION INC.

- A Player teachers drive each other to be As.

- Proof that company is more profitable with As than Bs.

- Teachers required to do professional development to become and remain A Players.

13. EMC (SALES REGION WITH 177 EMPLOYEES, 2005 CASE STUDY)

The region I inherited was 12th of 14 regions, and after Topgrading we shot to the #1 region.

—Greg Alexander, Regional Sales Manager
(now Managing Director, Sales Benchmark Index)

Industry: Leading Storage Hardware Solutions
Highlights:

- Improved from 27% to 95% A Players sales representatives, using Topgrading.

- Emphasized importance of Topgrading sales management before sales representatives.

14. GENERAL ELECTRIC (300,000 EMPLOYEES)

The tandem interview process is one of the best tools in our arsenal for getting an in-depth understanding of high-potential managers. (2011 quote)

—Bill Conaty, SVP Human Resources (retired 2009)

Industry: Multinational Conglomerate
Highlights:

- Improvement from an estimated "less than 50% to over 80% managers promoted turned out to be A Players."

- Smart & Associates client where managers trained achieved excellent results promoting people.

15. GHSMART (37 EMPLOYEES)

ghSMART attributes its success primarily to the talent of its team. ghSMART has been extremely selective, hiring fewer than 1% of the applicants for ghSMART who make it to the interview process, making it one of the most selective professional services firms.

—Geoff Smart, CEO

Industry: Professional Services (assessments/coaching executives)
Highlights:

- 100% of those hired with Topgrading methods have turned out to be A Players; a start-up, so there are no pre-Topgrading statistics.

- Topgrading methods:

  - Two in-depth assessments.

  - $100,000 referral bonuses.

  - Professionals are only accountable for superior client satisfaction; financial goals are up to the professional.

  - Extremely high retention.

16. GSI (2,500 EMPLOYEES)

Topgrading was not just useful but essential to our success.

—Scott Clawson, CEO

Industry: Grain Storage
Highlights:

- 90% of those hired for the executive team have turned out to be A Players/A Potentials. The executive team Clawson inherited had 22% As (suggesting that the actual hiring/promoting success was probably less than that).

- Outside Topgrading professionals used to assess C-suite executives and replacement candidates.

- "Work in progress," as Topgrading is rolled out throughout the company.

- Challenge balancing need for fast change (private equity owners) and not overwhelming people with change initiatives.

17. HAYES LEMMERZ (6,746 EMPLOYEES GLOBALLY)

Note: In 2012, Hayes Lemmerz was acquired by a strategic owner, Iochpe Group, parent of Maxion Wheels. Curt Clawson retired and long-term Hayes Lemmerz executive Fred Bentley became President and CEO, Maxion Wheels.

The company emerged from Chapter 11 one of the strongest automotive suppliers, and Topgrading contributed to that success. Hayes Lemmerz competes in one of the toughest markets in the world; the global automotive OEM supply industry. We slug it out all over the world in head-to-head competition against the Asians, Europeans, Indians, and Latin Americans. In this tough industry with demanding customers, powerful suppliers, and relentless competition from low-cost countries, we have to have the best people to be successful. Therefore, Topgrading is a central part of our culture and the most important of our core competencies. We can't win if we miss on people. I urge you to Topgrade so you too can get an edge on your competition.

—Curtis Clawson, President, CEO, and Chairman, Hayes Lemmerz (recently retired since acquisition by Maxion in 2012)

Industry: World's Largest Auto/Truck Wheel Company
Highlights:

- Of 137 management hires in recent years, 74% have turned out to be A/A Potentials.

- Of 96 promotions in recent years, 85% have turned out to be A Players/A Potentials.

- Combined, 79% of managers hired and promoted in recent years have turned out to be A Players or A Potentials.

- Business results in EBITDA: 2008-$157.2M; 2009-$54.5M; 2010-$154.9M; 2011-$193.3M.

- How to Topgrade through Chapter 11.

- How to succeed despite imbalance in currency and tariffs.

- Best example of Networking to attract As in down economy, Chapter 11.

18. HILLENBRAND INDUSTRIES (EXCERPTS FROM 2005 CASE STUDY)

Hillenbrand has been transformed with Topgrading. . . . Topgrading is never a finished program. . . . Clearly the shareholders were served by Topgrading faster rather than slower.

—Fred Rockwood, former CEO

Industry: Holding Company
Highlights:

- Percent A Players in upper management improved from low to 81%.
- Advantage of Topgrading fast, not prolonging replacement of underperformers.

HILLENBRAND

19. HOME INSTEAD SENIOR CARE (ONE OF 900 FRANCHISEES, GLOBALLY)

Topgrading enabled us to triple the projected sales for the Wichita office; A Player caregivers impress clients, who refer us, and A Players refer other A Players for us to hire.

—Michael Steinberg, Franchise Owner

Industry: Caregiver
Highlights:

- Improved from 25% to 88% A Player caregivers hired.

- Excellent examples of Job Scorecard, Career History Form, and Topgrading Interview Guide for entry (hourly) workers at www.TopgradingCaseStudies.com.

- 40% turnover beats industry average of 100%.

20. JT FOXX ORGANIZATION (60 EMPLOYEES)

Not Topgrading almost cost me my company; using Topgrading has caused my business to skyrocket.

—J. T. Foxx

Industry: Diversified Consulting and Coaching
Highlights:

- Improved from 2% to 80%+ A Players hired.

- Small but highly complex business requires As.

- One A Player does the work of 5 Bs.

21. K&N MANAGEMENT (500 EMPLOYEES)

Our Rudy's "Country Store" & Bar-B-Q restaurants increased average unit sales from just over $3 million in 2000 to $8 million in 2011. From its inception in 2007 through 2011, Mighty Fine Burgers, Fries and Shakes increased annual unit sales from just over $2 million to *more than $3.5 million in 2011, triple the unit sales of its best competitor. These results would not have been possible without Topgrading.*

—Ken Schiller, President and Co-Owner

Industry: Restaurant Chains
Highlights:

- Improved from 21% to 86% A Players hired, total company.

- Centralized hiring with Topgrading Director and HR conducting tandem Topgrading Interviews.

- Value of simplified process for entry jobs, but necessity of performing all steps rigorously.

22. LABSPHERE (65 EMPLOYEES, GLOBAL LEADER)

Topgrading helped Labsphere's transformation and success, and for sure contributed to my promotion to head a company 3 times larger. Your seminar revolutionized my thinking (built up over a 30+ year career) about how to hire, train, evaluate and develop our people resources. Over time, we trained more than 25% of our workforce—all managers, supervisors, and directors—on Topgrading principles and made Topgrading a vital part of our culture.

—Kevin Chittim, CEO
(recently promoted to CEO of another
division of Halma plc., OceanOptics)

Industry: Light Measurement Products
Highlights:

- Improved from 30% to 70% A Players hired/promoted in the total company.

- Three consecutive years of record profits (first year after adopting Topgrading, sales +19%, profit +73%; second year, sales +47%, profits +91%; third year (current), sales +23%, profits +36%).

- CEO posts his Job Scorecard outside his door.

- Portfolio CEOs share Topgrading experiences with each other.

23. LOS NIÑOS (300 EMPLOYEES)

Topgrading is the #1 reason for our company's success. Because of Topgrading we've hired people who share our core values—especially to provide wow customer experience, and it's also the main reason we have won many "best company" awards. People on our team become like a family, since we hire like-minded people who share the same values.

—Scott Mesh, CEO

Industry: Special Education Private Company
Highlights:

- Improved from 50% to 85% A Players/A Potentials hired, total company.

- Numerous "best company" awards attract A Players.

- Group exercise with teacher candidates helps screening.

24. MARINEMAX
(1,300 EMPLOYEES, TOTAL COMPANY, DEALERSHIP GENERAL MANAGERS)

There's nothing that's done more for our company than Topgrading. MarineMax is a huge fan of Brad Smart's Topgrading system. We began the process in 2002 and we're totally convinced Topgrading has significantly improved our bottom line. We are in the people business,

*and now with Brad's gift, Topgrading is the heart of our culture and a
primary focus of MarineMax.*

—Bill McGill, CEO

Industry: Largest Boat Dealer Company in the World
Highlights:

- 95% of store managers hired since 2009 have turned out to be A Players or A Potentials; pre-Topgrading hiring/promoting to store manager success was 25%.

- How to remain profitable selling a luxury item (yacht) in severe recession.

- Severe cutbacks in number of employees can work, if A Players are retained.

25. MARINEMAX REGION (175 EMPLOYEES)

*Unlike many others in the business, we've not only survived but
we've managed to be profitable; Topgrading has been crucial because
we've done well with fewer people, but almost all A Players.*

—Brett McGill, Region Executive

Industry: Largest Boat Dealer Company in the World
Highlights:

- Improved from 30% to 100% A Players in management; 30% to 80% A Players in all jobs in recent years.

- How to survive in a down market with A Players.

26. MINT.COM (40 EMPLOYEES, GLOBAL CUSTOMERS)

In a previous start-up I worked for, hiring was done haphazardly. At Mint.com, I've had very rigorous hiring. We use a technique called Topgrading, which reveals patterns in behavior. In the history of Mint, I've only fired two people and one left voluntarily.

—Aaron Patzer, Founder and Owner
(until Mint.com sold to Intuit)

Industry: Personal Finance Applications
Highlights:

- "Do it yourself" Topgrading successful.

- Start up with Topgrading—90% of people hired turned out to be A Players.

- Topgraded business sold after 2 years for $170 million.

27. NETSURIT (145 EMPLOYEES, SOUTH AFRICA)

Topgrading has definitely improved Netsurit's performance. Prior to Topgrading we made 3 serious management mis-hires, and the replacements have all been A Players. We've Topgraded the whole company and our sales and profits have skyrocketed.

—Orrin Klopper, Co-Founder

Industry: Outsourced IT Services
Highlights:

- Improved from 9% to 75% of those promoted to management turned out to A Players or A Potentials, with Topgrading.

- Recognized as one of the top companies at the Microsoft Partner awards, winning the "Microsoft Small Business Specialist of the Year 2010."

OUTSOURCED IT MANAGEMENT

- The A Players have definitely improved the quality of the services provided.

- There's been a dramatic reduction in employee turnover.

28. NORTH AMERICAN NURSING EDUCATION, INC. (4,500 EMPLOYEES; THIS COMPANY CHOOSES TO REMAIN ANONYMOUS FOR SEVERAL REASONS, AMONG THEM NOT WANTING TO INSPIRE COMPETITORS TO TOPGRADE; THEREFORE THE NAMES OF THE COMPANY, THE INDUSTRY, AND INDIVIDUALS HAVE BEEN CHANGED)

I believe that a focus on talent with Topgrading as a foundation has been foundational to our growth and success over the past seven years. From a financial perspective, we are primarily a capacity utilization business; every seat we fill in a school generates revenue. From a quality perspective, we are focused on delivering outstanding student learning results across all our schools. Our capacity utilization has set records over the past three years (since Topgrading) while academic achievement metrics have increased steadily. As we have increased the percentage of A Players in our organization, employee satisfaction ratings have also consistently improved as we ensure we have more of the right leaders in place.

—Alice Johnson, Vice President, People Development

Industry: Nursing Education
Highlights:

- With Topgrading, the percent A Player deans improved annually between 2004 and 2011, from 19% to 87%.

- Excellent example of tweaking Topgrading for entry levels.

- There is great value in analyzing every mis-hire.

- There is great value in coaching a new hire right away.

- Annual talent reviews assure low performers improve or leave.

29. NURSE NEXT DOOR (2,000 EMPLOYEES)

We've grown from 1 to more than 50 locations and have experienced 50% to 100% growth in revenues annually since Topgrading 5 years ago.

—Ken Sim, Founder

Industry: Home Care
Highlights:

- Pre-Topgrading hiring success unknown; 85% A Players hired (caregivers and corporate office) with Topgrading.

- Caregiver turnover declined from 50% to 25%.

30. ONYXMD (30 EMPLOYEES)

Once we had our A player executive team in place, we moved through the rest of the organization, replacing a team of mostly Cs with As. That ended up requiring a 100% turnover on our Sales team to accomplish. Now we're beginning to see some amazing results and are on track to become one of the top 10 players in physician staffing in the next 2 to 3 years.

—Jamal Pilger, COO

Industry: Physician Recruitment

Highlights:

- Improved from 10% to 90% of people hired in the total company turned out to be A Players/A Potential with Topgrading.

- 100% turnover prior to Topgrading; 0% this year.

- Company success in early stages had come from recruiting 90% As from Networks.

31. ANONYMOUS FORTUNE 500 PHARMACEUTICAL COMPANY (50-PERSON SALES DIVISION OF GLOBAL PHARMA; ANONYMITY REQUESTED BY COMPANY)

Although in a recession in which all sales forces in the industry were selling less, I'm confident that our Topgraded sales force sold much more than if we hadn't Topgraded.

—Regional Sales Director

Industry: Pharmaceutical Equipment
Highlights:

- Improved from 33% to 75% sales representatives hired turned out to be A Players.

- How to hire top performers at low ($45k) salary base.

- Excellent sales rep job scorecard.

- Details of estimated cost of mis-hired sales rep to be over $1 million.

- Excellent graphics for sales and turnover results.

32. PROSERVICE HAWAII (110 EMPLOYEES)

We are the largest Human Resources Outsourcing company in Hawaii. As we implemented Topgrading, we went from very high turnover with new hires (because we were disciplined about wanting a high-performing culture) to very low. This took us two years to really perfect, but over that time we rolled out Topgrading at every level of our org. We powered through the recession and are continuing to grow 20%+ annually (only slowing down because we are big and dominant in our small market, with 65% plus market share).

—Ben Godsey, President

Industry: Outsourced Human Resources Administration
Highlights:

- Improved from 45% to 91% of those hired and promoted (all jobs) turned out to be A Players, with Topgrading.

33. RED DOOR INTERACTIVE (65 EMPLOYEES)

There is no doubt Topgrading has made Red Door Interactive more successful. With more A Players, we can achieve higher margins on our services. And clients appreciate the results driven by the high caliber of people we hire and retain. All we have to sell is people.

—Reid Carr, CEO

Industry: Online Marketing Services
Highlights:

- Improved from 20% to 90% A Players hired, total company with Topgrading.

- Employee satisfaction with promotion processes 4% prior to Topgrading, and 80% with Topgrading.

- Awards build the recruitment brand (to attract As).

34. RON SANTA TERESA (400 EMPLOYEES, VENEZUELA)

In the Ron Santa Teresa Rum Company we started applying Topgrading three years ago in one of the roughest business environments in the world—Venezuela, where crime, corruption, and social deterioration are rampant. Thanks to Topgrading we've transformed the company and our community, but most importantly we've altered the philosophy of our surroundings. Topgrading is meta-strategy; talent must precede your purpose if you're determined to overcome the daunting challenges of survival as a business and then thrive in the international arena.

Business and social results have followed, as operations margins rose from 12% to surpass the 17% industry standard. Local human development index is more than 40% better than it was in 2003. In 2011, the company was selected as the third best place to work in Venezuela and the 23rd out of 1,900 Latin-American companies.

—Alberto C. Vollmer, CEO

Industry: Rum Manufacturing
Highlights:

- Improved from 25% to 74% of people hired in the total company (except hourly in the rum plant) turned out to be A Players, with Topgrading.

- 76% success Topgrading in all management positions.

- 90% of those hired come from Network.

35. ROUNDY'S (18,000 EMPLOYEES)

There is no doubt about it—the company as a whole has performed better because of Topgrading. A Player executives do a better job of setting direction, 4 times as many A Player store directors of course get better results, and when we've Topgraded entry employees and the social media rave about how positive and energized the whole store is, record sales no longer surprise us!

—Bob Mariano, CEO

Industry: Midwestern Grocery Chain of 160 Stores
Highlights:

ROUNDY'S®

- Improved from 20% to 80% A Player store managers hired.
- Best method to pick top team (CEO Network of A Players worked with in the past).
- 100% executives replaced; 100% executives hired are A Players.
- Average of 95% customer service ratings of entry-level employee.
- Store Director Job Scorecard at www.TopgradingCaseStudies.com.
- Excellent entry-level (abbreviated) Topgrading methods at www .TopgradingCaseStudies.com.

36. SIGMA MARKETING (85 EMPLOYEES)

When I came to Sigma just over four years ago, the company was badly hemorrhaging. We needed to make wholesale changes in our staff and change the culture from a "debating society" to a more sales and client focused environment. Over this time, we changed out 65% of our employees and went from 45% "A" players to 90%. Our new and Topgraded talent has helped us achieve four solid years of revenues and EBITDA. I believe that Topgrading will live beyond our tenures at Sigma and help propel the company's growth for many years to come.

—Kenyon Blunt, CEO

Industry: Integrated Marketing Services
Highlights:

- Improved from 45% to 90% A Players hired/ promoted throughout the company with Topgrading.

- Diligent adherence to Topgrading saved the company.

- Topgrading Snapshot makes hiring easier, better.

37. SOUTHERN TIDE (30 EMPLOYEES)

There is no doubt that Topgrading contributed to our 6000% growth in revenues since we began Topgrading.

—Jim Twining, CEO

Industry: Men's Apparel
Highlights:

- Improved from 15% (hired without Topgrading) to 67% A/A Potential (hired with Topgrading) since 2007.

- *Inc.* magazine's 500 fastest-growing companies—#1 in apparel, #73 overall.

- 2011 *Forbes* magazine: #27 on their list of top 100 America's Most Promising Companies!

38. SYNERGIA ONE (1,300 EMPLOYEES, 19 COUNTRIES)

Synergia One is definitely more successful because of Topgrading.

—Fred Mouawad, Chairman and CEO

Industry: Outsourced HR Functions (diversified group of companies predominantly operating in the gems & jewelry, food-service franchising, and publishing industries)
Highlights:

- Improved from 60% to 87% As promoted, across the entire company, with Topgrading.

- Improved from 57% (pre-Topgrading) to 83% (with Topgrading) A Players hired across the entire company.

- Successfully Topgraded in 19 countries, with vastly different businesses.

39. TEKMORE (1,000 EMPLOYEES; NAMES CHANGED—LACK OF CORPORATE SUPPORT FOR TOPGRADING)

Thanks to Topgrading and the improved team, operating profit tripled over the two years as TEKMORE gained the confidence of major customers around the world.

—Claude Hanson, CEO

Industry: High-Tech Manufacturing
Highlights:

- N/A to 95% A Players hired in management.

- N/A to 95% A Players promoted.

- How to Topgrade in a turnaround.

- How to Topgrade a division without Corporate support ("Stay under the radar!").

- Value of a "second opinion" by a Topgrading professional.

40. TRITON (350 EMPLOYEES)

Topgrading has definitely enabled Triton to perform better as a total company.

—Frank Evans, CEO

Industry: Pawn Broker and Financial Services Stores
Highlights:

- Management hiring and promoting success improved from
0% to 88% A Players.

- District Manager turnover was
reduced from 98% to 32% (far
better than industry average).

- Total staff hiring and promoting improved from 2% to 80% who turned out to be A Players.

41. VIRTUAL TECHNOLOGY
(100 EMPLOYEES, 2005 EDITION CASE STUDY)

With 95% to 100% success hiring As, our turnover is down and sales and profits have skyrocketed.

—Jack Harrington, CEO

Industry: Flight Simulators ("Video games for military")

Highlights:

- Upon Topgrading, 19 of 20 (95%) hired turned out to be As, total company.

- In the most recent year, 25 out of 25 (100%) turned out to be A Players.

- Fast-growth high-tech company.

SAMPLE EXECUTIVE SUMMARY AND INDIVIDUAL DEVELOPMENT PLAN

CYBER LEARNING INTERNATIONAL

Name of Candidate: Erik Dorsman
Position Applied for: Chief Talent Officer, Cyber Learning Int'l
Tandem Interviewers: Brad Smart (consultant)
                         Chris Mursau (consultant)
Date of Tandem
Topgrading Interview: June 9, 2012

Career History and Goals

Erik is considered a strong candidate for CTO—not quite an A Player but one who appears to have A Potentials.

In high school Erik was the "All-American Boy," a top 5% student, First-Team All Conference Soccer, Eagle Scout, and senior class vice president. He worked hard at everything he did, and was successful, except for failing to get elected co-captain of the soccer team. Showing self-awareness today, he admits that he wasn't elected because he was too intense and pushy with his teammates. This in one form or another has been a recurring issue for him, though fortunately he has conscientiously worked to overcome this weaker point with success.

Erik went on to Hope College, where his father was a professor. Only 5'8", Erik could play varsity soccer (a major consideration for him) in this Division III school, and with a father-professor, the costs were minimal. Erik also earned money as a resident assistant; in this role he faults himself for not bonding more with the students and for being too much the "cop," catching students with beer, etc.

He earned a 3.91 GPA, was named to the All-Conference Soccer Team, earned a Computer Science award, and showed some entrepreneurial inclinations: he had worked for a lawn-mowing service that folded, so he and a friend started their own company as a summer business, and it was successful. His biggest regret—not being elected co-captain of the soccer team, and the reason was the same as in high school—he was too intense and pushy, telling teammates to try harder, but in retrospect he wishes he had been more positive in his motivational methods, building more positive relationships that might have enabled him to coax teammates to try harder.

He earned a BS in Computer Science with a Secondary Education Certificate, anticipating becoming a teacher/coach . . . which he did after graduation in 1992. Following college he was a teacher for 6 years in a lower-income area (South Bend, Indiana). Erik earned top performance evaluations from the principal and says he bonded with the most motivated students. However, he regrets that he really did not reach out to connect more with the less motivated students. He said that he could have scheduled home visits to motivate both students and their parents. And he could have shown more interest in them personally . . . but didn't.

Evenings, weekends, and summers he had fun participating in a successful hobby—coaching soccer. He coached goalies at a Division I school. He shows self-awareness in saying that although his soccer coaching was demonstrably successful, he again was too much the pusher and not enough the positive motivator.

Not liking teaching and wanting administration and the opportunity to use technology to improve education, Erik attended Indiana University from '94 until '96 part-time, completing his MS Instructional Systems Technology. He made up to $38,000 summers running a soccer camp he started—another example of entrepreneurial and leadership potential. There is a pattern throughout his life, clearly shown during these years of teaching full-time, coaching successfully part-time, earning a master's degree, and (during summers) making good money as an entrepreneur: hard work, dedication, passion, and results-orientation.

Erik has been with EMI since graduate school, and he has progressed steadily, earning promotions. In the early years he headed IT, rising to director, and his main success was building a solid infrastructure to serve all the charter schools. For a teacher/coach to enter and build the IT function almost from scratch was a major accomplishment, showing resourcefulness.

He worked hard, and he faults himself for focusing so much on his immediate tasks that he did not reach out much to build relationships with key people in other areas of the company or vendors. And he admits he was too intense with his team, though he says it was a cohesive, effective team. Overall he received high performance ratings and achieved on-time, on-budget, high-quality goals.

From 2002 to 2005 he was vice president, the same basic job with added responsibility for overseeing annual plans for the senior team. He took control of budgets, came in under budget, and installed effective programs. He built a team of some A Players and a couple of lesser performers who were let go.

Erik admits that as a new executive he was too passive, realizing the company was in trouble but hesitating to speak up. He sided with his supervisor, the president, who wanted fast growth without much analysis of failures. Erik's peers pushed for far more analysis of such issues as picking locations for charter schools and marginal academic performance, and wanted moderated, controlled, and more successful growth. Erik has demonstrated a value system more consistent with the "other" faction and admits that a consideration is not wanting to irritate his supervisor.

Since 2005 he has been in his present role, VP People Development. The new CEO is totally talent-oriented, and together they have Topgraded the company. It's a work in progress, but Erik abandoned the IT career path for an exciting new one, one he believes will serve him well as he moves toward general management.

As he did once before, Erik took over a blank slate and built the function from scratch. He reports that teacher hiring has improved from 30% to 50% and principal hiring has improved from 15% to 75%. (His supervisor, Jeff Clarkson, says the pre-Topgrading percent high performers was higher.) His goal is for 90% A Players, with 80% of principals promoted from within.

He faults himself for not embracing Topgrading sooner and for carrying a C Player too long. He says that he now has all A Players (or those with A Potentials) reporting to him. He guessed that his supervisor Jeff would give him an Excellent overall rating (true), compliment his leadership and analytic abilities, drive for improvement, and value as a trusted counselor (all true), and criticize him for overplanning and for not being sufficiently assertive with peers (also true).

Clarkson also compliments Erik on being an extremely dependable and valued coach to him and peers, a "thought partner," and very systematic ... so much so that although deadlines are met, he feels Erik is too hesitant to change and move in a new direction, and in that sense his strength (being systematic) is overused at times, and becomes a weaker point.

He also faults Erik a bit for not displaying more dynamism initially, though he says Erik eventually exudes it. And he says Erik continues to hold back in groups . . . having to be called on to voice what are usually excellent insights. Finally, his supervisor thinks it would be beneficial for Erik to become more knowledgeable in finance, given his general management interest.

Erik's goals are to be CTO of a bigger company and to eventually move into general management of a technology-assisted company in the learning industry.

Strengths	Weaker Points
• Enthusiasm/Passion • Resourcefulness/Initiative • Accountability • Selecting A Players • Judgment/Decision Making • Redeploying B/C Players • Integrity • Leading Edge • Track Record • Analysis Skills • Conceptual Ability • Pragmatism • Education • Experience • Self-Awareness • Self-Objectivity • Written Communications • Tenacity • Highly Dependable • Planning/Organization • Listening • Coaching	• Team Player (at times good, but at other times needs to offer more opinions) • Change Leadership (drives successful change, but could get more buy-in to have the change be quicker and better) • Experience (fine for position applying for, but needs more business education for eventual general management) • Stress Management (regresses to introversion) • Likability (generally very well liked, but initially a bit cold)

Individual Development Plan (IDP) Suggestions to Erik Dorsman

(Note: The Executive Summary need only list the developmental suggestions: 1. Write your own IDP, 2. Revise your IDP with your supervisor quarterly, etc. The newly hired person writes the "why" when," etc. Simply show this sample IDP to the new hire, along with the suggestions, and the new hire will do the "heavy lifting" of creating the detailed IDP.)

Note: Erik, this section summarizes developmental ideas that came from you in the tandem Topgrading Interview and came from the other Topgrading sources. To have a developmental action in your IDP, you should fully embrace it—it's your plan.

1. Write your own IDP.

    After the meeting with your tandem interviewers, meet with your new supervisor to discuss this report and get his or her thoughts. Then write your own IDP saying what you intend to do, why, when, and how the results will be measured.
    - **Why:** smooth assimilation (onboarding), immediate productivity, and accelerated long-term development
    - **When:** within 2 weeks
    - **How Measured:** if done on time and supervisor approves it

2. Review your IDP with supervisor quarterly.

    Initiate meetings quarterly to check "how you're doing."
    - **Why:** to keep focus on development, particularly on improving weaker points
    - **When:** quarterly—Erik initiates
    - **How Measured:** calendar

3. Conduct e-mail 360 surveys in 3 months and 9 months.

    The 3-month survey will allow enough time for you to make impressions (yet early enough to help you correct negative impressions), and the 9-month survey will essentially "take the pulse" of the organization for the same purpose.

    Include strengths and weaker points (above), and set goals of at least a 7 on a 10-point scale for the weaker points.
    - **Why:** some of these weak points have been chronic, and it will take a multifaceted approach to overcome them; systematic feedback in the form of surveys will provide feedback to you and to your supervisor, helping to maintain the constructive focus
    - **When:** 3 months and then every 6 months, indefinitely
    - **How Measured:** survey completed on time

4. Retain your goal of general management.
    - **Why:** this truly is your goal; you joined CLI with the expectation of being groomed for general management and your supervisor (John Smith) supports the goal

- **When:** ongoing
- **How Measured:** your satisfaction with progress, discussed in quarterly development meetings with John

5. Improve financial expertise, taking a minimum of a 5-day course this year, Finance for Non-Financial Managers (a developmental activity to research and consider when family focus would seem to permit it—executive MBA)
   - **Why:** finance is the "language of business," and general managers must be very expert in order to succeed (and they are legally responsible for financial decisions); also, CLI uses sophisticated financial models for tracking performance, normal financial decisions, and due diligence for acquisitions
   - **When:** 5-day course completed this year
   - **How Measured:** successful completion

6. Integrate talent strategy with Corporate and each division strategy.
   - **Why:** to learn more of the financial and strategic nuances of the enterprise and each division . . . to perform better in present job and to prepare for general management
   - **When:** begin immediately, and ongoing
   - **How Measured:** E-mail 360 surveys of peers

7. Use two mentors in your onboarding.
   - **Why:** as you know, you only make a first impression once, and you have joined a politically complex company. To lead change will be challenging. John Smith has already told you he will be a daily mentor, but he travels a lot. He has someone in mind (Pat Jones) you could approach to help guide you when John is traveling
   - **When:** meet at least weekly with a mentor
   - **How Measured:** Erik to keep a log

8. Help with due diligence on some acquisitions.
   - **Why:** advance financial expertise to lead to general management. No promise, but Smith suggests you might be considered to run a small acquisition when you are ready
   - **When:** John Smith will decide
   - **How Measured:** discuss annually

9. Work with an executive coach.
   - **Why:** to continue progress on developmental issues of bonding, speaking up in meetings with peers, creating a more dynamic and inspirational first impression
   - **When:** monthly coaching?
   - **How Measured:** opinions of John Smith and results of e-mail 360 surveys

Note: Performance goals of Topgrading your team and the company will be discussed separately as part of the performance-management system.

Appendix H

TOPGRADING RESOURCES

1. Free Topgrading Snapshot and Career History Form at www .TopgradingSnapshot.com
2. At www.Topgrading.com:
   a. Free *Topgrading Tips* newsletter
   b. Free video: *How to Use the Topgrading Career History Form*
   c. Free video: *How to Use the (Full) Topgrading Interview Guide*
   d. Discounts for not-for-profits
   f. Major Topgrading Products in the Topgrading Shop
   g. Topgrading Workbook (167 pages; used in Topgrading Workshops)
   h. Topgrading Toolkit (all Topgrading explanations plus 7 hours of high-def demos of all 12 Topgrading Hiring Steps; used for internal training)
   i. Topgrading (forms) License (license all the copyrighted Topgrading forms and guides)
   j. Workshops, speeches
   k. "Second opinion" Interviews and Executive Coaching by Topgrading Professionals
   l. Affiliations

Smart & Associates offers three different levels of affiliation with our company:

A. **Team Member Professional.** Smart & Associates maintains a staff of "in-house" consultants who also have their own private consultancies. Team member professionals are thoroughly vetted through all of the Topgrading methods and become featured, with their picture and contact information, in the Team section of www.Topgrading.com. Team members serve clients by conducting Topgrading workshops, performing Topgrading Interviews, coaching executives, and consulting with clients regarding Topgrading implementation and related activities. Team members maintain the very highest professional standards, typically serving the CEO as the client contact. These same team members are available to the other affiliates listed below to perform Topgrading services.

B. **Certified Trainer Affiliate Program (CTAP).** This program enables consultants and trainers to become certified to conduct Topgrading Workshops and receive commissions for selling Topgrading products and services. A CTAP may also choose to contract with Smart & Associates to provide services to their clients on their behalf, earning substantial commissions. The process for certification requires people to attend one of our two-day Topgrading Workshops, conduct the Topgrading steps through the hiring of three people (e.g.: so if there were three finalist candidates, there would be three Job Scorecards, multiple documented Telephone Screening Interviews, nine tandem Topgrading Interviews, multiple documented reference calls, nine Executive Summaries, etc.) while periodically being coached via telephone by a team member. Following the furnishing of documentation of these steps, our certification expert will review them for completion and do an oral interview to make certain that all aspects of Topgrading are well understood and capable of being delivered by the candidate in Topgrading Workshops and consulting with companies. Finally, a test is administered by that same certification expert, completing the certification process.

C. **Basic Affiliation Program (BAP).** Members of this program simply earn commissions by directing traffic to our Web site from links we provide to them. When clients purchase products from our Web site, commissions automatically are tracked and accrue to the referring BAP member. BAP members may also refer clients to use services not vended via our Web site and earn commissions. These opportunities are handled on a case-by-case basis by our Affiliate Sales Manager. Commissions are paid monthly using online software. BAP affiliates do not perform Topgrading professional services.

For more information about Smart & Associates affiliation programs please review material at www.Topgrading.com and then call us at 847-244-5544.

Index

TALK WITH SMART & ASSOCIATES ABOUT WORKSHOPS, INTERVIEWS, AND LICENSES

Please call us if you would like to discuss any of the following:

- Internal Topgrading Workshops: Topgrading companies have found that two-day Topgrading Workshops are more effective than one-day workshops. Day 1 is Topgrading principles, case studies, and fun exercises, and Day 2 is coached practice in the Topgrading Interview, analyzing all the notes, arriving at valid conclusions, and providing feedback and coaching to the interviewee (just as you would do with your newly hired A Player).
- Topgrading speeches, short presentations, or Webinars. These can be a one-hour keynote and/or a Webinar designed for a company.
- Using the Smart & Associates Professional Team to conduct Topgrading Interviews of finalist candidates for key jobs. Almost always these are in-person, though with recent advances in video technology, using videoconferencing for interviews is sometimes done.

    Team Professionals have been Topgraded by Brad Smart, have conducted hundreds if not thousands of Topgrading Interviews, and every report is peer reviewed by Brad.
- Using the Smart & Associates Professional Team to conduct executive assessment and coaching of internal managers. We offer "second opinion" assessments of internal talent and coach B Players to become A Players.
- Using the global network of Topgrading affiliates, who are certified to conduct Topgrading Workshops. Smart & Associates Certified Topgrading Affiliates have been trained by Brad to conduct Topgrading Workshops. All have conducted at least 12 tandem Topgrading Interviews, and some have conducted so many that on their own (not repre-

senting Smart & Associates), they conduct Topgrading Interviews for their clients and Brad does not peer review their reports.

- Investing in a license to use Topgrading Forms and Guides including the Topgrading Snapshot, Topgrading Career History Form, and Topgrading Interview Guide. There are several options, including a free trial of the online forms and investing in a license to use Topgrading Forms and Guides. For example, companies typically "try out" the Topgrading Snapshot with purchase of individual Snapshots, and then have a license to use the Snapshot for unlimited usage. The cost depends on a lot of factors—number of employees, anticipated turnover, etc.

Dr. Brad Smart
PRESIDENT

w 847-244-5544
Smart & Associates, Inc.
37202 N. Black Velvet Lane
Wadsworth, Il 60083
BradSmart@Topgrading.com

Margaret Brask
OFFICE MANAGER

w 847-265-7415
f 847-265-7416
Margaret.Brask@SmartTopgrading.com

ADDITIONAL RESOURCES

Please go to Appendix H, page 331, to see additional resources available at www.Topgrading.com (many free) and learn about our different affiliate programs.